Contents

Contested Cities in the Modern West

A.C. Hepburn
Professor of Modern Irish History
University of Sunderland

palgrave
macmillan

First published 2004 by
PALGRAVE MACMILLAN
Houndmills, Basingstoke, Hampshire RG21 6XS and
175 Fifth Avenue, New York, N. Y. 10010
Companies and representatives throughout the world

PALGRAVE MACMILLAN is the global academic imprint of the Palgrave
Macmillan division of St. Martin's Press, LLC and of Palgrave Macmillan Ltd.
Macmillan® is a registered trademark in the United States, United Kingdom
and other countries. Palgrave is a registered trademark in the European
Union and other countries.

ISBN 0–333–71790–2

This book is printed on paper suitable for recycling and made from fully
managed and sustained forest sources.

A catalogue record for this book is available from the British Library.

Library of Congress Cataloging-in-Publication Data
Hepburn, A.C. (Anthony C.)
    Contested cities in the modern West/A.C. Hepburn.
        p. cm. – (Ethnic and intercommunity)
    Includes bibliographical references and index.
    ISBN 0–333–71790–2 (cloth)
        1. Ethnic conflict–Case studies. 2. Sociology, Urban–Case studies.
3. Urban policy–Case studies. I. Title II. Ethnic and intercommunity conflict
series (Palgrave (Firm))

HM1121.H47 2004
305.8–dc22   2003065843

10   9   8   7   6   5   4   3   2   1
13   12   11   10   09   08   07   06   05   04

Printed and bound in Great Britain by
Antony Rowe Ltd, Chippenham and Eastbourne

Ethnic and Intercommunity Conflict Series

General Editors: **Seamus Dunn**, Professor of Conflict Studies and Director, Centre for the Study of Conflict, and **Valerie Morgan**, Professor of History and Research Associate, Centre for the Study of Conflict, University of Ulster, Northern Ireland

With the end of the Cold War, the hitherto concealed existence of a great many other conflicts, relatively small in scale, long-lived, ethnic in character and intra- rather than inter-state has been revealed. The dramatic changes in the distribution of world power, along with the removal of some previously resolute forms of centralised restraint, have resulted in the re-emergence of older, historical ethnic quarrels, many of which either became violent and warlike or teetered, and continue to teeter, on the brink of violence. For these reasons, ethnic conflicts and consequent violence are likely to have the greatest impact on world affairs during the next period of history.

This new series examines a range of issues related to ethnic and intercommunity conflict. Each book concentrates on a well-defined aspect of ethnic and intercommunity conflict and approaches it from a comparative and international standpoint.

Rather than focus on the macrolevel, that is on the grand and substantive matters of states and empires, this series argues that the fundamental causes of ethnic conflict are often to be found in the hidden roots and tangled social infrastructures of the opposing separated groups. It is through the understanding of these foundations and the working out of their implications for policy and practical activity that may lead to ameliorative processes and the construction of transforming social mechanisms and programmes calculated to produce longterm peace.

Titles include:

Stacey Burlet
CHALLENGING ETHNIC CONFLICT

Ed Cairns and Mícheál Roe (*editors*)
THE ROLE OF MEMORY IN ETHNIC CONFLICT

T.G. Fraser
THE IRISH PARADING TRADITION

A.C. Hepburn
CONTESTED CITIES IN THE MODERN WEST

Colin Knox and Padraic Quirk
PEACE BUILDING IN NORTHERN IRELAND, ISRAEL AND SOUTH AFRICA

Colin Knox and Rachel Monaghan
INFORMAL JUSTICE IN DIVIDED SOCIETIES
Northern Ireland and South Africa

'The co-existence of several nations under the same state is a test, as well as the best security of its freedom ...'

Lord Acton, 'Nationality', in *Essays in the History of Liberty: Selected Writings of Lord Acton* (3 vols, ed. JR Fears, 1985, pp. 424–5)

'A strange city ... and a very beautiful one. And all refugees from all over the Earth are drawn to it ... And even though different tongues and languages mix in the streets, no-one hurts anyone else ...'

Stefan Chwin, *Esther* (Gdansk: Tykul, 1999. Cited in Jersak: 21)

'I come from the late city of Newark .... Look, the Irish ran the city, the Italians ran the city, now let the coloured run the city ... I got nothing against that. It's the coloured people's turn to reach into the till ...'

Philip Roth, *American Pastoral* (London: Jonathan Cape, 1997, p. 345)

Istanbul was Constantinople
Now it's Istanbul not Constantinople
popular song c.1953, words by Jimmy Kennedy

Maps and tables

Maps

Tables

Preface

This book arises from the curiosity of an historian of Belfast about the nature and extent of urban ethnic conflict in other settings. Like most historians I believe that every case needs to be studied for its own sake because it will be different to some degree. But we cannot tell how different it is without obtaining some sort of comparative measure. Historians have been slow to develop comparative history. A major reason for this has been our scrupulous desire to base analysis on a detailed assessment of the available evidence. In practice this admirable aim imposes serious limitations. To carry out this study on such a basis would have required a working knowledge of nine distinct languages for the case studies and a further six for the other cities discussed in Chapter 1. In the absence of such formidable linguistic skills – and indeed of more attainable ones – this work has been based mainly on secondary sources, almost all of them in English. There needs to be more reworking of 'secondary data' in modern historical studies if phenomena which are in fact common across a number of different political and cultural contexts are to be comprehended fully. This approach, too, has its limitations, for the writer is restricted to some extent by the questions which other scholars have chosen to explore. I would like, for instance, to have known more than appears to be known about socio-linguistic relations in nineteenth-century Danzig. But with this exception, the amount of detailed material in English on the various aspects of these cases is considerably greater than I had at first anticipated.

The widespread currency of rival names for a city is one of the most obvious indicators of its contested status. In this respect I have sought to take as neutral path as possible. The practice here has been to use the name by which the city is normally and currently known in English. Where particular historical periods are under discussion in which the city was better known by another name, this has been used. For example, up to 1945 Gdańsk is referred to as Danzig: it would be anachronistic to refer in English to the 'Free city of Gdańsk' or to the 'Gdańsk crisis of 1939'. For the same reasons I have used Trieste throughout, rather than the Habsburg Triest or the Slav Trst. Likewise I have held to the anglicised forms for Brussels and Jerusalem and, except where it appears as part of a French-language expression, have eschewed the accent in Montréal.

The book would not have been completed without a semester of research leave from the University of Sunderland. It would not have been started, during a particularly busy period of academic life back in 1997, without the magnificent escape-valve provided by a visiting residency at the Rockefeller Foundation's study centre at Bellagio, Italy. I am grateful to the Trustees and to staff and fellow-residents there, especially to Elihu and Ruth Katz for talking about Jerusalem and to my parallel resident Michael Keating. My horizons were initially raised beyond Ireland through participation between 1984 and 1990 in the European Science Foundation's project on 'Governments and Non-dominant Ethnic Groups in Europe, 1850–1940', and I would like to record my thanks to members of the sub-group which worked on urban ethnic identity, notably its leader Max Engman, and those who work has been of particular help in the current enterprise: Marina Cattaruzza, Gary B. Cohen, Colin Pooley and Els Witte. A visiting fellowship at the European University Institute in 1994, as part of the programme on 'National and Regional Identities in 19th and 20th Century Europe' directed by Heinz-Gerhard Haupt, Michael Müller and Stuart Woolf, provided further comparative perspectives. Likewise did a summer school at the University of the Basque Country in 1997, organised by Andres Barrera-Gonzalez, where Miquel Siguan explained to me why Barcelona is not a contested city. I benefited from the comments of participants in a seminar at the Joan B. Kroc Institute for International Peace Studies, University of Notre Dame, Indiana, in 2001. I am also grateful to the Peace Studies staff and others at Gujarat Vidypith, the university founded by Mahatma Gandhi in Ahmedabad, India, who showed such encouraging interest in Europe's contested cities at a conference in 1999, and to my hosts, Makrand and Shirin Mehta. I wish I had then been more aware of the intensity of the ethnic divisions which have since brought such tragedy to their own city.

I must also express thanks to colleagues and others who made available their knowledge of particular cities or advised on sources or approaches, including John Darby, Barbara Fennell, Colin Holmes, Alan Sharp, Derek Stubbs, Bill Wallace and Fritz Wefelmeyer. Michael Keating, A. Robert Lee, Donald MacRaild, Peter H. Wilson and Hans van Zon were kind enough to comment on various drafts of the book. I am especially grateful to Dr Katarzyna Jerzak for allowing me to consult her essay on Gdańsk novelists in advance of its publication. Several cohorts of MA students on my contested cities course at the University of Sunderland also made valuable suggestions: amongst whom I must single out for special thanks Tasos Karakatsanis, without whom I would not have known of Thessaloniki's contested past. Cherrie Stubbs was an encouraging and forbearing colleague as *Contested Cities* occasionally encroached upon other aspects of working life. I would also like to express thanks to my series editors, Valerie Morgan and Seamus Dunn, for their helpful comments and to them and to Alison Howson and Guy Edwards at Palgrave Macmillan for their own forbearance as deadline followed deadline. Felicity Hepburn, while living with *Contested Cities* for longer than it was reasonable to expect never doubted that one day it would be completed, and throughout provided the encouragement, support and wider perspective on life without which it never would have been.

A. C. Hepburn

List of Abbreviations

ABN	*Algemeen Beschaafd Nederlands* (general cultured Dutch)
AMG	Allied Military Government
BNA Act	British North America Act
CECM	Commission des écoles catholiques de Montréal
CLN	National Liberation Committee
EU	European Union
FLQ	*Front de Libération du Québec*
FTT	Free Territory of Trieste
IRA	Irish Republican Army
ITGWU	Irish Transport & General Workers' Union
LN	League of Nations
MUC	Montreal Urban Community
NATO	North Atlantic Treaty Organisation
NICRA	Northern Ireland Civil Rights Association
OF	*Osvobodilna Fronta* (Liberation Front)
PLO	Palestine Liberation Organisation
PQ	*Parti québecois*
PR	propotional representation
PSBGM	Protestant School Board of Greater Montreal
SS	Schutz Staffeln (protection squads)
UNO	United Nations Organisation
UNSCOP	United Nations Special Commission on Palestine
USA	United States of America
USSR	Union of Soviet Socialist Republics
UVF	Ulster Volunteer Force
VNV	*Vlaamsch Nationaal Verbond* (Flemish National Union)

1
Contested Cities: Social Change, State Action and International Intervention

> To me the giant city seemed the embodiment of racial desecration .... The longer I lived in this city [Vienna] the more my hatred grew for the foreign mixture of people which had begun to corrode the old site of German culture.
>
> A. Hitler, *Mein Kampf*, 1924 (Lehan:159)

Cities are frequently seen as centres of civilisation, as the cutting edge of human achievement, as cosmopolitan sites where new identities may develop and flourish. In this view, traditional barriers such as ethnic difference are eroded through proximity of living and working. But writers over the past two centuries have been just as likely to characterise modern cities as heterogeneous gatherings composed of communities which regard themselves, or are regarded by others, as distinct in terms of language, religious belief, skin colour or culture. From this perspective the question becomes 'how have cities sought to mitigate this potential for conflict?'. The rapidly-growing British industrial cities of the nineteenth century, for instance, recruited the bulk of their populations from nearby hinterlands, so that while the challenges of acculturation to urban living and the discipline of the factory may have been great, the challenge of acculturation to new neighbours was substantially reduced. In the first phase or mass urbanisation in Britain, for instance, only the Irish came from further afield.

But in other contexts, such as the cities of north America, or those of central Europe which so affronted the young Hitler, ethnic realities were more complex. Populations were often differentiated in their residential and associational life, their occupational and industrial profiles, and their marriage patterns. Sometimes, mutual hostility extended to

1

rioting and other forms of overt conflict. Many American cities have been so divided for a century or more as, to a lesser extent, are some of the larger cities of Europe. Such cases are frequently referred to as 'divided cities'. But in a smaller number of cases, animosity has been sharpened by the additional factor that neither group will recognise the political and/or cultural sovereignty of the other. We need a term other than merely 'divided' to distinguish these cases. Sometimes such a context has been described as a 'frontier city' but this suggests proximity to an international border, which may or may not be the case (Klein:12; Kotek 1996a:17). The term used in this book is 'contested city'. This is defined as a major urban centre in which two or more ethnically-conscious groups – divided by religion, language and/or culture and perceived history – co-exist in a situation where neither group is willing to concede supremacy to the other.

This book explores the variety of ways in which such problems have arisen and are coped with by the state(s) concerned, by the international system, and by the people of the cities in question. It also asks how such conflicts have been resolved, managed, or simply changed. The focus for the most part is on the nineteenth and twentieth centuries and is restricted to the western world, where contests have their origins, at least, in European history. Six cities are studied in detail. Gdańsk and Trieste, where external intervention has played a crucial role, are both failed examples of free cities under international rule, now apparently both resolved in favour of one of the parties. Brussels and Montreal have avoided extreme conflict and both grapple, mainly through the agency of state and regional policies, with the complex and sometimes quite technical problems of sustaining two not-very-friendly language groups in cities which need to remain unitary for most purposes. Belfast and Jerusalem, both in different ways unresolved cases, are cities where violence has for a long time been recurrent or chronic even when it has not been savagely acute.

Contested cities have developed in a variety of ways. In some cases the ethnic balance has changed for some reason, while in others existing ethnic admixtures have become newly problematic. Demographic change has been important. In Gdańsk, Trieste, Dublin, Belfast, Helsinki and Prague, for instance, the cities were originally urban settlements established by incoming people of one culture within a rural hinterland occupied by another. For long periods of time, often many centuries, this was not perceived as a difficulty. But at some point or other, conflict has tended to develop. Frequently the clash came during the late nineteenth century, as urbanisation brought the groups into closer contact. During this era the role of the state and of white-collar employment made matters such as language and education important to far more people than had previously been the case. 'The peasants coming to the city' was thus frequently the stimulus for change. Where this did not happen, perhaps because the main migrant stream was easily acculturated to the dominant urban community for some reason, conflict might be avoided. But at a later stage, as the city sub-urbanised and expanded into the countryside, the converse problem – 'the city coming to the peasants' – might add a further dimension to the conflict, as it did in twentieth-century Brussels. Another demo-graphic challenge, in a city where two consciously-distinct ethnic groups had previously established a *modus vivendi*, has been the in-migration of additional ethnic groups. The question then arises as to whether this new group will acculturate to the dominant group – perhaps the more expected outcome – or to the non-dominant group, or indeed to neither. This dimension was of particular significance in Montreal during the second half of the twentieth century, and appears in another form in the deepening division between ultra-orthodox and secular Jews in contemporary Jerusalem. Another kind of third element is a dominant imperial elite, ruling over both of the main ethnic groups. Habsburg Trieste, Tsarist Helsinki and Ottoman (and later British Mandate) Jerusalem are prominent examples.

Once problems of this sort arise in cities, they are less easily ignored than is the case in mixed rural areas. Economic diversification, the expansion of the social role of the state, and developments in transport and medicine all increase the degree of interaction between different groups. The language of everyday use then becomes more critical. Previous conventions as to which language was spoken where, or the use of a commonly-understood local *patois*, are likely to become less robust in the face of a more active centralising state (local, regional or national). Sometimes, as in Belfast or Jerusalem or the cities of the former Yugoslavia, religious difference can be as important an ethnic delimiter as language. The workplace and the school have been par-ticularly important *loci* for these issues. Whether separate educational provision should be made for non-dominant ethnic groups has been a frequent question, as has control over resources and curriculum. Equally, whether such provision should be at primary school level only, or should extend to secondary and university levels, has been an issue. Control of the economy has been equally crucial. What has been the relationship between ethnic-group conflict in cities and the mater-ial circumstances of the people concerned? What happens in a context where the political and social facts dictate conflict and separation, but proximity and economy require interaction? The case studies will explore the relationship between economy and ethnicity. Likewise the role of transport and communication will be examined.

Historians, perhaps, would be wise not to refer to the 'resolution' of contested city problems. Interventions of various kinds are often intended to bring about permanent change, and sometimes they appear to have done so. But experience of these case studies suggests that terms like 'resolution' and permanency' need to be used with great caution. Better, perhaps, to examine the variety of responses to contested city problems, and to regard all present circumstances as points on a continuum. Such responses may be categorised under three headings. First, external interventions, which break down into two sub-categories of interventions by international agencies and interventions – hostile or reconciliatory – by other states. Secondly, responses by the state. These may take the form of policy interventions by the central state, by a regional state where it exists, and/or by the local city government. Again, such responses may be reconciliatory or otherwise. Thirdly, ethnic communities in contested cities developed their own informal social processes in response to conflict. These range from essentially benign 'coping strategies' to genocidal aggression.

Contested cities are of course prime targets for hostile foreign intervention. Where the intervention succeeds, the local outcome is normally role-reversal. In 1939 ethnically-German Danzig, a Free City under League of Nations supervision, was the cue for the Nazi invasion of Poland. In 1945, on the other hand, the westward advance of the Red Army caused the majority of the population of cities like Danzig and Breslau to flee, to be replaced within months by a Polish population. Many of these incomers were themselves refugees from the USSR, fleeing from Wilno as it became Vilnius and from Lwow as it became Lvov (Davies:429). Sometimes, as in the case of Jerusalem in 1948 or Nicosia in 1974 the outcome, if not the purpose, of military intervention has been the partition of a city.

More frequently, perhaps, contested cities have changed hands as part of the spoils of war, in the context of a postwar settlement. In these cases the victorious allies, rather than the conqueror as such, may determine the outcome. Thus Trieste was transferred from Austria to Italy after the First World War, but not to Yugoslavia after the Second. Thessaloniki's capture by Greece in 1912 was challenged by Bulgaria, and required the endorsement of great power ratification before it was confirmed. Prague became the capital of a Czechoslovak state in 1918 as a result of the war, although it had already established a generation earlier, through other means, that its ethos was no longer German but Czech. Pressburg, on the other hand, became Bratislava, the regional capital of Slovakia, at the same time even though Slovak-speakers then comprised but a small minority of its population. In the case of Jerusalem the Balfour Declaration of 1917 carried more weight than commitments made to Arab leaders earlier in the war, so that Jerusalem under the British Mandate became more Jewish rather than more Arab. Conversely, external military intervention has sometimes introduced a long-term ethnic contest into a previously unproblematic situation. Montreal ceased to be an exclusively French city with the military defeat of French Canada by Britain in 1760. Brussels only became a majority Francophone city following the overthrow of the Austrian Netherlands during the French revolution and the subsequent failure of the short-lived United Netherlands experiment. The Brussels case is also an example of an international settlement – the Congress of Vienna in 1815 – being reversed by forces internal to the conflict.

As well as attempted resolution through conquest and/or great power dispensation, attempts have occasionally been made to resolve contested city problems through some form of internationalisation of the city. Such a move has usually been tried where the ethnic realities or 'facts on the ground', and sometimes the economic realities as well, are too far out of kilter with wider geopolitical realities to allow one or the other to determine the outcome. Thus in 1919 Danzig was ethnically German, but its hinterland was Polish. It was believed that its economic interests lay with Poland, while Germany had lost the war. A 'Free City', under League of Nations supervision, was the compromise outcome implemented by the Treaty of Versailles. In similar circumstances the Allies attempted to create a 'Free Territory of Trieste' after 1945. But Trieste was returned to Italy in 1954 when developments in the cold war and Yugoslav non-alignment meant that the wishes of the city's Italian majority could be privileged over those of the rural hinterland, as well as over economic considerations. In 1912–13 the great powers briefly considered making Thessaloniki a city-state under the leadership of the majority Jewish community. The internationalisation of Jerusalem has been proposed frequently in modern history and has remained the official United Nations position since 1947. These case studies will provide an opportunity to assess whether the free city is simply a failed model, or whether the apparent weakening of the nation state in the contemporary world may revive its potential as a problem-solving mechanism.

Some states have pursued a *laissez faire* policy towards their con-tested cities. More often they respond actively. The chapters which follow will explore some of the ways in which they have done so. First we need to distinguish between levels of government: national, local and – where it exists – regional. Sometimes, as in Belfast for most of the period 1922 to 1972 (regional and local), or in Jerusalem since 1967 (national and local), different tiers have pulled mainly in the same direction. In other contexts, such as Montreal – during the 1970s espe-cially – national and regional government have pursued different visions of the city's future. Local government helped to create a pre-dominantly Czech ethos in late nineteenth-century Prague before Habsburg central government was committed to such an approach. Likewise, local government in Habsburg Trieste was solidly Italian, in a city where the central administration remained German and a sizeable Slovene minority was beginning to assert itself. In the history of Gdańsk, where changes in sovereignty have been more frequent than changes in ethnic identity, the story has been more complex. In Brussels too, where governmental change at various levels charac-terised the late twentieth century as it did the early nineteenth, the roles of central and regional government need to be explored in some detail. We shall also need to consider the extent to which local govern-ment can alleviate wider conflicts over sovereignty.

The activities of the state may affect urban ethnic relationships in a variety of policy areas, including language policy, education policy from primary school to university level, planning and housing policy, and the structure of local and regional government itself (including powers, voting systems and boundaries). Immigration policy, economic policy and transport policy are also likely to have an impact in the context of a contested city. Sometimes, such policies have been quite frankly and explicitly designed to achieve ethnic change – the creation of 'facts on the ground' – such as the planning policy pursued by both central and local government in contemporary Jerusalem. In other cases, cities have put off what many would regard as essential modernisation. The Province of Quebec had no public department of education until 1964, and Montreal's education provision continued to operate through a Victorian system of denominationally-based school boards until the 1980s, in order to stave off the linguistic conflict which it was feared would follow any change. The continued operation into the nineteenth century of the confessionally-based *millet* system in the cities of the Ottoman Empire, such as Constantinople, Thessaloniki and Jerusalem, was another attempt to keep the winds of change away from a precarious structure.

Changes in the circumstances of contested cities have often been brought about by external or governmental intervention at some level. But organic facts on the ground – not just those deliberately constructed by state power – have also been important. Ethnic groups in contested cities have developed and evolved through a variety of non-state processes. Sometimes these have worked to alleviate conflict, and at other times they have exacerbated them. In Belfast, for example, the long tradition of savage, intercommunal rioting has played a major part in shaping the city's community relations, the operation of its labour market, its residential patterns and even its overall demographic trends. In Jerusalem too, this first became the case during the British Mandate era, before being compounded by later periods of open warfare. In both cases separation has been reinforced during the past generation by patterns of terrorist violence and state repression. Likewise, Belfast and Jerusalem have been the main cockpits, rather than in any sense the ameliorators, of conflict within their wider contexts. At a lower level of animosity, Brussels and Montreal have also been at the heart of wider national/regional disputes. Trieste and Danzig/Gdańsk, on the other hand, have been cities in conflict with their own hinterlands. Had Danzig not been German in culture it would have become part of Poland in 1919 rather than 1945. Had Trieste not been Italian, Yugoslavia's post-1945 boundary would have been drawn 20 miles further to the north-west.

By and large, the peoples of contested cities have tried to come to terms with their own divisions by pursuing courses of action intended to keep overt conflict within a mutually-understood structure of physical and behavioural boundaries, while at the same time pursuing strategies which maximise benefits to their own ethnic group. Non-dominant groups have often sought ethnic niches in the labour market, areas of work in particular industries and/or occupations which were left open to them for some reason. Equally, one of the strategies pursued by dominant groups has been to exclude rival communities from sought-after areas of work. Non-dominant groups in both contested and multicultural cities have also been constrained in their access to the housing market. Patterns and degrees of segregation have varied considerably, as have their causes but, in the case studies which follow, group residential patterns are always found to have some relevance. Patterns of ethnic behaviour in contested cities differ little in some respects from modes of ethnic relations found in all cities where there are ethnic divisions. Thus the labour and housing history of the Belfast Catholics or the Montreal Francophones is not entirely dissimilar to that of the Irish in Britain or Black and Hispanic groups in North American cities. The relationship between ethnicity, economy and housing is an important one, and will be followed through in most of the case studies which follow.

Economic and spatial pressures in large urban settings might be expected to encourage integration. One of the more remarkable features of urban ethnic conflict is the way that group boundaries have been preserved in the context of thousands of individual choices and life histories. Part of the explanation of course is the cultural and behavioural baggage which people bring to cities with them – histories, belief systems and languages being the main ones. Further differences may develop within the urban context, as additional group memories are accumulated. The multicultural cities of North America have in the main been characterised by patterns of 'neighbourhood succession' over the past century or more, whereby ethnic communities have tended to move onwards and upwards, leaving their old neighbourhoods to incoming groups, with relatively little sentimentality or struggle. In contested cities this is less likely to happen, because neighbourhoods and landmarks acquire symbolic significance. In contemporary Northern Ireland, for instance, Protestants have clung tenaciously to tiny urban enclaves within what has become Catholic territory, including certain streets and road junctions which are perceived to mark local ethnic boundaries, even where this flies is the face of demography and communal needs. In other cities, too, public spaces and residential neighbourhoods which are perceived as historic territory can assume a significance of their own. Jerusalem is of course the most prominent example of this. Even in this extreme case, however, where many sites do indeed have long-standing historic significance, we shall see that circumstantial as well as primordial factors have played an important role in establishing their contemporary salience.

We also need to explore ways in which ethnic boundaries have resisted erosion – and sometimes succumbed to erosion – as a result of individual choices. Language difference may, at first sight, appear to be an important and objective ethnic boundary marker. But in many of the cases studied there is evidence of a local dialect or *patois* with a high level of cross-communal currency. The *triestino* and *brusseleir* dialects are two such examples. More commonly, there have been long periods of time in many contested cities where the process of 'language shift' has operated, driven by urbanisation and social mobility. In such cases it was widely accepted that certain public activities would be conducted in one language, whereas private and domestic activities might be conducted in another. In cities like Trieste, Brussels, Montreal and Danzig it was accepted that social and occupational mobility required a shift to the dominant language. It normally took a significant increase in the number of migrants or upwardly-mobiles in a city to halt or reverse such a trend. If this point was reached, culturally-focused nationalism would typically assert the injustice of the situation and assert the equality – or often the superiority – of the non-dominant language. Language difference is, therefore, a rather less objective indicator of ethnic difference than might at first appear to be the case. Language shift and language maintenance are often communal strategies, the development or rejection of which has been determined by circumstances.

Language difference has to develop an ideological underpinning, which it may or may not do, before it can assume ethnic salience. Religious belief, on the other hand, has tended to generate a less permeable sense of difference. Of course religious difference does not necessarily have ethnic salience: Methodist, Catholic or Jewish congregations in contemporary England are not ethnic groups, although some English Catholics and Jews may regard their identities as broadly ethnic as well as specifically confessional. Thus, except in cases where language difference is underpinned by a differentiating ideology or values, religious difference in fact provides a stronger barrier against erosion of ethnic difference by, for instance, reducing the likelihood of widespread intermarriage and strengthening pressure for separate schooling. These case studies will examine the significance of the content of cultural differences in maintaining or eroding boundaries, including explorations of how and why it has not happened on an appreciable scale, and how individual instances of it have been accommodated. Likewise the significance, or otherwise, of levels of intermarriage across group boundaries will be analysed. To what extent have personal relationships across the ethnic frontier eroded or eased ethnic tensions, and how have contested cities sought to contain their potential impact?

All the above are communal 'coping' practices, evolved for the most part informally. We also need to examine conscious efforts to erode boundaries by means of potentially cross-cutting ideologies. The most prominent of these have been socialist ideologies and trade union movements. Socialist theorists have differed widely on these matters, some viewing ethnic minority movements as unnecessary diversions from class struggle or even as petty bourgeois reactionary movements, while others have linked national movements to class struggle or categorised them as 'liberation movements'. More important in these contexts, perhaps, have been practicalities. How have socialist political parties and trade unions sought to build support in contested cities? Trieste is perhaps the best example from among our case studies of a local leadership making sustained efforts to sustain support across the ethnic divide. Yet even in this case, ethnically-based divisions had become formalised within the structures of the labour movement before the First World War. In Belfast the non-nationalist labour movement was never able to attract large numbers of Catholics into its political or its industrial sector even before the emergence of a distinctly Irish Catholic/Nationalist wing of the movement after 1909. The roles, strategies and fortunes of political and industrial labour movements will be explored in the case studies, both in the formative pre-1914 period and more recently. 'The unity of labour' has been the slogan under which inter-ethnic collaboration has been most systematically pursued. Other examples, much more limited or recent in scope – sometimes pursued through the medium of political parties, sometimes not – have been appeals for religious collaboration, through 'women's movements', or simply through 'peace and reconciliation' rhetoric.

The six cases which this book will explore in detail have been chosen to represent a range of outcomes: varieties of unilateral resolution, struggles to achieve political pluralism, and ongoing conflict. They also reflect the interplay of international, state and social factors which shapes the character of each individual conflict. A comparative case study-approach has been adopted so as to identify not only the many common features of these conflicts but also the unique elements produced by the operation of chance factors. Other cases might have been chosen. Ethnic competition and contestation occur with equal frequency beyond the western world. Only lack of knowledge and space have limited the geographical scope of this book. In Europe, too, other examples might have been chosen. Prague, Bratislava, Helsinki and Dublin are all twentieth-century capital cities which converted successfully from the hegemony of one culture to that of another. As well as the case of Danzig/Gdańsk, which is examined in detail in the next chapter, Thessaloniki, Vilnius, Wroclaw and Algiers all saw the abrupt exodus of formerly-dominant communities, leaving the city for others to occupy as an outcome of war. In Nicosia, equally abruptly, military intervention prompted a more localised flight which resulted in the physical partition of the city. In Beirut, Istanbul and Sarajevo delicate, longstanding ethnic balances were also upset by social change and warfare. Barcelona, by contrast, is an example of a rather unusual kind, where the labels 'dominant' and 'non-dominant' are rather hard to apply consistently. Strasbourg, finally, is a case where the objective indicators of ethnic difference, both linguistic and to some extent historical, have been present, but a contest of the type we are studying has not emerged. Several of these cases are discussed briefly below.

Three new capitals: Prague, Bratislava and Helsinki

Unlike the eastern outposts of the German Empire, Prague under Habsburg Austria ceased, during the course of the nineteenth century, to be a machine for the assimilation of Slavs to the *Deutschtum*. This was visible, at its simplest, in the external face of the city, where compulsory street signs were originally in German, with Czech below. In 1861 this order of display was reversed, until in 1893 a Czech-dominated city council removed German signs altogether (Sayer:169). As with other linguistically-divided and rapidly-growing cities, reliable statistics on the changing ethnic balance are hard to come by (Table 1.1). First, language difference was not perceived to constitute ethnic difference before the mid-nineteenth century. Secondly, while the predominantly middle-class German community tended not to speak Czech most Czechs, at least until the late nineteenth century, needed to know German. Thirdly, the situation was complicated by the position of the Jewish community, which was broadly-speaking united in religion but divided by language. Anti-semitism was a feature of both the Czech and German communities, but Czech-German intermarriage was quite common among – though not between – Christians and

Table 1.1   **Prague: Population by main language spoken, 1869–1910** (city and four suburbs)

	Total population	German-speakers %	Czechs and others %
1869	204,488	?	?
1880	255,928	15.3	84.7
1890	314,158	12.2	87.8
1900	394,030	7.6	92.4
1910	442,017	7.0	93.0

Source: Cohen:92–3

Jews. The mother of the Prague novelist Franz Kafka (1883–1924) came from an upper-middle-class Jewish family, and spoke German. Kafka's father was a Jewish butcher from a small Czech-speaking village, who preferred to speak Czech. Franz's governess spoke only Czech, but he was sent to a German-language school and wrote in German (Sayer:166–8). The general level of private contact across the linguistic boundary was, until around 1900 at least, significantly greater than the level of public contact. The dominant German minority tended to be concentrated in the inner wards, while the outer wards and the industrial suburbs which were incorporated into the city after 1900 were almost entirely Czech. Other than this, there was little in the way of ethnic residential segregation in the city (Cohen:278).

As elsewhere in central Europe, society in Prague before the mid-nineteenth century was based on ranks and orders. Language was a means of communication rather than an ethnic marker. It is true that adherence to the Czech language and resentment at the growing power and wealth of German-speakers had been a focus for identity in late-medieval Bohemia. But the linear link which nineteenth-century Czech historians sought to establish between their movement and this earlier world, which had been destroyed at the Battle of the White Mountain in 1620, was highly tendentious. Modern Czech nationalism was plebeian. It was based on a language which had largely disappeared from literary and public life by 1800 and which owed its survival in large extent to rural Catholic priests. But in the nineteenth century a sense of 'linguistic kinship ... supplanted historical experience' (Sayer:185–91). Linguistic similarity meant that the people of nearby Slovakia (Upper Hungary), notwithstanding a millennium of separate history, could be imagined as part of the nation. Ironically many of the early intellectual protagonists of the Czech national movement, the *buditelé* (awakeners), were not native-Czech speakers. As Miroslav Hroch has noted, the first phase of non-dominant nationalisms in the nineteenth century was very often initiated by intellectuals who hailed from, or who were at least comfortably acculturated to, the dominant culture.

The popular challenge to German leadership in Prague began only around 1860. It was stimulated, as elsewhere, by the expansion of the role of the central state, by mass education, and by the consequent increase in the importance of written language and communication. Prague grew especially rapidly in the late nineteenth century and, while a part of its hinterland was German- rather than Czech-speaking, German migrants in search of big-city life tended to gravitate to

Vienna. Thus rapid population growth in Prague meant rapid *Czech* population growth and a shift in the ethnic balance: a city which may have been up to 30 per cent German-speaking in 1870 had become 94 per cent Czech by 1910. In her studies of Trieste, Marina Cattaruzza has shown how the rise in Slovene numbers across the same period reflected not increased Slovene migration into the predominantly Italian-speaking city but rather increased Slovenian consciousness and resistance to language shift. Certainly in the Prague case there is evidence of the same earlier link between language shift and upward mobility. It is apparent not only in the existence of linguistically-mixed individual families like the Kafkas, but also in statistics such as those which indicated that in 1891, almost a decade after the separation of the Charles University into separate German- and Czech-language institutions, 20 per cent of students who chose to study through German were in fact native Czech-speakers (Sayer:169). But overall the impression must be that the pattern in Prague differed from Trieste. The demographic weight of Czech-speakers coming into Prague was genuinely formidable, meaning that the pressure on the relatively small German-speaking lower-middle and working class was towards acculturation into what had been the non-dominant community, rather than vice versa (Cohen:281). Like the non-dominant Catholic middle class in Dublin, and unlike the much smaller one in Belfast (which had more in common with the situation of the Trieste Slovenes), the Czech middle class of Prague had by the end of the nineteenth century reached an ethnic take-off point. While control of the high points of finance and industry by the dominant minority was still obvious enough to be an irritant to them, the ethnic middle class was proportionately large enough to have reversed the overall trend. The liberalisation of political life which in Prague and Dublin, by the end of the nineteenth century, gave control of local government to formerly non-dominant groups was another force towards change in these societies, differentiating them to some extent from the situation in Germany or Hungary at that time.

By the end of the nineteenth century Prague was a city troubled by anti-Semitism and by Czech-German ethnic rivalries. But it was not characterised by significant ethnic residential segregation nor by ethnic violence. In 1918 it seemed to be working towards a new multi-cultural accommodation, capable of taking in its stride the transition to its new role as capital of a Czechoslovak state. In fact, by 1945 Prague has instead become a monocultural, monoethnic and unilingual city. From the start there was sufficient bitterness about the German-dominated past, and anxiety about the future, for the state to decide that German should not become an official language in Czechoslovakia and that even though Germans outnumbered the officially-recognised Slovaks in the new state no seats in government should be earmarked for them (Rubes:15–18). But Germans, though greatly reduced in number as well as status, still thrived in the economy and society of inter-war Prague. What ended the existence of their community was the emergence of radical and irredentist German nationalism in the nearby Sudetenland, together with the rise to power of the Nazi movement in Germany itself. These related developments denied Prague's Germans any chance of achieving the discreet near-invisibility which preserved the individual futures of Dublin's Protestants. Most of Prague's Jews, regardless of which language they espoused, were murdered in Nazi camps. Prague's Germans, along with their fellow-Germans throughout Czechoslovakia, were expelled from the country in 1946.

Prague's linguistic neighbour, Bratislava, is more a case of a city which had ethnic identity thrust upon it. Since 1993 it has for the first time been the capital of an independent sovereign state of Slovakia. Before 1918 it was for many centuries a part of the Habsburg Empire, governed for most of the time from nearby Vienna. It retained a strong German ethos, even during the post-1867 period when it was governed from Budapest. Apart from the close proximity of their two languages, direct Czech-Slovak links had existed only briefly, back in the tenth century. From 1919 to 1939, however, and again from 1945 to 1992, Bratislava was governed as part of Czechoslovakia from Prague. Between 1939 and 1945 a Nazi puppet government took its orders direct from Berlin. Known for centuries as Pressburg by the Austrians, as Pozsony by the Hungarians and as Presporek by Slovaks, it has only carried the name Bratislava since 1921. Only in that year, indeed, did the census for the first time record a Slovak majority in the population of the city. As late as 1910 the predominant ethos of the city was still German, while the largest population group described itself as Magyar. The self-defined Slovak proportion of the population was less than 15 per cent of a city with a total population of only 78,223. The Slovak population of the much bigger city of Budapest was almost twice as large. The slowly-developing national movement had argued for 50 years prior to 1918 over where a future Slovak capital should be located. Although Bratislava was the largest centre in the Slovakian region it was probably the least 'national', and many were bemused when it emerged as the regional capital within the new state of Czechoslovakia (Henderson: 1–4; Glettler: 295–319).

Prior to 1918 Pressburg was, like Budapest, a focal point for the assimilation of Slovaks to Hungary's dominant culture. This was only in part the result of the aggressive Magyarisation policies pursued by the Budapest government after 1867. It also had to do with the relatively small numbers, remote rural locations and very low literacy levels of Slovak society. In some rural areas illiteracy was the norm, while at 33 per cent and 20 per cent respectively, Budapest and Pressburg/Bratislava led the way in Slovak literacy. There was, unsurprisingly, very little in the way of Slovakian literary culture: state secondary education in Slovak had been discontinued in 1881, and the private schools used Czech-language text books into the early twentieth century. In 1907, at a time when 63 per cent of elementary schoolchildren in the Czech lands studied through Czech, 90 per cent of elementary schools in Slovakia taught through Magyar (Sayer:197). Similarly the religious texts of both Catholic and Protestant churches in Slovakia were in Czech. Evidence suggests that, across the whole period 1800–1914, the level of exogamy among Germans, Hungarians and Slovaks in Pressburg was in excess of 50 per cent. In these circumstances the emergence of a specifically Slovak national bourgeoisie was both slight and late. The strongest glimmer of Slovak ethnic consciousness in urban areas prior to 1914 was in the organised labour movement: in 1905 Slovak workers in Pressburg broke away from a labour movement which had been German in origin, to form an independent movement based on a policy of federal autonomy. The Hungarian social democrats put many obstacles, especially financial ones, in the way of the breakaway movement, and only financial support from Czech social democrats in Vienna enabled it to proceed.

Essentially, Slovak ethnicity before the First World War remained rural and relatively undeveloped. As late as 1921, a Czechoslovak census enumerator reported being told by a respondent in one village that 'if the bread is buttered on the Hungarian side I am a Magyar. If it is buttered on the Czech side, I am a Slovak'. The same census recorded that whereas 46 per cent of the population of the Czech lands lived in urban settlements of more than 2,000 inhabitants, fewer than 24 per cent of the population of Slovakia did so (Sayer:181, 197). The County of Bratislava had a slight overall majority of Slovaks in the population in 1900, at a time when the city itself was only 15 per cent Slovak. Yet the city was a considerable consumer of people: urban death rates were still high, so that even a slowly-growing city required substantial immigration in order to maintain its demographic trajectory. While it is true that a significant proportion of the population before 1914 were

German-speakers, often retired people from Vienna, the rural Slovak hinterland must have been an important source of migrants. This is further evidence of the city's continuing role in assimilating migrants to the dominant culture – which in the case of Pressburg, because of its proximity to Vienna, was German as well as Hungarian. Pressburg is therefore a city where national consciousness followed political independence rather than led it. As Glettler argues (1992:319), 'a comparison of the two cities [Bratislava and Budapest] shows that it was not until after the First World War, when they were separated by political borders, that a decisive change ... took place'.

It was, initially, Czech influence and support which aroused Slovak consciousness *vis-à-vis* imperial Austria and Hungary. Paradoxically, opposition to Czech domination was one of the factors which brought Slovak consciousness to a fuller maturity. During the inter-war period Slovak opposition to the Czechs developed, mainly as a rural phenomenon, to the extent that when Nazi Germany overran Czechoslovakia in 1939 it created the puppet regime of Slovakia as an independent state for the first time. Because of its relative remote location Slovakia experienced some industrialisation in the 1933–45 period as first the Czechoslovak government, and then the Nazi regime, developed an arms industry there. Under the Communists after 1948 this development took off in earnest: between 1948 and 1989 the agricultural proportion of the workforce fell from 60 per cent to 12 per cent. Thus, whereas the constitution of 1948 made the city of Prague a separate province while leaving Bratislava within a much larger provincial unit, by 1968 the latter has become the second city in the country and was officially designated capital of the Slovak Republic (Henderson:116). While the breakaway movement which cut Slovakia entirely free from the Czech Republic in 1993 was initiated by 'the rural values of the closed society that [President Vladimir] Mečiar represented', Bratislava remained 'largely hostile' to these values, and when the centre-left leader Rudolf Schuster toppled Mečiar in 1999 with 57 per cent of the national vote, the level of his support in Bratislava was as high as 75 per cent (Henderson:70).

Like Prague, Helsinki was a city created by speakers of one language, in which a previously-subordinate minority came to challenge the domination of that language, before continuing to predominate in the capital of a newly-independent state after 1918. The social processes, as we shall see, were similar, but different geopolitical circumstances produced some interesting variations in outcome. Swedes had settled in numbers in southern Finland from the late medieval period, with their main centre at Åbo/Turku. Further east, Helsingfors/Helsinki was founded by the Swedish crown in 1550 as a trading centre. It remained a small, Swedish-speaking town at the centre of a Swedish-speaking province, with a population of only 3,072 as late as 1800. In 1808 Finland was conquered by Russia, and became a Grand Duchy within the Tsarist empire. The capital was immediately moved from Åbo to Helsingfors, which was developed along grander lines, and the University followed suit in 1827. Finland gave no particular trouble, and Russia was able to run it with what, by its standards, was a relatively light hand for most of the period down to 1917. The majority population of Finnish-speakers had no expectation or previous history of statehood, and neither they – nor to any great extent the economically-dominant Swedish minority – hankered for a return to rule from Sweden. Only from 1899 onwards was a serious programme of Russification attempted. The traditional Finnish Diet, representing only a small minority of the population, was replaced in 1907 by a parliament elected by male householders, but its powers remained few. The success of the Bolshevik revolution in Russia in November 1917 caused the Finnish parliament to declare immediate independence. A short but savage civil war followed in 1918, during which Red terror was followed by White victory and counter-terror (Schoolfield:65, 207–8, 223, 255–63).

A century of Russian rule had left very little impact on Finland (Hamalainen:6). But the Russian dimension to Finland's life, and the manner of its ending, had some important effects on the emergence and development of ethnolinguistic rivalry between Finnish- and Swedish-speakers. By the 1860s the Russians had come to realise that some mild encouragement of Finnish *vis-à-vis* Swedish might help to weaken any vestigial attachment of the local elite to Sweden. Conversely, the fact that Russia rather than Sweden was the imperial overlord took at least a little of the edge off Finnish hostility towards Swedish culture while, as we shall below, giving rather more of a boost to Finnish national patriotism amongst Swedish-speakers. The Russification period is a little more difficult to assess. The same social forces in late-nineteenth-century Europe which produced the phenomenon that manifested itself as Russification, Germanisation, Magyarisation, 'peasants into Frenchmen' and so forth, also produced counter-forces among non-dominant groups such as 'advance through Czech' and 'Irish Ireland'. Thus a state policy of Russification in Finland coincided with the rise of ethnolinguistic movements amongst both the Swedish-speaking and Finnish-speaking populations. Tension between these two latter groups was considerably reduced by their common opposition to Russification (Hamalainen:15–18). But perhaps Russia's greatest impact on Finland's internal ethnic rivalries was in the manner of her departure from the scene. The Bolshevik rise to power caused the Finnish Reds to take a more conciliatory approach towards their eastern neighbour, while non-socialists increased their demand for full and unilateral Finnish independence. The Finnish civil war of 1918 was a brutal and bloody business, followed by 8,000 executions and 80,000 internments (Schoolfield:263). But it was not an ethnic war. It is true that the Reds were almost exclusively ethnic Finns and, as the fight continued they did not suppress any opportunity to type-cast the Whites as 'Swedish'. But the victorious Whites were in fact middle-class urban Finns and rural Finns of all classes, led in the main by ethnically-Swedish officers. The outcome of the civil war, therefore, had the effect of generally strengthening the standing of Swedish-speakers as patriotic Finns and, in specific terms building them into the structure of the new state as civil servants and army officers to an extent that would not otherwise have been possible. The link with Bolshevik Russia caused Finland's Reds to be seen as unpatriotic. A thoroughgoing revisionism within the Social Democratic Party was able to redress the latter problem in the early 1920s, but the continued high status of Swedish-speakers in the new state was a matter which was only resolved after some bitterness over the two following decades.

At the end of the period of Swedish rule in 1808, the small town of Helsingfors and its province of Nyland had been peopled predominantly by Swedish-speakers. The city grew steadily during the nineteenth century, to 91,000 by 1900. We do not know the ethno-linguistic proportions of the early migrants, but it is clear that Finnish-speakers coming into the city before 1850 were by and large 'Swedicised'. There was little sign before 1850 that Helsingfors would develop into a Finnish-speaking city. But around mid-century there developed an enthusiasm among Swedish-speaking intellectuals for the Finnish language, including even some who could not speak it (Schoolfield:60-61,126). This was a common phenomenon in European minority nationalist movements, identified by Miroslav Hroch (1985:23) as 'Phase A'. It was given added salience in the Finland context by the fact that the Swedish-speaking community was cut off from previous political links with Sweden and committed to a future as part of Finland. 'We are not Swedes; we can never become Russians; let us therefore be Finns' is a statement attributed to this group (McRae 1997: front papers). But by the 1880s a more characteristic ethnic division had emerged, with ethnic Finnish nationalism becoming more assertive of its role in public life and society, while a Swedish party had also emerged, based on ethnic defence – 'a little party of officials who want to keep the jobs for themselves', as they were described by their opponents (Schoolfield:135-37).

High levels of Finnish bilingualism means that the data have to be handled with caution, but it is clear that after 1850 migration from Finnish-speaking areas into Helsingfors predominated. Whereas in 1850 Finns were the group more likely to be bilingual, by 1900 42 per cent of Swedes were bilingual, as against only 30 per cent of Finns (Schoolfield:140). The linguistic transition in Helsinki (as we may now call it) displays a pattern and timing common to many of Europe's contested cities (see table 1.2). Helsingfors ceased to work as a machine for the Swedification of urban migrants, and by the end of the century was, for the first time in its history, a predominantly Finnish-speaking city.

Like Prague, Helsinki displayed a pattern in which the formerly-dominant group predominated in the central and older parts of the city, with the non-dominant group predominating in the expanding industrial suburbs. But a different political context meant that it took longer for the implications of this demographic shift to work through. In 1873, for instance, when the city was one-third Finnish-speaking, only three out of forty-eight councillors were native Finnish-speakers. The city council continued to be elected on a restricted franchise until 1917. Economic power remained in Swedish hands until well into the twentieth century. In the University of Helsinki in 1900 two-thirds of the student body was Finnish-speaking, but two-thirds of the faculty was Swedish-speaking and two-thirds of classes were conducted in Swedish (Schoolfield:156). A British writer in 1915 found that the

Table 1.2   Helsinki: Population by main language spoken, 1870–1980

	Total population	Swedish %	Finnish %	Russian %	Other %
1870	32,111	57	26	12	5
1881	42,800	52	34	10	4
1891	65,500	46	45		
1900	93,600	42	51		
1910	143,400	35	59		
1980	483,000	89			

Sources: Schoolfield, pp.139–40; McRae 1997:93; www.library.uu.nl/wesp/populstat/Europe/finlandt.htm

Finnish- and Swedish-speaking peoples in Helsinki 'mix little and do not speak very nicely of each other', yet had no 'radically different conceptions of life or values' (McRae 1997: front papers).

The 1920s and 1930s marked the high point of ethnolinguistic conflict in Helsinki. The establishment of a new relationship between the two languages had been delayed by the previous era of Russian domination and the circumstances in which it had ended. Party politics mitigated the conflict to some extent, as Finnish Nationalists were opposed by a surprising alliance of convenience between the Swedish People's Party and the reconstructed Social Democrats. The language issue, though bitter, never assumed a violent form, notwithstanding the appearance for a while of a Finnish fascist movement. The ethnolinguistic bitterness of the inter-war period was, in essence, unfinished business of the independence period.

Since 1945 linguistic conflict has become a relatively minor part of life in Finland. Whereas in the mid-nineteenth century Finns needed to be bilingual in Swedish in order to operate effectively in the city, by 1950 the situation was reversed: only 33 per cent of Finnish-speakers, but 83 per cent of Swedish-speakers, reported being bilingual in the other's language (McRae 1997:100). In 1977, 67 per cent of Helsinki Swedes thought that the most serious conflict in society was over matters of work and class, against only 16 per cent who identified language (McRae 1997:160). Since the 1960s it has become a fairly standard convention for a group talking in Swedish to switch to Finnish if a Finn joins the group. Analysts have in fact identified a widening gap between the constitutional/legal norms of the state, whereby Finnish and Swedish have equal status under the various language laws implemented since 1919, and the practical social reality: increasingly less, it seems, do Swedish-speakers in Helsinki and elsewhere claim their right to deal with public officials and others through the medium of Swedish. Although there is a significant Swedish-speaking working class, and although the absolute number of Finnish-speakers in the upper echelons of Helsinki society now considerably exceeds the numbers of Swedish-speakers, it is still probably the case that the minority Swedes are – like the Protestants of Dublin – on balance a privileged group (McRae 1997:160, 100, 112, 127–28).

The spoils of war: Wroclaw and Thessaloniki

In contrast to the evolution of Helsingfors into Helsinki, the transformation of 'German Breslau' into 'Polish Wroclaw' in 1945 was a sharp and sudden change, although the city's historians go beyond these two competing perceptions of their subject to draw attention to Czech, Austrian and Jewish themes in the city's history. They show 'how the political and cultural connections of the city have been transformed many times over', before the harsh dichotomy took its final shape (Davies & Moorhouse:11). Breslau, the capital of Silesia, was a semi-independent dynastic possession of the Habsburgs until it was taken by Prussia in 1741. A city with a considerable cultural heritage, it also developed in the later nineteenth century as Germany's third-largest city and the regional capital of a major industrial area, with a population of around 100,000 in 1849, rising to 629,000 in 1939 (Davies & Moorhouse:250, 375). Like Danzig, which we examine later in more detail, Breslau was mainly German in character. But in a Prussian state where King Frederick II (1740–86), at least, preferred speaking French to German, it was not a matter of concern that Polish was also a language of everyday use, unquestioned until the early nineteenth century. We do not know what proportion of the population would have regarded themselves as 'Polish' during this period, although 16 per cent of Breslau university students were so described in 1817. Religion is a less reliable ethnic indicator in this case, but the Catholic proportion of the city's growing population rose from 26 per cent to 39 per cent during the first half of the century (Davies & Moorhouse:250, 375, 244–45). This was primarily at the relative expense of Protestants, for the Jewish population remained at around 1 per cent until the later nineteenth century, when in rose to around 7 per cent.

Throughout the nineteenth century regional dialects of both German and Polish continued to thrive, at a literary as well as a popular level. But there can be no doubt that linguistic nationalism began to grow after 1815. There is less agreement among observers about the linguistic face of Breslau. One German writer noted in 1840 that, although Polish was heard on the streets, 'Breslau is thoroughly German city, the Poles are guests here'. But in 1857 a German novelist complained that Breslau was 'very much polonised' and lacked 'the desired purity', while a Polish counterpart three years' later rejoiced that 'one can hear our speech at the very gates of the Silesian capital'. It is true that the eastern suburbs of Breslau, across the Oder, retained a more Polish ethos, but as the tide of nationalism, both Polish and German, began to rise Breslau steadily developed an especially brash culture, characteristic of frontier cities. 'It was more assertively German than other large German cities ... where there were no frontiers or minorities to worry about' (Davies & Moorhouse:304). The city's biographers summarise neatly a trend typical of many contested cities during this period: 'Poles ... had somehow to find a *modus vivendi*. Some of them simply lost their Polishness. Some found a balance between the two parts of their identity. Others reacted so fiercely against imperial German attitudes that they became militant Polish nationalists .... [But] social advancement in the rapidly expanding economy was largely dependent on the acceptance of a German identity' (Davies & Moorhouse:295, 302).

The re-creation of a Polish state in 1919 weakened Polishness in Breslau, siphoning off possible immigrants to work and study in Polish cities, while the Versailles settlement was a provocation and stimulus to German nationalism in the city. In 1920, and again in 1938, public buildings which symbolised Polish culture in the city were destroyed by mob action. In the Reichstag elections of Spring 1933 Breslau was one of only seven constituencies in Germany to return an absolute Nazi majority. It was at the centre of demands for the return of the nearby Sudetenland to the Reich. Perhaps not surprisingly, Breslau was one of the very last parts of Germany to surrender in May 1945. Although it had always laid claim to Danzig, Poland made no serious demand for Breslau prior to the Second World War. Yet by the end of July 1945 it was clear that this is what would happen.

Poland's late claim to Breslau had its origins partly in encouragement from the Soviet Union, and partly in response to the Soviet Union's own westward expansion into formerly-Polish territories. The western Ukrainian city of Lvov, for instance, had been predominantly Polish since the fourteenth century, and part of Austria from 1773 to 1918. During the inter-war period it was 50 per cent Polish Catholic and 30 per cent Jewish. In 1945 many of its Polish inhabitants fled to what was about to become Wroclaw. The Polish University of Wroclaw for instance, which opened its doors in September 1945, was staffed initially by exiles from Lvov (Davies & Moorhouse:429). That this could happen required not only diplomatic and demographic pressure from the Soviet Union but also concurrence from the Western powers. The 'Oder line', which Prime Minister Churchill and American President Truman had intended to insist on at the Potsdam negotiations with the Soviet Union in July 1945, would have partitioned Breslau along its river, retaining most of the city in Germany. In the event, Churchill fell from power half way through the Potsdam conference, and Truman accepted the revised 'Oder-Neisse' line, which left all of Breslau/Wroclaw firmly inside Poland. If Churchill is to be believed, he would not have accepted such an Allied concession, in which case it may be said that the national fate of Breslau/Wroclaw was decided in the polling booths of the United Kingdom!

In December 1945 Wroclaw's population of about 200,000 was less than 20 per cent Polish; by March 1947 the city was scarcely any larger, but now 90 per cent Polish. The bulk of the German population was expelled, to be replaced by Polish expellees from the east. Many of the latter were encouraged and assisted by grants from Poland's 'Repatriation Board'. Within a few years, even the German cemeteries had disappeared. 'One city has died', wrote a leading American journalist some years later, and 'in its place, and in its histories, there lives another'. German Breslau appears to be a thing of the past, like Danzig, like the formerly Italian towns of Trieste's Croatian hinterland, and like Palestinian Jaffa. But exile associations and newspapers have continued to attract support in sizeable numbers. 'I would rather have a fourth or fifth partition of Poland than [accept] that Breslau will stay Polish forever', declared a speaker at a Silesian exiles rally in 1985. In 1991, however, as part of German re-unification, the German state at last gave *de jure* recognition to the Oder-Neisse line, thereby accepting the reality of 'Wroclaw'. It seems likely that irredentist sentiment will fade with the current generation, rather than grow. But we cannot be certain that another jerk of history's rack will not reopen this and similar questions (Davies & Moorhouse:412, 415–19, 429–31, 475, 484).

Even less likely to be re-opened, perhaps, is the less well-known case of Thessaloniki. Founded by the Macedonian kingdom in the fourth century BC, it was later for many centuries second only to Constantinople within the Eastern Roman/Byzantine Empire. From 1430 until 1912 it was part of the Ottoman Empire. It was the central city of Macedonia and, at various times, the main trading centre for the Balkans. During the early modern period the Turks encouraged Jewish immigration from Spain and central Europe as well as from the Ottoman heartlands. By the sixteenth century half of the city's 30,000 inhabitants were Jews, with Turks pushing the Greeks into third place. Thessaloniki was retained by the Turks following the Greek War of Independence in the 1820s. The Greek/Christian population suffered considerably, but by 1841 it is estimated that the population of the city may have exceeded 60,000, with no major change in its ethnic balance since the sixteenth century (Zafiris:20–38).

Steady population growth continued through the nineteenth century, and Thessaloniki remained an important part of the Ottoman State. Mustapha Kemal 'Ataturk' was born and raised in the city, and the Young Turk movement began there is 1908. Nonetheless, the Greek State at last managed to take control of the city following the Balkan Wars of 1912–13. The first official census, taken by the Greeks in 1913, showed that an overall population which had now risen to 157,889 was still 39 per cent Jewish, 29 per cent Moslem and only 25 per cent Greek (Papagiannopoulos: 198). These figures are probably accurate enough, although the Greek calculation of the Bulgarian population in the city, at less than 4 per cent, may have been influenced by Bulgaria's competing claim to the city. The European Powers took considerable interest in the future shape of the region, and for some time the British delegation at the London Conference in 1913 toyed with a scheme for the internationalisation of the city, possibly under the leadership of the Jewish community, which had endeavoured to keep a neutral stance in the Balkan conflict. Thessaloniki's future was ultimately decided in favour of Greece, partly by the great powers deciding that Bulgaria could be compensated elsewhere, and partly by the Greek victory in the second Balkan war, following the assassination of the Greek King George in the city in March 1913.

Prior to its incorporation into the Greek state Thessaloniki was scarcely a cosmopolitan city. Only the organised labour movement showed any glimmering of a multi-national character, whereas residential segregation between the three main communities was high and association restricted to necessary business interactions (Gounaris:157, 171–2). But it was certainly a polyglot city: it had, for instance, sixteen newspapers, of which five were published in Ladino [Hispanic Jewish], four in Greek, three in Turkish, two in French, one in Bulgarian and one in Rumanian (Papagianopoulos:195). The Jews, followed by the Greeks, predominated in the city's economy, while the more prominent Muslims were civil servants or rentiers (Gounaris:164; Petridis:181). Inevitably Greece intended to reshape Thessaloniki as a Greek city. It was assisted in this by two harsh developments. Firstly, a major fire destroyed about two-thirds of the city in 1917. Previously a city of Levantine appearance, it was rebuilt on European lines. Even more important was the aftermath of the First World War, which brought ethnic Greek and Armenian refugees from Bulgaria, Russia and eastern Turkey, and, in greater numbers, from Asia Minor into the city. Under the terms of the Treaty of Lausanne in January 1923 the Greek and Turkish governments agreed to a compulsory exchange of populations which brought one and half million ethnic Greeks into Greece. A Thessaloniki population of 170,000 in 1920 rose during the mid-1920s to almost 500,000 before settling at 237,000 in 1930. The Greek proportion of the population had risen from 25 per cent to over 80 per cent in 15 years (Zafiris:36; Mitchell:74). In 1924 the Greek government established the country's second university in Thessaloniki (Petridis:191).

Uncontested cities? Barcelona and Strasbourg

Barcelona's story has been very different again. An important city since the thirteenth century, it is the capital and cultural centre of Catalonia, with a population of over 100,000 in the early nineteenth century, rising to 1.8 million in the late twentieth. Catalan is an established literary language with between six million and eight million regular Catalan speakers, making it by far the largest non-state language in Europe.[1] Prior to 1976 the Spanish state had, for much of modern history, pursued policies of discouragement, sometimes very stern, towards the Catalan language. It is now a city of two languages, the one that is locally-dominant not being the language of the central state. Migrants from other parts of Spain bring the nationally-dominant language with them, but generally they have lower social and economic status in the city. Perhaps because, unlike in Montreal, the incomers lack power, while the two languages are both members of the Romance language sub-group, leading experts deny that Barcelona is a contested city (Siguan). David Laitin has made a helpful distinction between 'rationalisation' or 'standardisation' of language and 'language hegemony'. In France and in the United Kingdom French and English respectively have achieved a hegemony, whereas the position of Castilian in Spain is more limited. It is the standard national language, but it does not dominate to the extent that strongly-supported state languages normally do.

The modern Catalan movement has its roots in the 1860s/1880s period. Napoleon had attempted to encourage Catalan, although as long as the Catalan commercial elite benefited from access to wider Spanish markets they had little interest in emphasising difference. But the late nineteenth century saw rising discontent among this group.

---

[1] In 1936, the year of the outbreak of civil war in Spain, the number of books published in Catalan had risen to 865, while 27 newspapers were published in the language. In that year 12 per cent of all Spain's publications were in Catalan. During the following decade the Franco regime imposed a complete ban on the public use of Catalan, with any Catalan publications being destroyed. A less extreme, but still discouraging policy towards Catalan was maintained until the end of the Franco era in 1976 (Laitin:301–2).

Madrid failed to provide either tariff support for its developing industries, or investment in the railway system and other infrastructure in a way that was favourable to the Barcelona region. This, combined with standard late nineteenth-century factors such as urbanisation, the spread of jobs requiring literacy, and the widening of general education produced a strong Catalanist movement, centred on Barcelona, and grounded in support from the industrial and commercial elite and from the expanding lower-middle class. Regarded as a right-wing movement at the end of the nineteenth century, and opposed by much of the labour movement as conservative, clericalist and backward looking, the Catalanist movement broadened its base of support during the first years of the twentieth century to draw in a significant proportion of the skilled working class. As the industrialisation of Barcelona developed and the city grew, immigration from southern Spain became increasingly important. Whereas only 5 per cent of Catalonia's population was from outside the region in 1910, this changed quite dramatically from the 1920s onwards, so that by 1970 48 per cent of the province were incomers. Many of them lived in accommodation on the fringes of Barcelona and other centres, often purpose-built but of poor quality. Sometimes the location of these buildings was deliberately marginal, to keep the incomers insulated from mainstream city life. It was not easy, and it was not made easy, for these migrants to integrate as Catalans, nor was such a development encouraged by the Spanish state for most of the twentieth century. There had always been a tendency in industrial Catalonia for the mass of unionised and factory workers (below the supervisory and skilled grades) to identify with a Spanish-wide trade union and labour movement. The migrants greatly strengthened this trend, both by their numerical presence in the movement and by the Catalanist backlash which their presence provoked. Thus it may reasonably be argued that class cleavages in Barcelona became 'ethnicised' (Berger & Smith 80–91; Laitin:299–314). Class, reinforced strongly by migration patterns over an 80-year period, has in fact operated as a powerful cross-cutting cleavage in Barcelona, and is one of several reasons why the city does not entirely meet our 'contested city' criteria.

Objective linguistic difference, then, does not always lead to conflicts of the type studied in this book. Strasbourg, now a French city of some 250,000 people adjacent to the German border, has had a chequered political history. It was captured from the Holy Roman Empire and annexed by France for the first time in 1681. Returned to the German-speaking world after France's defeat by Prussia in 1870, it was restored to France in 1918, and again briefly returned to Germany during the Second World War. Historically the main Franco-German language line has lain some miles to the west of Strasbourg, along the crest of the Vosges mountains. The language traditionally spoken in Strasbourg and its immediate hinterland has been Alsatian, a dialect of German. Yet most of the evidence from the history of the past 150 years is of local support for Strasbourg's association with France rather than with Germany. There has been little change in attitudes since the Strasbourg history professor Fustel de Coulanges wrote in 1870 that 'if Alsace remains French, it is solely because she wishes to be so'. A German civil servant, writing at around the same time, in effect confirmed this assessment when he minuted that 'the French sentiments of the people of Alsace and Lorraine prove to me all the more strongly that we are duty bound to bring back the German race to the German Empire' (P.Smith *et al.*:60–1).

One important reason for Strasbourg's continuing identification with France notwithstanding its linguistic heritage is that, since 1945, any kind of autonomist or pro-Germany movement has been associated with Nazism. But another is to do with timing. Although it is true that, since the early nineteenth century, whichever state has ruled Alsace has sought to impose its national language through the education system and other means, only in the past 50 years has the balance of usage as between state language and dialect been reversed. Until 1945 French (or at other times German) was a language associated with school and with officialdom, but Alsatian was the language of everyday life. This has changed partly because it was possible in the political climate after 1945 for the French state to press French more strongly. There was a famous billboard campaign in the postwar years which included the slogan 'C'est chic de parler français', while as late as the 1970s it is said that children in some Strasbourg schools were punished for speaking Alsatian inside or outside the classroom. The often-noted concern in the region about the poor local standard of French also reflects a concern to ensure that Strasbourg and its province are accepted as part of the real France. But other factors, common to the decline of many minority languages, have also operated in recent generations. It is no longer just in the school or the government office that the language of the state is read and heard but also in the printed and broadcast media, the workplace and the increasingly-cosmopolitan urban centres of the region, especially Strasbourg itself. Whereas in 1950 more than 75 per cent of copies of the main regional newspaper were printed in the bilingual edition, by the 1980s more than 75 per cent of copies were printed in French. Although Alsatian was still reported to be known by the great majority of country people in a 1981 survey, its use was acknowledged by only 29 per cent of people in Strasbourg, and only 8 per cent in the city centre (Gardner-Chloros:5–29).

In the Strasbourg case, therefore, it seems that political factors have been of far more importance that linguistic or social ones. These factors include both matters of wider political context – German state sovereignty has only ever been achieved through invasion and conquest – and also of local political attitudes. In Strasbourg and its region, sentimental attachments to a regional language have not developed a political salience strong enough to make demands for regional autonomy a potent political issue. There was never any equivalent of the Sudeten Germans in Strasbourg or Alsace, and again the city does not meet our criteria for contested city status.

2
Surrender: from Danzig to Gdańsk

...[The Danzig compromise]...is going to produce a crop of
troubles for the future peace of Europe. Half-measures at the
time may offer a refuge from action but action must sooner or
later be faced.

Lord Birkenhead, 1919 (Holton:20)

People think of history in the long-term, but history, in fact, is
a very sudden thing.

Philip Roth, *American Pastoral* (London, 1997), p.87

By telling stories I...wanted to show...that that which is lost
does not have to disappear without a trace.

Günter Grass, Nobel Lecture 1999 (Jerzak:4)

Kashubia is a remote hill region to the west of the Polish city of Gdańsk.
Today it is the subject of glossy internet advertising for 'the Kashubian
lake district'. A century ago it was still an isolated rural area, a by-word in
Danzig for rustic backwardness. Half a million Kashubians spoke a dialect
which was more Slavonic than Germanic, but they were a people for
whom any sense of identity beyond the immediate region was only
beginning to emerge. The fact that their language was spoken by all
classes in the region, with the beginnings of a literary tradition, gave it a
strength which distinguished it from other Polish dialects (Stone:521–9).[2]
Cut off from its eastern approaches by the massive Vistula delta, Danzig
looked west to Kashubia as its main hinterland. In the opening passage,
set in 1899, of Günther Grass's classic novel *The Tin Drum* a Kashubian

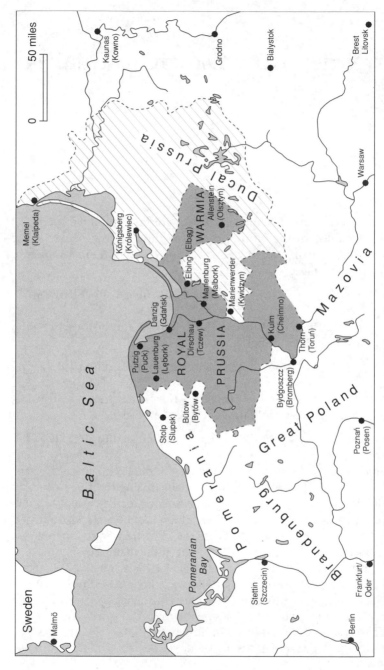

Map 2.1 The Southern Baltic Lands in the Seventeenth and Eighteenth Centuries
Source: K. Friedrich, *The Other Prussia: Royal Prussia, Poland and Liberty, 1569–1772* (Cambridge: University Press, 2000)

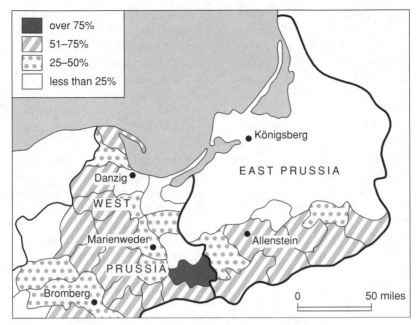

Map 2.2   Language Use in Germany's North-eastern Borderlands, 1910
Percentage of population speaking mainly Polish
Source: W. W. Hagen, *Germans, Poles and Jews: the Nationality Conflict in the Prussian East, 1772–1924* (Chicago: University Press, 1980), p. 80

peasant woman named Anna Bronski sits gathering potatoes. She is wearing the traditional great skirts of the region. A Polish stranger appears, chased at a distance by two Prussian policemen. He hides under Anna's skirts and, as she gives the policemen false directions, he furtively impregnates her. The family later moves to Danzig where Agnes, the child of this bizarre but symbolic union of Kashubia with Poland, marries Matzerath, a German soldier from the west. But she also continues her

---

[2] Kashubian is 'a Polabian dialect of the Pomeranian group of Slav languages … all of which are/were related to Polish'. By 1928 there were an estimated 110,000 Kashubes living in their homeland, and they were 'neither German nor Polish' (Tighe:59). Grass's translator describes the Kashubes as 'a Germanised West Slavic people, speaking 'a transitional dialect between Polish and West Pomeranian', numbering 'some 150,000' native-speakers until 1945 (Grass, 1959:567). Florian Ceynowa (1817–81) pioneered the Kashubian literary tradition. Even as late as the 1960s, the novelist Pawel Huelle (b. 1957) remembers wondering 'If they do not speak Polish here, then where are we?' (Jerzak:7).

youthful liaison with her cousin Jan Bronski, who has identified with Poland. Bronski avoids service in the German Army during the First World War, and is later executed by the Nazis for his role (in fact a cowardly one) in the defence of the Polish Post Office against German forces in September 1939. The central character, Agnes's son Oskar, does not know whether his true father is the German Matzerath or the Polish Bronski. The innocent pastoral identity of Kashubia – neither 'German' nor 'Polish' – is denied survival as individuals and families are forced to adopt national identities which, as often as not, destroy them.

This story highlights several common themes in the study of ethnicity and urbanisation: linguistic shift, the subjective character of national identity, violent conflict, and the triumph of the national over the local in the twentieth century. It also illustrates particular circumstances of geography and language which give individual case studies certain unique or distinctive features. Danzig's Kashubian hinterland was not only different in culture from the German city, but also culturally (as well as physically) remote from Polish heartlands. The Kashubians' embryonic national consciousness depicted in the novel – and it is a family background shared by Grass himself – helps to explain some unusual features of the Danzig case. Migrants travelled to Belfast, Jerusalem or Montreal and, from the mid-nineteenth century, to Prague and, later still, to Brussels, with an ethnic consciousness that was already well-developed. In such cases their arrival in large numbers brought about a change in the predominant culture of the city or, in the case of Belfast and Montreal respectively, a short- and long-fuse ethnic counter-attack. In the case of Prague, and many other cities of German origin, once the peasants came to the city cultural and ethnic change tended to follow. Prague, still German in its prevailing ethos in 1850, was indisputably Czech long before 1914.

In the case of Danzig such a change did not occur. Although ruled from German Berlin for only a fraction of the time that Prague was ruled from German Vienna, Danzig's ethos was almost as German in 1914, and indeed in 1939, as it had been a century earlier (see Table 2.1). In seeking an explanation for this, factors other than the important Kashubian dimension must also be taken into account.

Hohenzollern rule in the later nineteenth century had a shorter way of dealing with non-dominant ethnicities than did the multicultural Habsburg Empire. Danzig's golden era had been two to three centuries earlier, and its nineteenth-century expansion was relatively modest. To the east of the Vistula delta lay not Polish heartlands, but an East Prussia which had long been heavily Germanised at the expense of the

Table 2.1   Danzig/Gdańsk: Population and language, 1850–1992

Year	Total pop.	German	Polish	Kashubian	Other
1850 city	60,000				
1880 city	109,000				
1910: city	162,000				
future Free City	329,916	95.6	3.1	0.6	0.7
1921 city	195,000		2.6		
1934-5: city	295,000	c.33% Catholic, but Church German-controlled			
Free City area	400,000 est	87.5% est 12.5% est.			
1945 city	70,000				
1950 city	170,000	No data, but very strong Polish predominance			
1960 city	286,000				
1992 city	465,000				

Sources: Tighe; Levine 1973; Szermer; *Cambridge Encyclopaedia*, 1994

pagan, and now extinct, Old Prussian peoples. Finally, the geopolitical context of east-central Europe was especially important. Between 1793 and 1945 Danzig came under four different jurisdictions. All of these changes were brought about by outside intervention. When Danzig did become Gdańsk, in the spring of 1945, the change was sudden, brutal and total. In this respect its story is a rather different one from the other cases examined in this book. Its long and complex history also provides an opportunity to explore events prior to the nineteenth century, before Europeans began to assume that the ethno-linguistic nation should necessarily form the basis of the state.

Teutonic knights and the Polish-Lithuanian Commonwealth, 997–1793

Gdańsk is some two hundred miles east of the modern German border, and one hundred miles west of Russia. It lies on the northern rim of a great plain that runs from the Netherlands through north Germany and along the southern shores of the Baltic to Russia. Apart from the three major north-flowing rivers – Elbe, Oder and Vistula – and a once-dense-forest, much of which is now long gone, it is a landscape with very little in the way of natural barriers. Boundaries between peoples have been fluid and hard to defend in this region. This was recognised as early as the year 805, when the Emperor Charlemagne built a great wall, the *Limes Sorabicus*, mostly along the line of the Elbe, as a border between Latin-Germanic Christendom and the Slav world (Tighe:7). The Baltic Sea was, from very early days in history, a by-pass to this land-mass, giving Danzig a direct trading link to the Germanic west and beyond. Like other cities on the Baltic's south-eastern arc, it was developed by German-speaking peoples. But Danzig was situated on a branch of the Vistula delta,[3] which also gave it economic links to a Polish-speaking and east European hinterland. This location at the coastal interface of north-eastern and north-western Europe was the key to its commercial significance.

In some ways Danzig has scarcely been a contested city at all. Polish and German historians of the nineteenth and twentieth centuries have differed on this, but it seems clear that, if it did not begin life as a city in which German language and culture went unchallenged, it soon became one. The main early flow of population was from the seaward side. In another sense however, Danzig was a much-contested city. The first recorded reference indicates that it was a settlement of some size by the end of the tenth century. For a long while after that, Polish Kings and Holy Roman Emperors vied for domination, but localism held out and in 1236 Danzig's charter was granted by a local Pomeranian ruler. The city expanded as a trade centre, flourishing especially once it was admitted to the Hanseatic League in 1261. Neither the Imperial nor the Polish crowns held sway, but a trend was already beginning to emerge which was to determine and sustain Danzig's character over many centuries. The expanding trade of the city attracted a growing number of traders and settlers from the German west, whose language and culture quickly subsumed any local Slav influences. The German 'Danczik' rather than the Polish 'Gydanie' was already the name by which the city had come to be known (Tighe:13; Szermer:16–17).

About the same time a very different kind of Germanising influence appeared in the south-eastern Baltic. The Teutonic Knights was a military crusading order which had been supplanted in the Holy Land by rival orders. During the late thirteenth century the Knights moved into East Prussia, virtually exterminating the Old Prussians and drawing in their wake large numbers of Germanic agriculturists. These Baltic cru-

---

[3] Danzig is situated very close to the sea, at the point where the Mottlawa River flows into the Vistula. In 1840 an enormous ice floe blocked the lower Vistula and caused it to cut a new channel to the sea five miles east of Danzig. By reducing the pressure of water and silt in the old channel, which came to be known as 'the dead Vistula', and thereby increasing the land area, this change benefited Danzig's port development (Cieślak:336; Tighe:46).

saders operated under the authority of the papacy alone, acknowledging allegiance to no temporal power. Their members were recruited from many areas of northern Europe, but the overall ethos and language was German. In 1308 the local Danzig and Pomeranian rulers made the classic error of forces struggling to resist centralisation: in an effort to get the Polish crown off their backs they called in outside help. The Teutonic Knights were only too happy to help, but their price proved to be the execution of the city's local leaders and the subjection of Danzig to an external control far greater than anything the Polish crown could have imposed. The Knights were, however, wise enough to preserve the golden egg. They expanded and fortified the city and laid out much of its modern shape. The city's German-speaking and Germanised Slav character continued to develop. Estimates of the city's population around 1300 vary from 2,000 to 10,000, but there is a measure of agreement that by 1400 the figure had grown to about 20,000. In 1410 the revived Polish-Lithuanian crown inflicted a great military defeat on the Knights at Tannenberg and, by the time of the Peace of Thorn/Toruń in 1466, the Knights were sufficiently weakened to be restricted to the province of East Prussia, losing Danzig altogether. The Knights became secularised in 1525, converted to Lutheranism, and their leader took the title of Duke of Prussia (Burleigh:60; Tighe:20–4; Szermer:18–30).

From the late fifteenth century there were therefore two Prussias. In the east, weakness obliged the Duke to accept Polish overlordship over his territory until the Elector of Brandenburg won full sovereignty in 1657.[4] East Prussia was to remain part of Brandenburg-Prussia and, later, Germany until 1945. Danzig, on the other hand, became the main city in a separate jurisdiction, which became known as Polish or Royal (as distinct from Ducal) Prussia.[5] Between Brandenburg and the territories of the Knights was the much poorer and thinly-populated region of Pomerania, which retained a more localised culture until much later,[6] while those German peoples who migrated further into Slav territory, into Great

---

[4] Ducal Prussia was inherited by the more influential Brandenburg line of the Hohenzollern family in 1618, when the Prussian line died out.

[5] The name 'West Prussia' was introduced by Frederick the Great in the 1770s, and carried the implication that the territory was rightfully part of Brandenburg-Prussia. It was therefore a partisan term.

[6] Pomerania was an ethnically-mixed area by the end of the middle ages. Its ruling family was Slav, but they accepted incorporation into the Holy Roman Empire. When the family died out in 1637 Sweden gained control of most of the territory, which was gradually won from them by Brandenburg between 1720 and 1815.

Poland, did so in smaller numbers, and became Polonised (Burleigh:204; Hagen 3–4; Friedrich:1–5). After 1466, for more than three hundred years, Danzig and the entire province of Royal Prussia formed part of the Polish-Lithuanian Commonwealth, with important regional and urban privileges, both economic and constitutional. Together with its smaller neighbours, Thorn and Elbing, Danzig was claimed as a free city within the Holy Roman Empire by the Imperial Diet, but it continued to regard Royal Prussia as a better guarantor of its liberties.

Throughout the early modern period German was the language of Danzig's ruling elite, and of business and administration, but it was also the regular language of the majority of the population in the city. Slav dialects seem to have been in use as a second language, mainly among the craftsmen and day-labourers, but Polish names were not at all in evidence among the city's elite (Tighe:34; Cieślak:288). In the rural areas of the province the picture was very much more mixed, with both Polish Catholics and German Lutherans among the land-owning class. Partly for this pragmatic reason, the working language of the Royal Prussian *Langtag* was changed from German to Latin and Polish during the course of the sixteenth century. To this limited extent, language did remain a bone of contention between the German-speaking burghers of Danzig and the nobility thereafter. Religion was a more important cultural indicator than language, but recent work has shown a relatively high level of tolerance in Prussian society (Friedrich:38). There were conflicts between Lutherans and Calvinists in Danzig, but the local Lutheran practice of electing clergy chosen by local congregations suggests a measure of compromise with Reformed Church practices. In principle Catholics had full rights in the city, although in practice they were not permitted to participate in the government (Cieślak:276–7). Until the eighteenth century the Catholicism of the Counter-Reformation was pursued with less vigour than was the case in western Europe.

Of course religion was at the heart of the early modern sense of identity for the majority of the population. But amongst the educated elites such as those which conducted the affairs of Danzig, other dimensions assumed a higher importance. Citizens of Danzig regarded themselves as firmly linked, historically and politically, to the Polish-Lithuanian Commonwealth. For them, the crucial distinction was not between Germans and Poles but between the rights and freedoms which they possessed in the city of Danzig and the province of Royal Prussia, and the hereditary, authoritarian and increasingly militaristic regime which prevailed in the neighbouring Hohenzollern territories.[7] As Karin Friedrich has noted, '[Royal] Prussians were neither Germans nor Poles.

The [Royal] Prussian nation defined itself politically as a community of citizens who embraced the constitutional agenda of the multi-national Commonwealth, even if burghers and nobles could not always agree upon the finer points' (Friedrich:15, 217). The Polish-Lithuanian Commonwealth, with its elected monarchy, was neither a centralised nor a national state. Its uniting myth was not ethno-linguistic nor, for the most part, religious. In the sixteenth century writers began to trace a link between the peoples of the Commonwealth and the Sarmatian tribes which had inhabited the Ukrainian steppes during antiquity. Evidence for the link is slight and tentative, but it was an important feature of historical writing and educated thinking throughout most of the Commonwealth's existence. Its romantic, independent conservatism was especially attractive to the unruly nobility, the *szlachta*, who comprised as many as 10 per cent of the Commonwealth's population. As time went by they sought to appropriate the myth to themselves, a kind of Sarmatian master race within the Commonwealth. By the end of the seventeenth century various elements had been added to the *szlachta* version of the myth including eastward expansionism, generalised xenophobia and militant Catholicism (Ascherson:230–2). But recent studies of the myth-making writers of the period have shown that, at least before the eighteenth century, the myth had wider functions. Some seventeenth-century historians sought in it the basis for a common history of the Slavonic and Germanic peoples. The concept of Sarmatian citizenship thus permitted Danzig citizens and other Prussian burghers to associate themselves with the constitution and political system of the Commonwealth without having to identify themselves as Poles. This is not to deny the existence of any antagonism between Germans and Poles prior to the partitions, but the Royal Prussian elites, both rural and urban, saw themselves as citizens of the Commonwealth and not, politically, as Germans or Poles or Catholics or Protestants. The ambitions of Lutheran Sweden in the 1650s did not lead Lutheran Danzig to shift its allegiance from the predominantly Catholic Commonwealth, while the final confirmation of Hohenzollern/German sovereignty over

---

[7] The burghers of Königsberg, the main city of Ducal/Hohenzollern Prussia, had taken a similar view. Although Königsberg included 'a Polish colony' it was very much a German-speaking city. Nonetheless, its leaders strove as hard as they could for as long as they could to sustain their links with the Polish-Lithuanian Commonwealth in opposition to Hohenzollern absolutism. Political associations in the early modern period were 'founded on political calculations and reason', not on nationality (Mallek:35).

Ducal Prussia in the same decade actually widened the rift between the two Prussias (Friedrich:17, 55–6, 93–5, 217).

For much of this period the burghers of Danzig saw no good reason to exchange the liberties of the Commonwealth for the uncertainties of an authoritarian regime. The economy had boomed, and the city had grown. As early as 1500, with trade across the Baltic and with north-western Europe expanded, the city's population reached 35,000, far bigger than the other main cities under the Polish crown.[8] By 1650 the population may have been as high as 77,000. But the impact of the Thirty Years' War and of Sweden's subsequent military incursions, together with the continuing growth of the Atlantic trade, weakened Danzig's commercial supremacy. There were long-term dislocations of trade with the west, compounded by several devastating outbreaks of plague, including one in 1709 which claimed 24,000 lives. By the mid-eighteenth century the population had fallen to below 50,000, although it was still probably the largest city in eastern Europe (Friedrich:121, 133; Tighe:36; Szermer:58; Jerzak:3). The Great Northern War of 1700–21 shook the economy of Danzig, highlighted the political and constitutional deficiencies of the Commonwealth regime, and accelerated foreign intervention in the region. From the 1730s to the 1760s elected Polish monarchs attempted financial and political reform by introducing centralising measures which the urban elites of Danzig and the other cities saw only as undermining their ancient privileges (Friedrich:18). As Enlightenment ideas spread, a narrower definition of Polishness and, paradoxically, a more insistent style of state Catholicism accompanied the material threat to rights and privileges. The annexation by Brandenburg-Prussia in 1772 of all Royal Prussia except the cities of Danzig and Thorn further aggravated this relationship. The burghers were no more willing to surrender their privileges to a Polish rump-state, which was now desperately attempting to centralise, than they had been in easier times. In Thorn it was declared that anyone appointed to the city council must be 'at least of the German nation', yet it was to Russia and England rather than Brandenburg that the two cities looked for allies. The burghers were still more concerned to protect their urban privileges than to embrace their ethno-linguistic kin. Only when the deed was done, and Brandenburg-Prussia annexed Danzig and Thorn in 1793, did their tune change: sentiments of German-Prussian state loyalty began to flow from the pens of the hapless burghers of Danzig. But their local rights and privileges had

---

[8] These were Poznan, Cracow and Warsaw.

disappeared, and they found themselves for the first time part of an authoritarian nation-state (Friedrich:217–20).

Prussian and German rule, 1793–1918

As the aspirations of the Hohenzollern state grew during the eighteenth century, it had come to covet Danzig and the territories to the west of it as a land bridge to its dynastic possessions in East Prussia. When Prussia, Russia and Austria carried out their first partition of Poland in 1772, Frederick the Great gained control of most of Royal Prussia and the lower Vistula, but Russian objections prevented the annexation of Danzig. During the following two decades, however, Prussia was able to use its virtual encirclement of Danzig to apply a damaging economic squeeze. The government of rump-Poland made one last-gasp attempt to reconstruct the Commonwealth, but the centralisation, and loss of local privileges which this implied, further weakened the Danzig elite's commitment to it. When the changed international climate of 1793 enabled Prussia to lay siege to Danzig, the city's elite quickly gave way. Some spontaneous resistance delayed things for a few weeks, but Danzig was soon taken into the Prussian state (Cieślak:255–62).

The population of Royal Prussia in 1793, including Danzig, was estimated at around 647,000, of whom 57 per cent were Protestants. Almost all of the latter group were German-speakers, as was a minority of the Catholic population. The Polish and Kashubian minorities of Danzig and it surroundings lacked any kind of leadership. They possessed little in the way of a middle-class or artisanate, and while the *szlachta* had some (self-interested) elements of Polish national consciousness, this tended to make the peasantry less rather than more nationally-minded. Pomerania and Danzig took virtually no part in Poland's national uprising of 1794. A few young Poles managed a street demonstration in the city in 1797, but by and large the first few years of Prussian rule, as Europe's *ancien regime* sought to come to terms with the challenge of Revolutionary and Napoleonic France, were conciliatory and, with hindsight, something of a honeymoon period. The Polish language enjoyed certain rights, and Polish-speakers were appointed to public positions (Tighe:40–3; Cieślak:289). The city's population is estimated to have grown by 22 per cent, to 44,000, during the first 12 years of Prussian rule (Cieślak:286).

Opinions differ among historians as to how far Danzig was reconciled to Prussian rule by the time of the city's next siege and capture – by the French – in 1807. Polish troops comprised the majority of the city's garrison during the few years of French rule, but it is indicative of the balance of feeling in the city that, rather than hand it over to the new Grand Duchy of Warsaw which he had created, Napoleon designated Danzig as a free city, comprising 15 square miles and about 80,000 people (Tighe:43; Cieślak:303–9). Later, once Napoleonic Europe began to collapse, only the French and Poles fought hard to defend Danzig. When they pulled out at the beginning of 1814 Prussian and Russian troops entered the city from opposite sides. In a situation which was to be replicated in Trieste 130 years later, the two armies manoeuvred for advantage for more than a month before British intervention ended in a Russian withdrawal in favour of the Hohenzollerns' return. The Danzig merchants made one last effort to regain free city status in Restoration Europe. But Britain took the view that the only safeguard against the threat of a Russian Danzig was the restoration of Prussian Danzig, and the latter arrangement was confirmed by the Congress of Vienna in 1815 (Cieślak:317–19).

After three sieges and enforced changes of rule in 20 years, Danzig once again entered a period of stable government (Tighe:20-40; Hagen:17). With the restoration of European peace, it at last came out from behind its city walls and its land area trebled. The incorporation of suburbs increased its nominal population to 55,400 by 1821. But the economic stagnation caused by the trade dislocations of the wartime period in fact continued throughout the following generation. By 1849 the population of 64,000 was no higher than it had been two centuries earlier, while 10 per cent of that figure was made up of the expanded military garrison (Askenazy:98). Any other increase was the result of in-migration for, although the birth rate was sometimes as high as 40 per thousand, the death rate in this era was even higher.

It is not easy to obtain ethno-linguistic data on the city's population, and indeed it would be of limited meaning prior to the more nationally-conscious era of the late nineteenth century. Religion is probably the best objective guide available to us, bearing in mind once more that Protestants tended to be more or less exclusively German-speakers or other westerners, while Catholicism was a strong, but less precise indicator of Polish or Kashubian linguistic identity. Table 2.2 shows a relative increase in the Catholic minority population from the 1790s to 1821, and then a reversal of this trend in the next generation. During the Revolutionary and Napoleonic period there was an increase in migration from Kashubia and other predominantly Catholic and

Table 2.2   Religion in Danzig, 1796–1910
(% distributions)

Year	Protestants	Catholics	Jews	Others	Total population
1796	75.9	21.4	1.7	0.9	37,462
1821	71.0	23.7	4.1	1.1	55,370
1849	72.9	21.8	4.0	1.3	58,280
1861	70.0	23.0	3.6	3.4	70,000
1910	64.0	33.0	1.4	1.6	162,000

Source: Cieślak:321, 355; Tighe:49

Polish-speaking areas. After 1815, as industrial and commercial stagnation set in, growth came mainly from the expansion of Danzig as an administrative centre, which attracted German-speakers from other parts of the Prussian state. The military garrison, of course, was also German-Prussian in ethos. By the 1830s memories of both the local privileges of Commonwealth Danzig and of the existence of a Polish state were dying out, to be replaced by widespread acceptance of a Prussian-German outlook by both residents and new arrivals, even those from non-German-speaking areas. Kashubian speech was still commonly used in homes and in private-sector work, but German was the language of education, administration and literary culture, and also the language of compulsory military service for men. The apparent increase in the Jewish population during this period is simply the outcome of the incorporation of suburban villages into the city (Cieślak:320–4).

Nearby villages were also the main source of domestic servants and labour for small businesses, which made up more than 10 per cent of the workforce. Most of these rural–urban migrants were of Polish or Kashubian background. Joanna Schopenhauer, the travel writer and mother of the distinguished philosopher, wrote of how the children of the German-speaking elite often learned of Polish or Kashubian cultures in this way.[9] By the mid-nineteenth century about 60 per cent of the city's children received some schooling, of whom about 10 per cent continued into secondary education. Polish was taught at both primary and secondary level for a while, but it had ended everywhere by the 1870s. This was the case throughout Prussian Poland, except for religious

---

[9] Recounted in her memoirs, *Jugendleben und Wanderbilder* (Danzig, 1928), cited in Cieślak:279.

education. Such protests as there were appear to have come from individual teachers rather than from any more broad-based movement (Cieślak:279, 298, 341, 355; Kulczycki:209). Polish national consciousness in Danzig and Pomerania was considerably slower to develop that was the case in Russian Poland or in the more predominantly Polish territories of Prussian Poland. The city experienced none of the upheavals which affected so many parts of Europe in 1848. There was a Danzig branch of the Polish League, which was recorded as having 228 members in 1849, before being dissolved by the authorities. Details of its leading members do suggest the existence of a small Polish section of the Danzig elite at this time, including merchants, Catholic clergy, artisans and even some soldiers (Cieślak:352–3, 399).

The second half of the nineteenth century saw important changes, stimulated by economic and politico-military developments in Prussia/ Germany and other western industrialised states. These brought about a three-fold increase in the city's population, from 64,000 in 1849 to 175,000 in the city proper in 1914. The birth rate, which fell from 43 per thousand to 31, at last came to exceed the death rate, which fell from 45 to 30 per thousand. Although Danzig's overall growth was relatively modest, its population balance is similar to other European industrial cities of the period. At the beginning of the twentieth century only around 46 per cent of the population had been born in the city; 33 per cent came from the Pomeranian and Kashubian hinterland; and 21 per cent came from further afield, mainly from German-speaking territories. But this growth in population during the later nineteenth century in fact represented a considerable decline relative to other cities in both Poland and Germany (Cieślak:375; Askenazy:99). Emigration of Danzig-born people was the main factor. Religious – rather than linguistic – data has to be our guide to what was happening. Table 2.2 indicates a reversal of the early nineteenth-century trend, so that the Catholic minority population – mainly, we may be confident, Kashubians and Poles – began to grow at a considerably faster rate that the Protestant majority. After 1850 Danzig had a far less static population that the raw population data suggest. It was a city with a large outflow, predominantly of German-speakers, to the industrial west, which was not fully compensated for by in-migration of German-speaking officials and others. In 1905 about one-quarter of those born in the city were believed to have left, mainly for better employment prospects in the industrial cities of western Germany. The non-German minority was growing, mainly through in-migration from the Kashubian hinterland, and partly through the incorporation of nearby villages into the city. Between 1896 and 1913 as much as 20,000 hectares of land in and around Danzig may have transferred out of German hands. The census data are not entirely reliable on matters of language, but the city's Polish-language historians estimate that the Polish proportion of the population at the end of the nineteenth century – within which they would have included the Kashubians – was about 15 per cent (Cieślak:353–61; Tighe:57–8; Szermer:68).

By the end of the nineteenth century language, and the ethnicity for which it had become the main indicator, was a matter of great contention. Throughout the Prussian east, the governments of Bismarck and his successors became concerned about what was known as the *ostflucht*, the flight from the east. Large numbers of Prussian Poles also migrated, but the depletion of the German-speaking population was relatively much greater. Until the 1860s the ethnic balance in the Pomerania-Danzig borderlands was about even, but by the 1880s Poles and Kashubians outnumbered Germans by two to one. Extensive efforts were made to stem this flow: inducements were offered to German-speaking farmers to remain in or move to the east: it was made difficult for non-German-speakers to take over 'German' land; and migrant labour from Russian Poland was discouraged from entering or remaining within the eastern marches of the Reich. All this had a very limited effect, and was in some ways counter-productive. Expansion of public-sector administrative employment, supported by Danzig's important role as a military and naval centre, were more effective means of sustaining German language predominance (Tighe:50, 57; Cieślak:356–7).

If ethnic consciousness on the part of both Germans and Poles existed in the early nineteenth century in a way that it had not a half-century earlier, it intensified very much more in the period between 1870 and 1914. In 1876 a new cultural organisation, *Ogniwo*, was established to stir Polish national consciousness and resist Germanisation. Other specialist cultural, sporting and business associations followed and were now strong enough to survive police harassment. About 150 Polish-language books were published in the city during the century. In 1901 Danzig became the headquarters for a co-operative bank which sought to sustain the Polish rural population of Pomerania by resisting the efforts of the Prussian Colonisation Commission to buy up all vacant land for Germans. Only when the Poles discovered that the nationally-unaware Kashubians were as happy to sell land to Germans as to Poles did they begin seriously to court Kashubia for Poland. In

1891 a Polish-language daily newspaper, the *Gazeta Gdańska*, was established in Danzig. It devoted special efforts to reversing the Germanisation of the Kashubian population in both Danzig and Kashubia itself, for a while publishing a special Kashubian-dialect edition. In the years just prior to the First World War the burgeoning seaside resort of Zoppot/Sopot, now a Gdańsk suburb, attracted visitors from all parts of Poland and played a significant part in disseminating Polish national consciousness in the Danzig region (Cieślak:399–402; Tighe:56,60–1).

Thus Danzig became the urban centre for Polish activism in Kashubia and eastern Pomerania, including banking, the press and tourism. So, even though Germanness in Danzig itself was not seriously threatened by demographic change in the city in the way, for instance, that had happened in Prague, Polish counter-consciousness was sustained by the changing climate in the wider region. Attempts by government and pressure groups to reassert German language and culture were widespread. Bismarck's *Kulturkampf*, though primarily concerned with the balance of power between Catholics and Protestants in Germany at large, impacted on the situation in the Danzig region: control of education passed to the state in 1872, Polish prayer books were confiscated, and Polish sermons came under the scrutiny of German bishops. In 1887 German language tuition was made compulsory and Polish was banned from elementary schools throughout Prussia. In 1907 almost 100,000 Polish school children throughout the east went on strike, including about 12,000 in the Danzig regency (a region considerably wider than the city itself). The Polish masses had been notoriously slow to embrace the nationalism of their social superiors: the school strike movement of 1901–07, according to its historian, was less a manifestation of popular nationalism than the main stimulus for it (Kulczycki:ix,110, 219). German nationalist organisations had a symbiotic relationship with Polish cultural reassertion, including bodies such as the National Germanic League of Clerks and the Agrarian League (both 1893).The most significant was the *Ostmarkenverein* (The Eastern Marches Society, 1894), better known, after the initials of its three founders, as the Haketa. The latter had 20,000 members by 1901, and operated as a pressure group which both shaped new government initiatives and smoothed the way for them (Tighe:52–5).

Since 1772 Danzig had suffered severe disruptions in trade patterns as a result of frontier/sovereignty changes and related wars. During the second half of the nineteenth century it became a significant industrial city, thanks in no small part to government orders. The numbers of those employed in port or industrial work increased almost five-fold, to account for more than half of the workforce. Trade unions developed along similar lines to the main centres of western Europe. By 1900 free trade unions with social-democratic political links had emerged, and about 30 per cent of workers were unionised (Cieślak:343–5, 355, 394–5). There is no evidence of any ethnic dimension in labour conflict but, as in Trieste (1905), Belfast (1909) and elsewhere, the Danzig labour movement came to divide along ethnic lines. A Polish trade union was formed in Danzig in 1906. As well as conventional industrial work, it engaged in cultural and national consciousness-raising through Polish language classes and related activities. It encountered some hostility from the existing (German-language) unions, and by 1914 had only 300 members out of an estimated total of 8,560 trade unionists in the city. During the later stages of the war, however, it expanded its activities across rural Pomerania (again, there are similarities with the Irish Transport & General Workers' Union in these years) so that its membership grew to about 120,000. In 1919 this body argued strongly for the inclusion of Danzig in the Polish state. Labour movement solidarity was maintained, however, to the extent that German and Polish unions came together in Danzig to oppose the removal to Germany of various items of equipment from the shipyard. In politics, the Social Democrats were unable to challenge the Liberals' predominance in the city prior to 1918. Subsequently the party split over the question of support for the war, and soon afterwards the success of the Bolshevik Revolution in Russia led to the establishment of a Communist Party in Danzig (Cieślak:395–8).

In 1910 the estimated population of the city of Danzig was 175,000. More precise census data available for the wider Danzig administrative district (pop. 329, 916), which was later to become the territory of the Free City (see map 2.3), suggest that the proportion of the population which perceived itself as German-speaking may have been as high as 95 per cent, with 3 per cent being Polish-speaking and less than 1 per cent Kashubian.[10] While rival estimates of the population of the city itself range only between 85 and 95 per cent German, probably with no more than a certain amount of micro-level residential segregation, the distrib-

---

[10] Equivalent statistics for West Prussia as a whole (i.e. Danzig and eastern Pomerania, including Kashubia, total population 1.6 million) were: Germans 57 per cent, Poles 35 per cent, Kashubes 7 per cent and Others/bilinguals 1 per cent.

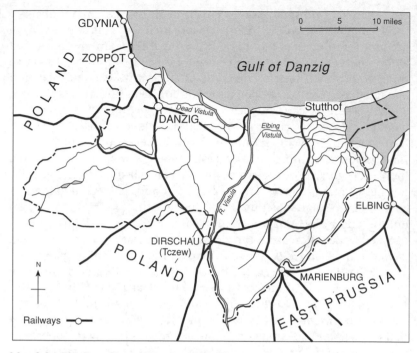

Map 2.3   The Free City of Danzig, 1919–39
Source: R. Donald, *The Polish Corridor and its Consequences* (London: Thornton,
Butterworth, n.d. c. 1929) p. 124

ution in the outer areas of Danzig district varied considerably, outlying
areas to the west and north being between 60 and 100 per cent Polish,
while areas to the east of the city were less than 10 per cent Polish
(Cieślak:403–5; Tighe:61–2; Szermer:68; Wandycz:230). Thus both
Germans and Poles in Danzig saw their case as a strong one and, unlike
the situation 125 years earlier, they saw the matter in entirely ethnic
terms. With the failure of Germany's spring offensive in 1918, the re-
creation of a Polish state and the return of much German territory to
Poland was widely predicted.

From Germany to Free City and back, 1919–45

In 1919, with Germany defeated and Soviet Russia in chaos, the
western powers wanted to build a strong, restored Polish state. The
Poles, sandwiched as they were between two large and hostile neighbours, argued that this required not only a corridor to the Baltic

through rural Kashubia but also a major port. This could only have been Danzig. But here, as in many cases, economic, strategic and geographical considerations were in conflict with ethnic demography and democratic will. The Polish demand, while it accorded with Woodrow Wilson's principle that Poland should have access to the sea, was in direct opposition to the other key Wilsonian principle of national self-determination. The French, anxious to weaken Germany as much as possible, pressed strongly for Danzig to go to Poland. In contrast the British government, archetype of imperialism and 'secret diplomacy', argued for an outcome closer to the self-determination principle. This was not as paradoxical as it seemed: the British view was based not on the principle of self-determination as such, but on a more traditional diplomatic assessment that to put a large and thoroughly German city under Polish rule would bring not justice but dangerous instability.

The earliest allied thinking in February 1919 had been that Danzig should indeed go to Poland comprising, as it would have done, considerably more than half the coastline of the proposed 'Polish corridor'. Ignoring the tidal wave of ethnic nationalism which had swept Europe for half a century and provoked the Great War, British Naval Intelligence argued that, within a few years, Danzig's German inhabitants would be as 'contented with Polish suzerainty as their predecessors. and as the German merchants of Riga under Russia' (Nelson:157). These views were endorsed unanimously by the Peace Conference's Commission on Polish Affairs. It saw six reasons why Danzig should go to Poland. These included Polish need for port access to the sea; the fact that German rail transit rights across the corridor to East Prussia's small population was a far less significant extra-territorial risk that to cut all of Poland off from a port; the economic interests of Danzig's German merchants; the firmly Polish character of Danzig's local and regional hinterland; the likelihood of renewed population growth for the city as the port of Poland; and the expectation that such population increase would inevitably take the form of rural-urban migration of Poles from that hinterland. By early March 1919 there was a widespread expectation at Versailles that Danzig would go to Poland (Kimmich:6–8).

This expectation was shared, but not welcomed, by James Headlam-Morley, of the British Foreign Office's Political Intelligence Department. A relatively junior official, his advice proved to be of great significance. He argued that 'to assign to Poland a town such as Danzig, which is almost purely German in population ... will undoubtedly arouse the most bitter animosity, not only among the Prussian

military party and the chauvinists, but among the whole of the commercial community'. It would also be foolish, he thought, to assign
Danzig to a new state 'as to the character and government of which we
are still completely in the dark'. Some form of autonomy, he thought,
was essential: 'what I maintain we cannot do is simply to annex
Danzig to Poland without consulting the inhabitants, in such a way as
to make the German population subject to Polish compulsory military
service, religious and educational legislation'. He did, however, agree
that 'the natural future of Danzig is with Poland, and if we go slowly,
carefully and prudently, I should hope that eventually the recognition
of the enormous advantages which would come to the place from the
development of Polish commerce will outweigh national feeling ...'
(Headlam-Morley:23, 40, 41, 44). Lloyd George shared this view,
arguing the danger that Danzig and other German towns in the contested area could become '*Germania Irrendenta*'. Thus, in March 1919,
the first Allied attempt to settle the Danzig issue, on the basis of Polish
sovereignty, ended in failure.

The debate continued into April 1919, France's Clemenceau still
favouring the full transfer of Danzig to Poland, while Lloyd George
argued for a free port. The USA havered. The debate was narrowed to
three options: the creation of a free state of Danzig; the assignment of
Danzig to Poland; or the assignment of Danzig to Poland with some
compensatory territory on the lower Vistula for Germany. None of the
victors argued for the restoration of Danzig to Germany. It was at last
agreed on 22 April 1919 that Danzig would become a Free City. Its constitution and borders would be guaranteed by the League of Nations,
which would also appoint a High Commissioner to oversee relationships between Germany and Poland. There would be a Danzig-Poland
customs union and free access by Poland to all port and waterway facilities; the Poles would control river and rail administration in the Free
City as well as post and telephone links with Poland and Danzig's
foreign relations. Equal treatment for Poles in the Free City, including
schooling and freedom of association, would be guaranteed. All
German nationals resident in Danzig would have the option of automatically becoming Danzig nationals, or of retaining German nationality and removing to Germany within two years (Nelson:196;
Kimmich:27–30). The German government declared the settlement to
be 'in the sharpest opposition to all the assurances given in the state-
ments of President Wilson', and contended that the economic arrangements were intended to Polonise German territory (Nelson:331). The
Polish government was equally unhappy about not gaining political

control of Danzig. Headlam-Morley acknowledged, at least to himself, that if acute national rivalries returned to Europe the arrangements for Danzig and the two Prussias would in strategic terms prove 'quite impossible'. But he thought it a positive advantage that enforcement would require a League of Nations strong enough 'to impose peace and disarmament' (Headlam-Morley:171). His analysis was correct, but his prognosis proved tragically wrong. The Commonwealth politician J.C. Smuts told Woodrow Wilson that 'we are building a house of sand' (Nelson:327).

At one point in the discussions Headlam-Morley and his American counterpart had suggested calling the new creation 'the Free Hansa City [Hansastadt] of Danzig', believing that this would distinguish the German character of Danzig from both the old 'Prussian Idea' and the German Reich. They thought that 'a German merchants community might have in the future, as such communities have had in the past, a very prosperous existence while closely associated with a foreign power'. The suggested title was 'too German' and was quickly dropped. But the idea of practical political and cultural independence, linked to what was intended to be a beneficial economic relationship to Poland, was implemented, and did derive from a perceived historical model. Headlam-Morley hoped that

> the prosperity of the town will increase enormously, and it will come into its rightful position of being a great port with a very large hinterland, and should be one of the largest cities on the continent. It ought also to be good for British trade which has, so far as I can understand, almost disappeared since Danzig was annexed by Prussia. (Headlam-Morley:69,77)

Danzig's German-speaking majority regarded the settlement as unjust and hypocritical. Almost all the major political parties in the city wished to remain with Germany: the right for nationalistic reasons, the left owing to unease about the developing right-wing ethos of the new Polish regime (Cieślak:409). Although the Allies had in fact acknowledged the German character of their city by reversing the original intention to incorporate it into Poland, Danzigers regarded their location within the Polish customs union as a political threat rather than an economic benefit. So the implementation of the Treaty of Versailles in Danzig began with protests, demonstrations and serious clashes between Germans and Poles in the city. The civic leadership of the ruling German National Party, however, co-operated fully with the

LN in implementing the settlement, realising that failure to do so, in the weakened state of defeated Germany, would result in Polish occupation of the city (Levine 1973:11). In elections to the Danzig Constitutional Assembly in May 1920 the German Nationalists won 34 seats, the independent Socialists 21, the Social Democrats 19, the (German) Catholic Centre Party 17, and other German parties 22. Polish parties, with 9,400 votes, won 7 of the 120 seats (Cieślak:413).

The legal status of the Free City of Danzig was not entirely clear. The view of Germany and of Danzig appeared to be upheld by the High Commissioner who said that Danzig was indeed a sovereign state. But Poland's rights in the territory called this into question. Formal responsibility for foreign affairs, control of the railways and waterways, control of its own post office in the city, and the inclusion of the Free City in Poland's customs area – with most of the customs revenue going to Poland – amounted to significant limitations on the Free City's sovereignty. Danzig was also obliged to allow unrestricted labour migration by Polish citizens. Thus, although the number of enfranchised citizens of Danzig voting for the Polish ethnic ticket actually declined during the 1920s, the number of Polish citizens in the city increased, from about 5,000 in 1923 to 17,000 (6 per cent) in 1934, to which must be added about 3,000 Polish Jews (Mason:5–7).[11] Half of the employees of the (Polish-managed) railway system in the Free City were Polish citizens or Danzig Poles (Cieślak:423). On the Port and Waterways Board, the Polish delegation agreed a target with the Free City in 1923 that in future half of the employees should be Polish. For 10 years all new appointments went to Poles, though by 1937 only 41 per cent of officials and 29 per cent of the 683 manual workers were Polish (Cieślak:419–20). Both this employment dimension, and the reporting line between Polish customs officers in Danzig and the Warsaw government, were matters with high public visibility which helped to make the Free City a cauldron of ethnic conflict rather than a model of co-operation.

The LN High Commissioner in the city had very limited jurisdiction over matters judged to be internal to the Free City. His job was to settle disputes between the Free City and the Polish government. There were

---

[11] This is Mason's estimate. The Polish architectural historian Szermer (p.73) states that there was substantial re-Polonisation during the Free City era, bringing the number of Polish inhabitants of the city to around 50,000. Older-established Jews who were Danzig citizens were more likely to identify themselves with Germany than with Poland.

indeed many such disputes, and in practice the more important among them were almost always appealed to the Commissioner's superior authority, the Council of the League of Nations. As the commitment of the powers and the general standing of the League of Nations weakened during the 1930s, its importance in the affairs of Danzig declined. The Danzig Germans always had limited confidence in it, and as the Poles lost confidence in its capacity to act they weakened it further by seeking bilateral agreements with Nazi Germany (Cieślak:425–6).

Just as Polish power infringed legally and fiscally on Danzig's independence, so party political culture and administration in the Free City continued to be integrated into German politics. The city was governed by an elected parliamentary body, the *Volkstag*, which in turn appointed a governing cabinet, known as the Senate. The German National People's Party, the German Communist Party and later on the Nazi Party were simply local branches of parties based in Germany; the Centre Party and the Social Democrats were nominally autonomous, but in practice closely involved with their equivalents in Germany. Germans appointed to the Danzig civil service were automatically granted Danzig citizenship, and the majority of senior city officials were in fact German citizens who moved freely between postings in Danzig and in the *Reich*. Free City policy, in the 1920s as much as in the Nazi period, was co-ordinated between Danzig and Berlin. Throughout the 1920s and beyond, until cut back by recession, the Free City was also supported by substantial financial aid from Germany (Kimmich:89–93, 107–8).

There were a number of competing Polish organisations in Danzig during the inter-war period, notably the *Gmina Polska* (Polish Community), founded in 1921, and the *Związek Polaków* (Union of Poles), formed in 1933. Rival trade unions also developed in association with these two bodies. Through the agency of the Polish Commissioner-General in Danzig they were brought together as the *Gmina Polska–Związek Polaków* in 1937, with a combined membership of about 10,000. The new grouping adhered much more closely to the views of the Polish government than the independent-minded *Gmina Polska* had previously done. Underpinning these splits was a class and geographical base – the *Gmina Polska* represented the old-established Polish colony in Danzig, predominantly working- and lower-middle class, while the membership of *Związek Polaków* consisted more of Polish citizens, predominantly recent arrivals who tended to be of higher social and educational status. The splits were damaging to the small Polish political parties in the Free City. Rival candidates were run in elections for the *Volkstag* from 1927 to 1933. Support for Polish parties fell from 9,321 votes (6.1 per cent) in 1920 to 5,764 in 1927, before recovering to 8,311 in 1937. Thus, although the Polish-speaking population of Danzig undoubtedly increased during the Free City era, support for Polish parties never regained the level attained in 1920 (Cieślak:444–8).

In 1921 the Danzig *Volkstag* agreed to maintain some Polish primary schools and a Polish-language stream in some others, mainly in the rural areas. Numbers in these schools rose to 1500 in 1936, falling to 800 by 1939 as many Poles left Danzig for Poland. Poles believed that these schools were poorly resourced, and that the city authorities endeavoured to appoint inadequate teachers or 'renegades', while discriminating against teachers who taught in 'the Polish spirit'. There was no state provision for Polish-language secondary education. This was provided for about 300 pupils by a Polish community body, the *Macierz Szkolna* (School Matrix), which also provided seven primary schools in the Free City (748 pupils in 1936). In 1938 there were 1,750 Polish boy and girl scouts in the Free City. Many of the prominent teachers in these institutions were to be murdered by the Nazis during the first year of the war. There was no Polish further and higher education provision, and no provision in northern Poland either. Thus large numbers of Polish citizens and Danzig citizens of Polish ethnicity studied at the Danzig Technical University: about 600 students (36 per cent) at the highest point in 1930 (Cieślak:450–55).

In the economic sphere the anachronistic nature of Headlam-Morley's vision of a restored Hanseatic Danzig was quickly revealed. In 1920 the pro-Soviet dockers of Danzig had refused to unload arms destined for Poland's war with the Soviet Union. This action by German dockers, firmly non-ethnic and class-based though it was, alerted the Polish government at the outset to the vulnerability of its new port access. In 1924 the Poles secured financial backing from France – which was provided for entirely anti-German political reasons – to build a wholly new port within the Corridor at Gdynia, a small fishing village less than 15 miles north of the centre of Danzig (Tighe:83). Gdynia grew rapidly, but the onset of depression after 1929 highlighted the fact that there was not enough work for both ports. In 1931 the Danzigers protested vainly to the League of Nations that Poland should either use the Free City for the economic purpose for which it had been created, or allow it to be reunited with Germany. By 1933 Gdynia's turnover exceed that of Danzig, and by 1939 it has grown to a city of 127,000 people. The new fact of Gdynia, support by the ongoing Polonisation of the Kashubians and peoples of mixed ethnicity in the rural Corridor, was of political as well as economic significance. After creating Gdynia, Poland didn't need Danzig. But Danzig on its own was not what Germany wanted. The old Weimar strategy of using Danzig's ethnic demography to argue for ending the entire Corridor experiment would no longer wash now that the Corridor really was Polish. This left war and chaos as the only German strategy for reversing the Versailles settlement on its eastern frontier (Kimmich:162–4).

There was continuing support for the left among the German workers of Danzig, and the Social Democrats actually governed the city between 1927 and 1930. But between 1929 and 1932 unemployment doubled to 29,000, and the Nazi advance in Danzig became as formidable as in the *Reich* itself. Even before this, political debate in the Free City had tended to focus on whether or not candidates' views were 'tough enough' on Poland. Ethnic relations deteriorated, with attacks on Polish officials and symbols, and expulsions of Polish students from the Technical University (Szermer:73–4). Nazi party membership had reached only 800 by mid-1930, but grew to 9,519 by December 1932. Street fighting between Nazis and Communists was common from 1930 onwards. One Nazi was elected to the Free City's original 120-seat *Volkstag* in 1927, rising to 12 out of 72 in 1930. In June 1933, five months after Hitler came to power in the *Reich* with 44 per cent of the vote, the local Nazis won control of the Free City with just over 50 per cent of the vote, and 38 out of the 72 seats (Levine 1973:18–55).[12]

There was close co-ordination between the *Reich* party and the local movement. The early Nazi leaders in Danzig were mainly clerks in various large concerns who appeared, in the case of Danzig, to have been low on ability as well as social status. There were increasing tensions in the local movement partly centred, as elsewhere, on power struggles between the Party and the SA. Göring arrived to adjudicate, and a 28-year-old Bavarian clerk, Albert Forster, was sent to take charge of the local Gau. Assisted not only by the depression but also by the immediacy of the Versailles grievance and the Polish issue, his leadership and close collaboration with the Reich party helped the local movement to advance. Although impatient for action, Forster was responsive to the directions of the central leadership. After his arrival the local party began to follow the *Reich* party's new emphasis on the

---

[12] The size of the Danzig *Volkstag* was reduced from 120 to 72 members in 1930.

nationally-minded middle class and on rural voters, a sector of the Free City's electorate which amounted to 30 per cent of the population. Guided by personal meetings with Hitler, Forster followed a calculated policy. Although Danzig was perceived as perhaps the most gross example of Versailles hypocrisy regarding the principle of self-determination, a softly-softly policy was adopted. The relatively moderate, establishment figure of Hermann Rauschning, German war veteran and farmer from Poznan/Posen, was cultivated as the local Nazi figurehead, becoming President of the Senate of the Free City in 1933. Rauschning, who seemed to the British consul more like 'an old-fashioned English squire' than a Nazi, attracted rural voters and projected a responsible image in the Free City, while giving the Polish government the impression for a while that the Danzig Nazis were a party it could do business with. In the summer of 1933 Rauschning negotiated an agreement with the Poles that they would use Danzig and Gdynia equally – itself a reduction on Danzig's previous demands – in exchange for major concessions on the provision of Polish education in the Free City. But the Berlin foreign ministry was incensed that Rauschning had 'elevate[d] a national minority to virtual equality with the native populace'. He resigned his position late in 1934, and subsequently fled to the west (Levine 1973:52; Kimmich:144–6). Hitler still did not want a situation to develop in Danzig which might cause the League of Nations to authorise Polish military intervention in the Free City, so until the autumn of 1938 he continued an ambivalent policy, balancing his impetuous Gauleiter Albert Forster against the more pliant Senate president Arthur Greiser. The overall intention was to maintain a bilateral relationship with Poland which would minimise the role of the League of Nations in Danzig, and generally postpone the development of a crisis over Danzig until such time as Germany was ready for it.

Nazi Party membership in Danzig had grown to almost 22,000 when membership was closed in June 1934. The lists were reopened two years later, and by December 1937 there were 36,465 members, or almost 10 per cent of the entire population. More than 60 per cent of the membership was drawn from the white-collar and supervisory, lower professional and artisan classes. Labourers in civic or railway employment were also well represented but the industrial working class, at less than 12 per cent of total membership, was heavily under-represented (Levine 1973:122). Because of Hitler's wish to delay the Danzig issue, the bizarre picture emerged in the last elections held in German Danzig, in April 1935, of the Social Democrats taking a stronger line on reunion of the Free City with the *Reich* than did the local Nazis (Levine 1973:87). The situation could scarcely have been more favourable to the Nazis: the election was fought hard on the heels of the referendum in the Saarland, on German's western border, where 90 per cent of the electorate had voted to return to the *Reich*; the Nazi Party had sole access to the radio; opposition newspapers were harassed and known supporters intimidated; civic employees were used to distribute Nazi election material and civic funds were used to support the Nazi campaign. In these circumstances the rise in Nazi support from 50 to 59 per cent of the electorate, and from 38 to 43 members of the 72-seat *Volkstag* was modest. As the only opportunity ever granted to electors to pass judgement on a Nazi Party in power, it was less than the ringing endorsement the Führer would have liked, and it fell short of the two-thirds majority which the Danzig Nazis needed if they were to modify the Free City's constitution (Cieślak:429).

The endorsement might have been even less ringing has voters been fully aware of the extent of the city's economic crisis. Unlike Roosevelt's America or Hitler's Germany, a state the size of Danzig could not afford to respond to the depression with deficit financing. Indeed, the *Reich's* own unemployment and re-armament policies meant that the Nazi government was less ready to fund German Danzig than its predecessors had been. Following consultations with Hitler and his financial advisers the local Nazis devalued the Danzig gulden by more than 40 per cent. The crisis continued through the summer of 1935 as many Polish importers moved their businesses to Gdynia, and Danzig's share of Poland's trade by sea fell from 47 per cent to 37 per cent in the space of a year (Levine 1973:92–5).

Unlike the frightening speed of the transformation in Germany, Danzig was not completely Nazified until 1937. Non-Nazi work schemes were stopped, labour conscription was introduced, and unemployed workers were denied support if they declined opportunities to take work offered in the *Reich*. But Polish voluntary associations and political parties were permitted to continue, as were some of the German opposition parties and the Churches. The main reason for this was the continued presence of the League of Nations High Commissioner and the continued wish of Berlin to avoid confrontation with Poland. Only after the remilitarisation of the Rhineland in the summer of 1936 did Hitler allow his Danzig representatives to reject League of Nations authority in the Free City. Then, within a few months, the League's guarantee regarding Danzig became a dead letter. The Social Democratic Party was banned in September 1936, the German nationalists dissolved themselves, the Catholic Centre Party was banned in October 1937, and new political parties were forbidden. The Catholic bishop, Eduard O'Rourke (whose aristocratic Russian links were more central to his identity than his Irish name), continued to defend Catholic schools and voluntary associations, until his resignation in June 1938. His successor capitulated on these issues, and also took firm steps to ensure that the Catholic Church in Danzig – with a membership of 50 priests, and about one-third of the population of the Free City – remained firmly German and did not become a vehicle for the Polish cause. By 1938 all political opposition to Nazism had ceased and the Nuremberg laws against Jews were introduced. The British Foreign Office advised the new High Commissioner in 1937 that 'the establishment of a full National Socialist regime was probably inevitable, but he might be able to moderate the pace at which it was carried through' (Levine 1973:142).

Immediately after the Munich crisis, Germany's Danzig policy changed gear. In October 1938 Hitler proposed privately to Poland that Danzig might be returned to the *Reich* by bilateral agreement. The offer was flatly rejected. Following the German occupation of Prague in March 1939, Hitler told the *Reichstag* that 'Danzig is a German city and wishes to belong to Germany' (Levine 1973:147). The governing Senate in Danzig announced that the existing *Volkstag* represented the will of the people, and cancelled the 1939 elections. It was the end of constitutional government in the city. It was clear, however, that only through invasion and war could Danzig be taken back into the *Reich*. The location of railways and bridges, as well as the legally-approved Polish military and paramilitary footholds in Danzig, meant that as late as the spring of 1939 the balance of military advantage in any 'dash for Danzig' favoured the Poles. But from May 1939 onwards the Nazi governments in Germany and Danzig began a quiet, but none-too-subtle, build up of forces. German 'tourists' entered the Free City in large numbers to supervise the construction of military emplacements and bridges linking the Free City directly with German East Prussia. Military supplies arrived nightly at Danzig and at the nearby port of Elbing in East Prussia. Genuine tourists stayed away during the summer of 1939. On 1 September local SS units and others seized the city, a German warship in the harbour bombarded the Polish base at Westerplatte, in Danzig harbour, and the LN High Commissioner was ordered to leave. Most of the 50 postal workers who attempted to defend the Polish Post Office in the city were later executed on the false grounds that they lacked combatant rights (Cieślak:464).

Gauleiter Forster exchanged telegrams with Hitler declaring the Free City of Danzig to be restored to the German *Reich*. German armies overran Poland within a few days. Danzig suffered little damage, and became the administrative centre of a new *Reichsgau*, Danzig-West Prussia, which included Gdynia (now Gotenhafen) and the former Polish corridor. Gdynia, Danzig's trading rival and the visible symbol of Poland's economic hostility to the Free City, suffered especially badly under the new regime, losing almost half its population during the first two years of the war (Levine 1973:156). Danzig, however, with its German shipbuilding workforce and its relatively safe distance from early Allied bombing raids, was especially important to the war effort (Cieślak:467).[13] Instructions from the SS were to identify German and Germanisable elements in the population, and to expel the rest to the area of the General Government to the east. Bizarrely, Forster declared almost all the Polish population of Danzig-West Prussia to have been effectively 'Germanised'. The SS was not convinced by Forster's statistically-excellent record of achievement, but he was able to hold his ground until 1944, declaring that 'If I looked like Himmler, I wouldn't talk about race' (Levine 1973:159). Forster's false accounting only began to rebound on him during the last months of the war, when many of those he has certified as 'Germanised' joined the Polish resistance, and enabled the Red Army to enter many towns without a fight. Forster's optimistic assessment of his Germanisation policies did not betoken any conciliatory spirit on his part towards subject populations: Danzig's concentration camp, at nearby Stutthof, housed a total of 120,000 Polish, Jewish and other anti-Nazi elements during the six years of war, of whom more than 70 per cent died (Tighe:195; Szermer:79).

Danzig's Jewish community was destroyed by Nazi terror. For most of its existence it had been relatively small and well-integrated into German Danzig, although after 1900 it had developed something of a miniature version of the German–Polish divide in the city. Jews had been excluded from the city during the medieval and Commonwealth periods, but from bases in the suburbs had managed to develop some specialist trading functions. The Prussian state granted more legal rights, but local officials still tended to make difficulties, and full legal rights were obtained only in 1869. By this time the small Jewish community of two to three thousand people was actively involved in the cultural and business associations of the city. The great majority of them were

---

[13] British forces first bombed Danzig in July 1942 (Cieślak:468).

German in speech and culture, and saw themselves as 'Germans of the Mosaic persuasion' rather than as Zionists. Many volunteered and some gave their lives for Germany in the First World War. From the late nineteenth century *Ostjuden*, Jews from Russia and Russian Poland, also began to arrive in the city in numbers. The Jewish community provided relief for these newcomers, but excluded them from communal decision-making, in the hope of discouraging both Zionist influence and orthodox practices. This left a residue of bitterness within Danzig Jewry which never quite disappeared (Twersky:109–12; Bacon:25–8).

During the Free City period anti-Semitism became a more serious problem. Conflict with Christian Danzig was exacerbated by an increase in Jewish numbers: 60,000 *Ostjuden* passed through Danzig in the years 1920–25, of whom enough stayed to increase the Jewish population of the city from about 2,500 in 1910 to more than 10,000 in 1930, by which time Zionism was close to achieving a majority in the community. Only the imminent Nazi threat ended community division. Rauschning, the first Nazi president of the Danzig Senate, declared that anti-Semitism would harm Danzig, and the tactical moderation of Danzig Nazis continued at the formal, though not always at the street, level until 1938. By the time the Nuremberg laws were introduced in November 1938 almost half the Jewish community had left the city. The entire community then took a formal decision to evacuate the city, with the encouragement of the Nazi Senate. Of 6,000 remaining Jews, 2,000 Polish citizens were able to go to Poland, while 1,000 were able to make their own arrangements. For the remainder, funds were raised by the sale of the synagogue and its treasures (the latter to the USA) and used mainly to assist Jews to migrate illegally to Palestine. Some of these perished at sea, while almost all those who remained were sent to the death camps in the autumn of 1941. Only a handful of the community survived in the city (Bacon:28–36; Twersky:21–31; Cieślak:441).

In March 1945 Danzig itself came under siege from the Red Army. After leaving behind a taped radio broadcast in which he declared that 'Danzig remains German' and urged a fight to the end, Forster quietly departed by submarine. He was arrested in western Germany, sentenced to death by a Polish court in 1948, and later executed.[14] The great majority of the German population of Danzig left the city. *The Times* of 31 March 1945 estimated that 39,000 civilians died in the

---

[14] Sources differ as to Forster's fate, but his recent biographer, Dieter Schenk, appears to have established that he was hanged in prison in Warsaw in 1952.

final struggle. Many more died in attempting to reach the west, or were taken to camps in the Soviet Union from which they did not return. Large numbers also made their way as refugees to West Germany: an estimated 1.2 million civilians and soldiers, from all over the German east, were evacuated in a week by the German army from improvised jetties to the east of Danzig (Levine 1973:161; Tighe:194–5). As the Soviet commander at the gates of the city declared on 30 March 1945, 'further resistance is pointless' (Ward 94).

A new city: Gdańsk since 1945

In the spring of 1945 Danzig lay in ruins. The behaviour of the Red Army in the city matched the Nazis in savagery if not in the calculated scope of its brutality (Tighe:196–200). The population of the city proper, estimated at 247,000 in 1939, fell in April 1945 to about 120,000 (Szermer:91,162).[15] Not only had a large proportion of the population gone, but an estimated 60 per cent of the physical fabric of the city had been destroyed: 6,000 buildings, 33 schools, 20 bridges, 12 kilometres of tram track, two-thirds of the water supply system, part of the gas works and electricity system – all reduced to three million cubic metres of rubble. In the shipyards 70 per cent of the machinery was destroyed. Much of the surviving movable material was scavenged, officially or unofficially, by the Red Army (Cieślak:472; Szermer:83–4). In May 1945 a commission began to change all the place- and street-names to Polish. Schools became monolingual Polish almost overnight as did the language of administration. Protestant churches became Catholic churches, within which use of the German language was forbidden (Tighe:206, 212).

Not all the Germans left the city in April 1945. A Warsaw radio broadcast in September 1945 stated that 'until the Poles come in masses it will not be possible to expel the Germans' (Tighe:211). In Stefan Chwin's novel *Hanemann*, remaining Germans attempt to sell their salvaged possessions to incoming Poles at an improvised market (Jerzak:18). Many more Germans were deported during the second half of the year, following the Potsdam conference. In February 1946 the population of the city was estimated to include about 93,500 Poles and 34,000 Germans (Szermer:91; Cieślak:473). The remaining Germans

---

[15] The estimate, made by a Gdańsk researcher in 1961, that 139,000 inhabitants remained after the exodus of April 1945, is believed by others to be too high. About 20,000 of these, it is suggested were short-term transients (Szermer:91).

were mainly older people or of mixed ancestry. The new arrivals, on the other hand, who included refugees displaced by the westward advance of the Soviet frontier as well as urban migrants from Kashubia and central Poland, were mainly young. In 1950 the birth-rate in Gdańsk was almost 31 per thousand against a Polish average of 19. In the first 20 years after the war 130,000 children were born in Gdańsk (Szermer:92–3, 156–7). Pawel Huelle's novel *Who was David Weiser?* (1991) evokes wonderfully the experience of Gdańsk children growing up in the 1950s, playing amidst graveyards and ruins which seemed to them to belong to a different civilisation. But this is a story written a generation later, in the era of post-cold war *détente*. Those growing up in the fifties, sixties and seventies, too young to recall the horrors of 1939–45, knew little of Danzig apart from these curiosities, and received every encouragement through their education to perceive their city as rightfully and historically Polish. The German script on their domestic installations and mailboxes remained a mystery to them (Szermer:160; Jersak:6). They perceived the previous residents as occupiers in every sense, and were well insulated by cold war physical and ideological barriers from any challenge to this view.

Population growth in Danzig and throughout the Prussian east had been sapped by ethnic animosities and western industrialisation. After 1945 these constraints were removed. Gdańsk was now a Polish city, in Poland: by 1956 its population exceeded the pre-war total, and by 1980 it had almost doubled. The situation presented a unique challenge to urban planners. Gdańsk was not only devastated, but also faced open competition from several other centres which had become part of Poland. In particular Gdynia, which had started only 20 years before, under a separate and hostile jurisdiction, now became a partner in the same small conurbation. The two cities, or three counting the separate resort town of Sopot (formerly Zoppot) which linked them, came to be referred to as the *Trójmiasto*, or Tri-city. Only in their building restoration work on the devastated city did the Poles seek to reconstruct what had been there before. Architecturally this has been a great success, though even as late as 1968 much of the city centre was still rubble (Levine 1973:161, 216; Szermer:*passim*). The rebuilding proceeded slowly, but the end result was a quite remarkable reconstruction of what had been a handsome city. Outsiders noted the apparent paradox of the immense effort and expense being invested in restoring 'a German city'. With only slight exaggeration the Poles were able to point out that Gdańsk had been part of a Prussian/German state for only 270 years of its history, and that for much of the remainder of the period its bourgeoisie – mainly German-speaking though they were – valued their independence from a more centralised German-speaking state, and through their monuments were proud to celebrate in symbolic form their links with a Polish-Lithuanian Commonwealth which supported their trade and left them alone (Szermer:118).

Between 1970 and 1990 Gdańsk was best known in the west as the centre of opposition to the Communist regime in Poland under the leadership, ironically, of the industrial working class in the shipyards and related occupations. There is no indication that this had anything at all to do with the city's history of distance and separation from the rest of Poland. The reason are, rather, two-fold. First, the gap between the investment made in Gdańsk as the industrial showpiece of Poland and the lack of investment in housing and general living standards was no longer sustainable. Secondly, it seems that a stimulus to unrest may have been the 25,000 Polish political prisoners released from Soviet jails under the 1956 amnesty, most of whom had been re-settled in the Gdańsk area. Between 1945 and 1990 it has been estimated that the city lost around 400 dead in protests and demonstrations (Tighe:240).

Linguistic and other restrictions on the small, remaining German community have been lifted; Germany has at last given formal recognition to the border with Poland which was imposed in 1945. German heritage tourism in Danzig has developed strongly, but the city's economy in general has struggled. Danzig exile associations in western Germany are less active than they were in the 1970s, but calls to redress 'the ethnic cleansing of 1945' are still posted on the internet from addresses as far afield as Munich and Australia. What will happen in the future, now that cold-war barriers have been removed and Polish European Union membership is imminent? Günter Grass, in his late novel *The Call of the Toad* (1992), makes a satirical guess. A west German academic, returning to Gdańsk in the wake of *détente*, develops a business selling plots of land to exiled Danzigers so that they may be buried in Gdańsk. But then, why wait until you die? Retirement and holiday homes follow, the area becomes overpopulated and the economy collapses. The novel ends with an entrepreneurial Bengali rickshaw driver, who has been loitering on the fringes of the plot throughout, employing Poles and Germans alike to run between the shafts, showing tourists around the city that each of them claims as their own.

3
Resistance: the Survival of Italian Trieste

Are we going to stud Europe with Danzigs?

British Foreign Office minute on Trieste, 1943 (Whittam:359)

The country must follow the lot of the town and not the other way about

Carlo Schiffrer, Italian socialist and nationalist, 1946 (Sluga 2001:287)

Nuša is walking with long strides, letting the soles of her feet bang against the cobbles and leaning back against the gradient ... When I reach the Corso, she says to herself, I will walk like someone from the city.

(J. Berger, *G:A Novel*, 229)

Trieste's most celebrated writer is probably the novelist who called himself 'Italo Svevo' (1861–1928), and who was born Ettore Schmitz. A native of Trieste, Schmitz was Italian by mother tongue and political outlook, German by family background and schooling and Jewish by religion (McCourt:86). This cosmopolitan background was character-istic of Trieste in the pre-1914 era. Schmitz's particular ethnic mix did not include any known Slavic ancestry, but that of many others did. Bruno Coceani (1893–1978) for instance, the leading Fascist in the region, who became provincial prefect during the period of Nazi rule, 1943–45, was born Coceancig. Scholars have debated quite intensely in recent years whether Trieste's history has been primarily that of a bitterly-contested ethnic frontier of three hostile civilisations or a hy-brid, cosmopolitan 'Illyria' whose true enemies have been interfering

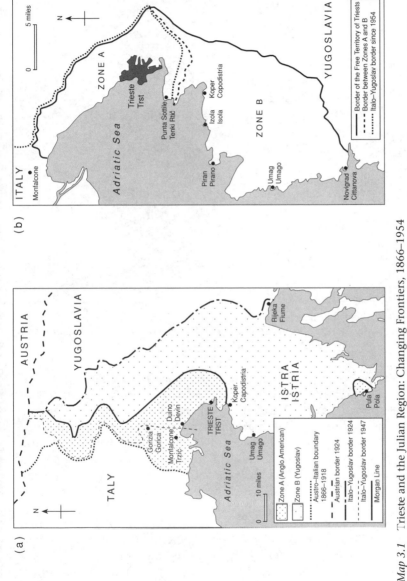

Map 3.1 Trieste and the Julian Region: Changing Frontiers, 1866–1954
Map (a) shows the Zones of control established in 1945, and Map (b) shows the smaller Zones as redefined in 1947

Source: R. G. Rabel, *Between East and West: Trieste, the United States and the Cold War, 1941–54* (Durham NC: Duke University Press, 1988) pp. xvi–xvii.

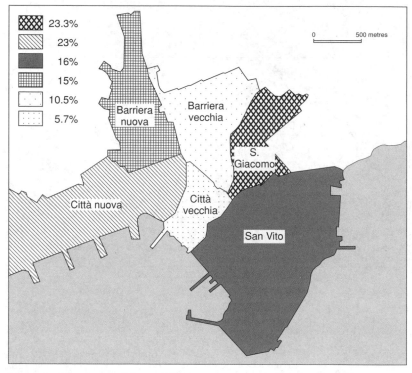

Map 3.2   Slovenes in Trieste, 1920
Source: M. Cattaruzza, in Engman *et al.*, *Ethnic Identity in Urban Europe* (Aldershot: Dartmouth Publishing, 1992) p. 219

outside powers. It is the main city of the Julian region, that band of territory in the north-east corner of the Adriatic where the Julian Alps meet the sea, known in Italian as Venezia Guilia and in Slovenian as Julijska Krajina. Spatial metaphors to describe its circumstances abound. Physically it is the main crossing-point between Central Europe and Mediterranean Europe. Ethnically it is the meeting point of the Germanic, Romance and Slavonic language groups. Politically and socially it is the crossroads where northern and southern Europe, and eastern and western Europe, meet. During the post-1945 decade Trieste succeeded Danzig as modern Europe's latest attempt to resolve urban ethic conflict by means of a free city experiment. While the latter's heyday was as a Polish emporium on the Baltic run by Germans, so Trieste's was, a little later, a Habsburg emporium on the Adriatic run by Italians. Waiting off-stage for much of history, like the Kashubians, was another third force, the Slovenes. The differences are: first, that while the Kashubians decided – or had it decided for them – that they were Poles, the Slovenes were never very sure about being Yugoslavs and were able to sustain and develop a distinct identity; and secondly, that the physical geography delineated maritime Trieste much more sharply from its hinterland, a rugged and barren limestone escarpment rising steeply and immediately behind the city. However, the most important difference between the cities, for our purposes, is that while German Danzig succumbed, Italian Trieste has survived.

Apart from a few years of Venetian rule in the late fourteenth century Trieste, Italian in language though it was, had no history of association with any other Italian-speaking state before it was added to the Kingdom of Italy in 1918. Before then it had for six centuries been a part of the multinational Habsburg Empire, governed from Vienna. Hitler blamed the Habsburgs 'for not having been able, in spite of centuries of rule, to Germanise Trieste and the Adriatic coast' (Rusinow:226). The Italian-speaking middle-class intelligentsia was determined from the late 1860s onwards that Trieste should retain and expand its *italianitá*. Slovene teachers in 1914 believed that 'the famed *italianitá* is based on crumbling foundations' and that within 30 years they might 'hoist the southern Slavic flag above the ruins of the historical remnants', shaking off Trieste's Italian ethos just as Prague had shaken off its German one (Cattaruzza 1992:201). In May 1945, when Tito's Partisans and the Yugoslav army began the liberation of Trieste from German occupation, it seemed for a few weeks that their prediction might be correct. This was not to be, however, and the western Allies quickly regained control of the city. The Free Territory of Trieste (FTT) compromise of 1947 was never fully implemented and, after nine years of Allied Military Government, Trieste rejoined Italy in October 1954.

Habsburg Trieste, 1377–1918

Trieste's antecedents were Roman and medieval. It became a Habsburg free port in 1719, and by the mid-nineteenth century it was the world's seventh-largest port (McCourt:29). In 1891 it was more firmly located within the Austrian economy, and free port status was ended. This was a realistic decision, for although the opening of the Suez canal in 1869 had realigned western Europe's oriental trade routes, the exclusion of Austria from the new German Empire meant that most international trade north of Austria's borders was routed through north German ports. More positive developments, such as the extension of the *Südbahn* railway from Vienna to Trieste in 1857, and the opening of a second line in 1909, appeared to point to Trieste's real future as the main port of Austria. Modern engineering skills had broken through the Alpine barrier between central and Mediterranean Europe, opening up the opportunity for Habsburg Austria to advance its development as a Mediterranean power. Trieste, the leading edge of this strategy, grew from a population of 45,000 in 1815 to a total of almost 230,000 by 1910 (Table 3.1).

In population Trieste had from medieval times been a predominantly Italian-speaking city. But its rural hinterland in all directions was solidly Slovene or, to the south, Croat. The historian della Croce wrote in 1698 that 'today ... outside the city walls ... they speak no other idiom than Slav' (Stranj:39). Only the small coastal towns of the Istrian peninsula shared Trieste's Italian pedigree. So once Lombardy (1859) and Venetia (1866) were transferred from Austria to Italy, the way was open for the development of an Italian nationalist movement in Trieste. Irredentism proper, calling for the direct transfer of Trieste to the Kingdom of Italy, remained a minority movement until the First World War. But Trieste's Liberal National Party, founded in 1868 and predominant in local politics until 1914, defended Italian cultural hegemony vigorously. Although Slovene and some Croat in-migration increased in the later nineteenth century, Slovene public schools were effectively banned in the urban area by the local state, while the use of Slovenian in street signs and in speeches in the city council was not tolerated (Cattaruzza 1992:203). The local dialect, *Triestino*, flourished

Table 3.1   Trieste: Population by main language spoken, 1846–1953

Year	Total population	Language of everyday use (umgangssprache) %			
		Italian	Slovene/Croat	German	Non-Citizens
1846	80,300	58.0	31.5	10.5	–
1880	144,844	61.2	18.0	3.3	17.5
1900	178,599	65.1	13.1	4.7	16.9
1910 revised	229,510	51.8	25.8	5.5	16.8
1921	228,583	85.0	11.1	3.9	n/a
1940	261,809				
1945	259,102	No data, but strong Italian predominance			
1953	272,188				

Sources: Cattaruzza 1992:213; Stranj: 39

(as it still does) among all classes and ethnic groups, but its effectiveness as a mode of communication was not enough to combat growing linguistic conflict (McCourt:87).

If Trieste's role as Austria's port and third city was to be sustained, it was therefore essential for the central state to find some way of counterbalancing local Italian supremacy. Although Germans retained high status, they amounted to no more than about five per cent of the population. The Austrians had indeed failed to Germanise Trieste. Vienna therefore pursued as best it could its usual post-1867 policy of equal recognition of nationalities. The more strident the claims of Italian ethnicity became, therefore, the more crucial it seemed for Vienna to preserve the position of the Slovenes in the city. Ironically therefore, Austria in effect encouraged a measure of Slavisation in Trieste, in the years prior to 1914, as a way of safeguarding the Balkans for the monarchy. *Municipalismo*, a sense of civic pride, both local and cosmopolitan, was encouraged for this purpose (McCourt:73). It was not just the requirements of state policy which led in this direction, however. The Slav minority in the city was also undergoing important changes, first demographic and then social and political. Historically the Slovenes constituted an overwhelming majority in the area surrounding Trieste and also in the outlying areas which lay within the city boundary. But the central city, which had always been Italian, grew rapidly as the nineteenth century progressed. Slovene predominance in the outlying districts changed very little, but its importance fell in relation to the size of the city as a whole, so that the city region, as it grew through the second half of the nineteenth century, appeared to have become increasingly Italian, prior to a revival in Slovene numbers first measured in 1910. Without explanation, however, these figures are misleading.

Migration into the city during this period was considerable. During the later nineteenth century it came mainly from the rural Slovene population of the area north and west of Trieste, and from the eastern hinterland as part of the agricultural depopulation characteristic of upland Europe at this time. After 1900, with the ending of free port status and the expansion of trade and industry, there was increased migration from the mixed Italian- and Croat-speaking districts to the south of Trieste, and from *regnicoli* (citizens of the Kingdom of Italy). Research on the local origins of immigrants during these two periods has shown that what was really happening was that, contrary to what the above table appears to suggest, there was proportionately far more migration of Slovenes to Trieste in the pre-1900 period, while after

1900 it declined relative to that of Italian-speakers and *regnicoli*. Prior to the 1880s it was broadly accepted by Slovenes that urbanisation and Italianisation went hand in hand. Only at the very end of the nineteenth century did Slovenes began a widespread drive to maintain and advance their own culture in the urban setting of Trieste. The first statistical manifestation of this was the Census of 1910 (Cattaruzza 1992:193).

The level of residential segregation between Italians and Slovenes was not high. Even in the outlying suburbs, once exclusively made up of old Slovene settlement, the expansion of the city after 1870 led to a dilution of the Slovene proportion to below 50 per cent. In the six districts of the city proper, the size of the declared Slovenian-speaking minority ranged from 5 per cent to 23 per cent. There is little evidence of micro-level segregation within districts. In the working-class San Giacomo district, for instance, Italian and Slovene workers shared the same apartment blocks and voted in large numbers for the multi-ethnic Socialist party. San Giacomo, like the suburban areas, was apparently occupied predominantly by Slovenes until about 1900, when local government policy connected it by tram and tunnel to the main city, and established several Italian-language schools there (Cattaruzza 1992:203–4). The other city district with a large Slovene minority was Cittanuova, the city's richest district. This neighbourhood included the premises of all the main Slovene organisations. It was also the district with the highest level of support for *Edinost*, the Slovene Nationalist Party. This high-status area was also where the small German elite mainly lived, and so had more of the Habsburg multi-ethnic ethos and less of the Italian cultural predominance which characterised much of the city. The Italian-dominated local government permitted public Slovenian primary schools only in the suburbs and rural areas. In the city itself the only education in Slovenian was provided by the private primary schools funded by the Society of St Cyril & Methodius and by a private commercial school. The municipally-controlled school system was a major tool for Italianisation. A total of 2,852 children attended the high-status German primary and secondary schools, of whom 34 per cent were Italian-speakers and 30 per cent Slovenian-speakers (Ara:269).

In the city's social pyramid the German bureaucratic and business elite was at the top. Forty-two per cent of German households had domestic servants in 1900, against only 19 per cent of Italian households and 10 per cent of Slovene households (Cattaruzza 1992:196). In 1910, only 37 per cent of German males were in manual employment.

Sixty-three per cent of the Slovene male workforce was based in the lower echelons of public employment, in labouring work in industry and the port, and in agricultural work in the rural fringes of the municipality. Slovene women worked predominantly in domestic services, especially as housemaids, including many Italian households. Slovenes were under-represented in the professional and white-collar classes, although after 1900 there was a distinct Slovene middle class in Trieste 'which included building contractors, house and property owners, haulage contractors, merchants, teachers, lawyers and wealthy master craftsmen' (Cattaruzza 1992:196). There was also growing white-collar employment for Slovenes in the *Ljubljanska Banka* (1901) and the *Jadranska Banka* (1905), established in the city with Czech/Slovene and Croatian capital respectively. The Italian community, in contrast, was fully distributed throughout the social structure. Fifty-two per cent of Italian men were manual workers in 1910, the remainder being distributed through the range of professional and white-collar occupations. Italians were found in all major occupational groups in broad proportion to their overall numbers in the population. This broad structure was one of the factors which enabled Trieste's Italian community to assimilate other ethnic groups into its environment for a longer period of time and to a greater extent that was the case elsewhere in Habsburg Austria (Cattaruzza 1992:196).

In terms of religious adherence Trieste appeared to be more united, all three of the main groups being Catholic. The position was in practice rather more complex. Italian Liberalism, which dominated municipal politics, was secular and somewhat anti-clerical. There was also a liberal wing of the Slovene national movement, but for most Slovene nationalists in Trieste in this period 'religious affiliation coincided with national identity' (Cattaruzza 1992:199). One of the strongest elements in the campaign against Italianisation at the turn of the century was the characterisation of the town's Italian bourgeoisie as anticlerical and ungodly. The Habsburg state was happy to foster this division: no Italian was appointed as Bishop of Trieste between 1850 and 1914. With the exception of one German appointment all were Slovenes. In 1912, 190 out of 290 priests in the diocese were Slovene, including 20 out of 70 in the city (Rusinow:27).

Attitudes to religious practice were only one part of cultural distinctiveness. Italian activists prided themselves on the way in which urbanisation and Italianisation in Trieste appeared to go hand in hand, spreading 'the delights of town life saturated with *italianitá*' (Cattaruzza 1992:203). Close observers however might have noted the growth of *Edinost*, the Slovene newspaper and National party, which in the 1870s depended almost entirely on the old Slovene villages for its membership, but which by 1897 recruited most of its members from the city proper. The development of a range of middle-class cultural organisations in the Cittanuova after the turn of the century was harder to ignore, as was the increasingly militant display of Slovene ethnic awareness. In 1904 the Slovene banks funded the conversion of the old Hotel Balkan into the *Narodni Dom* (National House) as a focus for these activities (Stranj:70).

The changing political culture of the city reflected these developments. Trieste was governed by a city council and, from 1861, was also given full status as one of the 17 provinces of Austria, with the council doubling as the provincial diet or *Landtag*. From 1873 Trieste also returned members to the *Reichsrat*, the imperial parliament in Vienna. Voting was restricted to only about 5 per cent of the population until reforms in 1909 increased the number of electors in the municipality from 9,000 to 41,000. The party political culture which operated through this system consisted of four main groups. The Conservative party, led by the mercantile and business elite, dominated representation in both the city council and the imperial parliament for much of the late nineteenth century. Although mainly Italian in language and culture, its outlook was cosmopolitan and it was strongly loyal to the Habsburg monarchy. The Italian (or National) Liberal party, *Partito Liberale Nazionale*, contested city council seats vigorously, but stood on an abstentionist platform for election to the imperial parliament until 1897. The abandonment of this policy won them both representation at Vienna and control of the city council, where they effectively supplanted the Conservative Party. With their main base in the intelligentsia and the professions, they were also believed to have strong links with the Italian Masonic lodges (Webster:335). The Slovene Nationalist Party, *Edinost*, was established in 1874, and until 1900 drew its support almost entirely from the outlying areas of traditional Slovene settlement. The fourth major political grouping, the Social Democratic Party, entered Trieste politics in 1897. In 1905 it split into separate Italian and Slovene sections. The Italian section remained firmly Austromarxist, but the Slovene section encouraged the development of strong Slovene cultural sentiments among its followers (Melik:156–61). The outcome of this complex political culture was that Trieste was represented in Vienna by a mixed ticket of Italians, Slovenes and Germans down to the mid-1890s, by a solid block of five Italian Liberals for the decade 1897–1907, and thereafter by Social Democrats, Italian Liberals and Slovene Nationalists.

In 1914, therefore, Trieste remained a city of predominantly Italian culture and political leadership with German influence greatly reduced. Trieste's Italian business elite, though not the broader stratum of the lower middle class, was still inclined to the view that its best interests lay in continued membership of an Austrian Habsburg state which delivered order and which maintained the carefully contrived pre-eminence of the city's port. The major changes had been the new capacity of Slovene ethnicity to survive, develop and assert itself in the urban setting, and the rise of a Social Democratic movement which appeared as if it just *might* have the potential to transcend the ethnic division that prevailed among the middle classes. There was, without doubt, a vociferous Italian irredentist movement in the city by 1914, but it was by no means clear that the mainstream of local Italian opinion was dissatisfied with the city's existing status. There were two unstable elements in this situation. The first was the apparent end of Slovene willingness to accept Italianisation as the price of urbanisation. Trieste was no longer just the only major Italian city in Austria but also, since it was so much larger than Ljubljana, it was also the largest Slovene centre in Europe.[16] The second unstable element was the condition of the Habsburg state itself. If it were not to survive, or if it were to further devolve power to the nationalities, then there might be no choice for Trieste other than that between Italy and membership of a new south Slav state.

Trieste and Italy, 1918–45

On the eve of the First World War Trieste had been Habsburg Austria's third largest city (after Vienna and Prague) and its only major port, some 310 miles from the capital city. With the collapse of Austria-Hungary in 1918, Trieste became the fourteenth-largest city in Italy, 410 miles from Rome. The economic unity of central Europe during the Habsburg era had gone: new political boundaries brought new customs barriers, and the benefit of Austrian subsidies to Trieste's railway links was largely lost. The total traffic by sea and rail through Trieste, which was 6.1 million tonnes in 1913, fell to 2.9 million tonnes in 1921 and remained at below half of its 1913 level for most of the 1930s. Venice, which was almost 20 per cent below Trieste's

---

[16] Trieste's population in 1910 included some 56,916 who identified themselves as Slovenes, according to the revised census. Ljubljana's total population in 1910 was 41,727 of whom 33,846 were Slovenes (Stranj:66).

volume of exports in 1913, exceeded it comfortably after 1929 (Moodie:216; Mihelic:36–40). It is true that inter-war Italian governments, both non-Fascist and Fascist, made considerable efforts to revive the city's fortunes, transforming it from a commercial into an industrial city (Moodie:220). Nonetheless, the city's best economic days were behind it. The new Yugoslavia had argued in 1919 that it could offer a better future to the port city, but in truth the replacement of Habsburg Austria by a string of protectionist successor states meant that Trieste's former role had largely gone whatever her future national location. The Trieste entrepreneurs were won over to Fascism in large numbers by its chimerical vision of an imperial Italy dominating the Balkans and the Levant through Trieste (Rusinow:114–15).

The transfer of Trieste to Italy in 1919 was politically unavoidable. First, by the secret London Pact of April 1915 with Britain, France and Russia, Italy had been promised Trieste, together with most of the remaining Austrian territory in the Julian region, in exchange for entering the war on the Allied side. Secondly, Italy was a war victor with more clout than the emerging Kingdom of the Serbs, Croats and Slovenes (Yugoslavia) so that the Italian majority in the city was given far more weight in the decision-making than the Slovene predominance in the surrounding countryside. The region which was transferred from Austria to Italy, known in Italian as Venezia Giulia, included just over half a million Slovenes and Croats, a narrow majority of the region's population (Stranj:33). In these circumstances postwar Italian governments were eager to confirm their rule over Trieste and its hinterland, including the Istrian peninsula.

This had not always been Italian policy. When Italy was pursuing a foreign policy based on trans-Mediterranean expansion, between 1878 and 1904, her main competitor was France. The Triple Alliance with Germany and Austria-Hungary was therefore a natural corollary. It implied closing the door on a Balkan-centred foreign policy and discouraging such irredentist rumblings as might appear in Trieste from time to time. But after 1904, following Italy's disappointing experience of African imperialism, her focus shifted slowly to the Balkans and to the Italian populations in Trieste and the Istrian coastal towns. Her diplomatic change of sides and involvement in the Allied war effort after 1915 was the confirmation of this change (Webster:333–9). Although Austrian naval forces in the Adriatic surrendered in 1918 mainly to local Slav committees of public safety, the Austro-Italian Armistice gave over the whole area to Italian military government, pending a general peace settlement (Rusinow:84–5).

All the main political parties in Trieste were disorientated by the new context. The National Liberals had achieved their irredentist mission, but their upper-middle-class leadership had to learn to work in the context of Italian universal suffrage rather than the Austrian curial system. A wave of industrial militancy swept both Italian and Slav workers, and the Socialists were in fact the strongest political party in Trieste at the end of the war. But their ethnic unity was maintained only by continued adherence to a redundant Austromarxism. In October 1918 they made a forlorn attempt to revive this policy by coming out for an autonomous Trieste under League of Nations protection (Rusinow:89). But within a year the old leadership had been ousted and the local movement became part of the 'maximalist' wing of Italian socialism, including a substantial Slovene element which Socialist prime minister Nitti regarded, rather optimistically, as a welcome step towards ethnic integration (Rusinow:97).[17] Italy's newly-appointed city commissioner saw in Italian nationalists and Fascists the only effective force for resisting this. For the middle-class and professional Slovenes who had supported *Edinost*, the situation was no easier. In 1918 they denounced as 'unnatural and unacceptable' the suggestion that Trieste might be separated from its economic and geographic hinterland and attached to Italy, but could only respond with ineffectual anger when it came to pass (Rusinow:91).

The American government had not been a party to the secret London Pact with Italy in1915, and at the Paris peace conference Woodrow Wilson proposed a line through the Julian region which was slightly more favourable to Yugoslavia than the London Line. Rather than agreeing to less, however, the Italians in fact demanded more territory. Once America returned to Republican isolationism in November 1920, Italy indeed obtained a more favourable settlement than even the 1915 London line. The concession they made to achieve this was that the predominantly Italian-speaking coastal city of Fiume (Rijeka), deep inside Croatian territory, was guaranteed as a Free State, with D'Annunzio's irregular forces to be expelled by the Italian Army. In fact, however, the strength of Italian irredentism in Fiume made it impossible for the last liberal Italian governments to implement the

---

[17] In Habsburg times the SDP comprised separate parties for the various nationalities in the Monarchy. The Austro-Italian SDP joined the Italian Socialist Party after Italy's occupation of Trieste in November 1918. The Austro-Yugoslav SDP continued for a while to support an independent Trieste, but it too joined the Italian Socialist party in September 1919 (Novak:39).

Free State effectively, and in September 1923 Mussolini's government took control of the city. The Italian middle class of Trieste, most of whom had placed their economic faith in Austria before 1914, were now prominent in their support of Fiumean irredentism, fearing that an independent or Yugoslav Fiume would further destroy Trieste's international trade (Novak:27–34).

The tensions in Fiume and the other Italian centres along the eastern Adriatic contributed greatly to the worsening of ethnic relations in Trieste. The first Fascist units were established in the city in April 1919, led by irredentists who had fought as volunteers in the Italian Army during the war, notwithstanding their Austrian citizenship. Once Francesco Giunta was despatched from Milan to take over the leadership of Trieste's Fascists early in 1920, the Fiume issue began to be effectively exploited to advance Fascism in Trieste. Giunta played down the local party's early emphasis on corporatism, distinguished Trieste Fascism from the unstable left-radicalism of D'Annunzio, and secured the support of Trieste big business for Fascism. When two Italian sailors were killed in the Yugoslav town of Split on 12 July 1920 Giunta organised a mass protest meeting in Trieste the following day, which ended with the burning down of the Slovenian national centre, the *Narodni Dom*, by Fascist mobs with the apparent collusion of the Italian Army (Rusinow:99–100; Novak:36). In September the crisis deepened as a general strike swept Italy. While government policy elsewhere was to let the strike take its course, in Trieste the response was more forceful, stimulated both by Fascist agitation and by the local authority's fear of a Slav/Communist revolution. The trade union headquarters was destroyed in a police raid, and the ethnically-mixed working-class area of San Giacomo threw up barricades which were blasted aside by artillery (Rusinow:105).

The first opportunity to measure public reaction to these dramatic developments came in 1921. The new Italian census of Trieste revealed that while the total population, at 228,583, had remained virtually unchanged since 1910, the number who perceived themselves as Slovenes or Croats had fallen from 26 per cent to 11 per cent of the population (Stranj:39). In politics, likewise, the size of the Italian electorate was increased by the enfranchisement of the *regnicoli*. A new nationwide anti-left coalition, the Italian National Bloc, took the form in Trieste of a Fascist-led movement, completely subsuming the old National Liberals. The 1921 turn-out of 70 per cent represented a fall from the 83 per cent levels of 1909–13, and may or may not have included an element of intimidation of Slav voters in some neighbourhoods. Certainly the lower turn-out of 57 per cent in 1924, after Mussolini had seized power, does suggest intimidation (see Table 3.2). In comparison to pre-war elections, the Slovene Nationalist vote had declined dramatically, while the Left's vote had improved substantially, lending substance to the view that many Slovenes had shifted their allegiance to a doctrine which appeared to offer a better prospect of taking them out of Italy than did old-style nationalism. The Italian Socialist party, however, had been split in January 1921 by the creation of the Italian Communist Party. The majority of the Triestine Left went Communist, including virtually all the Slovene group and many Italians, leaving the local Socialist Party as the smaller of the two groups and as exclusively Italian (Novak:41–2). After 1924 genuine democratic elections ceased in Trieste.

During the 1918–22 period there was still a considerable amount of support among Trieste's Italians for administrative autonomy in the Julian region. This was the case for many older people, for Socialists, for the Mazzinian Republicans and for the old National Liberals. The Fascists, however, were totally opposed to autonomy, and helped to resist it until Trieste's legal transfer to the Kingdom of Italy was secured in December 1920 (Rusinow:109-110). In social policy, Italianisation quickly became the order of the day at an early stage after the war. Remaining German-language schools were immediately closed. The private Slovenian-language schools financed by the St Cyril & Methodius

Table 3.2   Selected elections in Trieste, 1897–1924
Support for the main parties (as % of turn-out)

	Austrian Parliament 1897	City Council 1909	City Council 1913	Italian Parliament 1921	Italian Parliament 1924
Votes cast	25,319	33,894	35,440	34,108	32,118
Turn-out	70	83	83	70	57
National Liberals	56	34	44		
Republicans				13	11
Bloc/Fascists				44	55
Social Democrats	18	21	21		
Socialists				12	4
Communists				20	14
Slovene Nats	26	27	25	9	8

Sources: Melik: 160; Stranj: 77

Society were also closed down, and many suppressed schools reopened as Italian schools. From 1919–20, Italian taught by Italian teachers became compulsory in Slovene primary schools. Slovene education was allowed to continue in the rural Slovene areas, but only one Slovenian primary school was allowed to remain in the city of Trieste. Slovene secondary education in Trieste was stopped. In the pre-Fascist period therefore, state education policy was to 'ruralise' Slovene language and culture, and in effect set the clock back to the mid-nineteenth century (Ara:271–2). In civil administration, bilingualism continued to be the formal position until 1922 but in practice the authorities required, from the beginning, Italian translations of Slovene documents to be provided wherever such was needed for their convenience. Probably there were few in Trieste city for whom the need to provide Italian documentation was more than a mild humiliation, but in the rural areas it was more often a serious inconvenience (Rusinow:117–18).

Ethnic competition in the Trieste region had been a cornerstone of the Fascists' advance in Italy, and conditions for Slovenes in the region deteriorated rapidly once Mussolini seized power. Slovene émigrés and irredentists publicised Italian maltreatment so vigorously that Mussolini failed in his bid to achieve friendly relations with Yugoslavia, and in November 1926 he took an opposite diplomatic direction. His one-sided pact with Albania was a signal for a new bout of Italianisation and suppression in the Trieste region (Rusinow:199; Novak:42–3). In June 1927, a meeting of Fascist leaders from Trieste and the other five Julian provinces met to co-ordinate an Italianisation programme. They agreed that there was no 'aliens problem', but there was a problem of achieving full Italian and Fascist 'penetration' among the Slav population. The aim was therefore to 'eliminate from public life in the individual centres the Slav agitators', including the lawyers, the school teachers and the priests, together with the Slav press, cultural and athletic organisations. Publishers and political parties were soon suppressed. In rural areas placenames were Italianised. Syndicalist policies had the effect of undermining the Slovene co-operative system and damaging the finances of Slovene farmers and other businesses. The civil service in Trieste was fully Italianised, the number of vacancies being increased by the transfer of civil servants of Slovene background to distant parts of Italy (Rusinow:199–201; Novak:37). Schools were quickly identified as 'the fundamental instrument of the policy of assimilation', and from 1923–24 Italian was to be the only language of education for children entering the system. The essentials of this policy were accomplished by 1927–28. 'Extra hours' provision in minority languages was made difficult and then abolished, and private instruction in minority languages to groups of more than three students was forbidden. During these years it was often the lower ranks of Slovene Catholic clergy, especially in rural areas, who kept their language going. Italian policy during the Fascist period was in practice harsher in the Julian region than in other minority areas because of the local circumstances of close ethnic intermixing and past bitterness. Slav reactions therefore took a form which did not appear elsewhere, of burning of Italian schools and nursery schools, 'the two most visible and hated symbols of the Italian denationalisation policy' (Ara:274–84). During the Fascist period it is estimated that about 100,000 Slovenes and Croats, 20 per cent of the region's Slavs, left Venezia Giulia (Stranj:33).

Resistance in the Julian region came from three groups – the Italian Communist party, the Trieste Mazzinian Republicans, and Slav clergy and lay activists. Resistance was probably strongest in the rural areas where the priest was the main influence. In Trieste and the smaller urban areas the Communists were stronger and the enemy was characterised primarily as 'Fascism'. But most resistance activity in the pre-war period was in fact from Slovene and Croat activists for, as one writer later put it, 'the national factor put the ideological factor in the shade' (Rusinow:208). The Republicans were effectively rounded up in 1932, though some of them later reappeared in force in the regional Committee of National Liberation established in 1943. Fascist repression was answered with terrorist violence. Police were attacked and killed, schools and munitions factories were burned, and in 1931 the *Corriere della Sera* of Milan wrote of an 'atmosphere of war' in the Julian region. A major show trial before a special tribunal in Trieste in 1930 resulted in four executions and many long prison sentences. A more conciliatory era followed, as Mussolini's wider international aims led him to sign a non-aggression pact with Yugoslavia. The pact ended suddenly in April 1941, when Germany and Italy overran and carved up Yugoslavia (Rusinow:236–7; Novak:44–5).

The first organised resistance to the Axis in Italy and Yugoslavia came from the Slovenes. The *Osvobodilna Fronta* (Freedom Front) was Communist-led, but included the non-Communist Slovene nationalists and was active in Trieste by the end of 1941. Its policy was strongly Slav nationalist, and so its work complemented perfectly the simple Fascist representation of the situation as Italy/Fascism or Slavdom/Communism. The Italian Communists were effectively bound into this situation by the Comintern's popular front agreement of 1936 and by the immediate priorities of resistance. By the end of 1942 the OF was strongly established in the city's underground network and had a formal agreement with the Italian Communists. Ironically the Italian Fascist government's acquisition of Ljubljana province, which they were pleased about insofar as it kept their German Axis partners at a distance from Venezia Giulia, aided the *OF* by removing the international frontier between Trieste and Ljubljana and thus facilitating movement. The Italian government attempted to respond to *OF* operations by reprisals against farms and villages, and by the gratuitous diversionary tactic of a pogrom against Trieste's Jews in 1942–43. But by the summer of 1943 Slovene and Croat resistance in Venezia Giulia had escalated to the level of an alternative government in many areas. The progress of these Partisans throughout the Julian hinterland in 1944 had the effect of confining not only German forces, but also Italian resistance elements, to Trieste and the other coastal towns (Rusinow:276–80, 324).

The Hungarian minister in Rome had reported to Mussolini as early as 1939 that the song of the moment in the bars of Nazi Vienna was 'what we have we shall hold on to tightly, and tomorrow we shall go to Trieste' (Rusinow:268–9). In September 1943 Nazi Germany did indeed take over direct control of the region from the collapsing Italian Fascist regime. This posed some new problems. On the Italian side the choice for non-Communists was either to work with Slav Partisans to end the German occupation, thereby running the double risk of ending up in a state which was both Slav and Communist; or to collaborate with the increasingly-harassed Nazis against these longer-term threats. Several members of the Trieste business elite accepted the responsibility of running the city's local affairs for the Nazis, including the Prefect Bruno Coceani, who had deserted from the Austrian army in 1915 to join the Italian fight for Trieste. They later defended their actions on the grounds that to have Triestine Italians volunteering to collaborate in the government of the city was a better strategy for resisting Slav advance than allowing Nazi administrators to divide and rule, or even to annexe Trieste to Germany (Rusinow:327–8). They made no recorded protest against the Nazi concentration camp established at *Risiera di San Sabba*, in the suburbs of Trieste (Sluga 2001:81).

The Italian Resistance, on the other hand, dismissed Coceani's policy as doubly misjudged. In the unlikely event of Germany winning the war Trieste would certainly be Germanised rather than returned to Italy. In the more likely event of an Allied victory, the best insurance for Trieste's *italianitá* would be to have played a prominent role in the resistance and, as far as possible, to have identified Italians rather than Tito's Partisans with the liberation of Trieste. This was the task of the

Committees of National Liberation (CLN) set up in Trieste and the other Julian centres, most of which stood in the Mazzinian republican tradition. Their task was the most difficult of all, because both the realities of the Nazi occupation and the instructions from the central CLN for northern Italy (for whom the Trieste question was of secondary importance) required them to work with Tito's Partisans. Their strategy was to seek to maintain a high profile, and independent status. But as the Yugoslav partisans grew stronger in late 1944 they could afford to withdraw all Communists from the CLN and leave it in a weak state, especially in Trieste itself, from which it could not recover. Rusinow believes that even this was irrelevant, for the border formalised by the Italian Peace treaty of 1947 was really the result of a compromise between the political goals of one Allied Army and the military requirements of another. 'The Italians had no say' (Rusinow:328–30).

From Military Government to Italy again, 1945–present

In the summer of 1943 Roosevelt floated the idea of a free port zone comprising Trieste, Pola and Fiume (linked or not linked) to serve the economies of central Europe, along Habsburg lines. Britain did not rule out the free port idea, which thus began to emerge in a half-hearted and hesitant way as the preferred option (Whittam:346–70). Following a German military revival in Yugoslavia, Churchill and Tito met at Naples in August 1944. Tito disliked the proposal for an Allied Military Government in the Julian region pending a peace conference, and refused to commit himself on the postwar system of government to be implemented in Yugoslavia. A few weeks later he won from Stalin a 'unique concession' that Soviet troops would help drive the Germans out of Yugoslavia but would not remain in occupation. This put Tito in power in liberated Belgrade, but the Russians then left the Yugoslavs to deal with the Germans in north-west Yugoslavia. Had the Russians committed forces to this sector of the front, 'they and Tito could have entered Trieste by the end of 1944' (Whittam:363). Whether Churchill's 'per centages' agreement with Stalin, made on 9 October, which had agreed a 50–50 east–west balance of influence over Yugoslavia, influenced Stalin's choice, is not known. Even so, given the obduracy of German military resistance in northern Italy, Anglo-American hopes of reaching Trieste before Tito were not high. But, faced with competing resource priorities, and apparent American unwillingness to commit resources to the region, the Foreign Office in December 1944 suggested that Tito be permitted to establish his administration up to Italy's pre-1918 frontier with Austria, including Trieste. As late as 15 March 1945 Eden advised Churchill that Tito was already in control of most of the Julian region and 'on the withdrawal of the Germans might well control all of it before our armies can get there'. The British Ambassador on the other hand advised that if Trieste were lost the Italian government would fall, with the likelihood of a Communist government taking over in Rome. The death of Roosevelt on 12 April further delayed the prospect of securing American commitment to face down Tito with force if necessary. On 25 April 1945 Field-Marshal Alexander's Eighth Army crossed the Po and it was he, influenced by immediate considerations of military strategy, who took the crucial initiative to race for Trieste (Whittam:364–5).

On 1 May Tito informed Alexander that his forces were liberating the entire Julian region, right up to the Isonzo River, Italy's pre-1918 boundary. Yugoslav Army and local OF forces fought their way into the suburbs of Trieste, while pro-Italian resistance fighters emerged in their own neighbourhoods of the city. On the same day Alexander's troops crossed the Isonzo and pressed rapidly east along the coast to towards Trieste. On 2 May Allied New Zealand troops arrived in the city and, to the fury of the Yugoslavs, the besieged German forces made their surrender to the New Zealanders. Alexander's priorities were simply to control such territory as would secure his supply lines for the advance into Austria and to avoid a situation developing where his instructions would lead inevitably into an armed clash with the Yugoslavs (Whittam:367–8). He therefore presented Tito with 'the Morgan Line',[18] which marked off the western and coastal districts of the Julian region as far south as Pola, and including Trieste, as an intended area for Anglo-American Military Government. But Tito's forces and the OF already controlled the barracks and most of the main buildings in Trieste, and the liberation committees which were carrying out civilian administration in the region. On 1 May pro-Yugoslav posters written in Italian were displayed in Trieste, stressing the themes of Italo-Slovene fraternity, and linking Fascism and the CLN as the enemy. The future of Trieste and its region, it was suggested, lay as a seventh republic within the Yugoslav federation. After two weeks of military rule by the OF, a civilian 'Liberation Council' was appointed, which declared that Trieste would be regarded as 'a city of mixed inhabitants, each with respected rights regardless of their nationality'. But these developments

---

[18] Presented to Tito in Belgrade by Alexander's chief of staff, General Sir W.D. Morgan.

in the first days after liberation took place in a context of violent daily clashes between different ethnic and ideological groups, and some fatalities. Although the Liberation Council sought to strengthen its position by drawing the Italian middle class into co-operating with its administration, tension was instead raised higher and higher by rumours, which often enough were true, of mass disappearances of Italians, who were thrown to their deaths in the *foibe*, great natural pits in the nearby limestone karst.[19] Even the local anti-Fascist Italian leader Carlo Schiffrer noted in 1944 that fear concerning the possible occupation of the city by 'a ferocious Balkan militia ... was not to be taken lightly' (Sluga 1994:285–9).

The situation was resolved when Churchill persuaded the incoming American President Truman to agree a common course of action so as to bring about Yugoslav withdrawal from the city. On 21 May Truman allowed US forces to make a major display of air power, and on the same day Belgrade announced that it would agree to the establishment of an Allied Military Government (AMG) to the west of the Morgan Line, including Trieste city. Stalin allowed some days to pass before making any formal protest, and it was clear that Tito had failed to obtain from Stalin the pledges of support which he would have needed in order to face down the Anglo-American threats. All this was confirmed in the Belgrade Agreement of 9 June 1945, and on 12 June the AMG was established over all the territory between Italy's pre-1918 frontier and the Morgan Line, which became known as Zone A. Territory east of the Morgan Line, as far as Italy's inter-war frontier, remained under Yugoslav occupation and became Zone B (Whitam: 368–70). Slav Trieste had been brought to an end after 40 days by an Allied threat of renewed war. The *OF* was not party to the final negotiations, and the activities of Trieste's Liberation Council were slowly wound up by the AMG. In Slovene communes in Zone A, and in four Italian-majority communes where Communists were strong, though not in Trieste city itself, resistance to the appointment of civil

---

[19] These *foibe* deaths are remembered most poignantly in a memorial near the village of Basovizza, just outside Trieste. In 1993 this site was raised to the status of 'national monument', the same status as the *Risiera di San Sabba*, the former Nazi concentration camp in the city. Many Slovenes believe that Italian official memory has thereby given undue prominence to the *foibe* atrocities, which it perceives as Italian deaths at the hands of Slavs, whereas it used the state trial of 1975 to suggest falsely that the *Risiera* and the thousands of deaths which took place there were entirely the responsibility of German Nazis rather than Italian Fascists (Sluga 2001:169; Stranj:90).

administrations by the AMG continued into the autumn of 1945 (Sluga 1994:291).

Military intelligence and other analysts at this stage differed in their assessments of the community divide. Some made the simple equation of Communist with Slav. Others argued that Italian political opinion was as likely to be influenced by economic as by nationalistic considerations, and 'ideological [i.e. pro- or anti-Communist] and nationalist aspirations were very much intertwined'. In the absence of a more recent census of Trieste's ethnic populations, observers fell back on the Italian census of 1921 for their reckonings of the Italian-Slovene balance in the city as about six to one (Sluga 1994:292–3). There is no doubt that there was serious ethnic division in postwar Trieste, although it is also true that some Italian Communists favoured joining Yugoslavia, and that perhaps a greater number of Communists and other anti-Fascists favoured a third option of Triestine independence. But it is also true that it suited the AMG, and the western powers generally, to simplify Trieste's divisions along ethnic lines, and to equate Communism/anti-Communism with the same ethnic line. Thus the AMG would only allow national flags, but not the Italian Communist Party flag. In 1947 it would not allow the Union of Anti-Fascist Italians and Slovenes to hold their May Day rally in Trieste's main square, the Piazza Unitá, but restricted it to a 'Slav' area. 'The Slovene problem was of course the primary reason for our presence in Trieste', reported the British General Airey, head of AMG administration, in 1949, and 'I am determined that nothing shall be done to retard the healing process or to open old wounds by reviving lost causes' (Sluga 1994:294–5).

Negotiations towards a peace treaty with Italy were begun in September 1945. The city of Trieste was the main area of disagreement between the great powers, just as Fiume (Rijeka) had been in 1919. The Four Powers agreed that there should be a border drawn on 'ethnic' lines in the Julian region, but there was no agreement on where the line should be drawn. The Russians formally called for the city itself to go to Yugoslavia. Finally a compromise was agreed by the four-power Council of Foreign Ministers on 3 July 1946, embodied in a treaty signed in February 1947, which considerably reduced the size of both military zones. Most of the territory of the larger Zone B went to Yugoslavia, including the majority Italian towns of Fiume/Rijeka and Pola/Pula, together with a long band of rural territory to the east of the Isonzo river. But the ethnically-mixed areas formerly part of Zone A, including Gradisca, Monfalcone and the contested city of Gorizia, went to Italy. Most important, the city of Trieste and a narrow coastal strip running 10 miles north remained under the AMG in the new Zone A, while a larger but more thinly-populated area in north-west Istria remained under Yugoslav administration as the new Zone B (see p. 63). It was the declared intention that the reduced Zones A and B (total population now 377,000), while remaining under Anglo-American and Yugoslav military government respectively for the present, should develop permanently as an internationalised 'Free Territory of Trieste' (FTT), with democratic local government, subject to the overall authority of a Governor to be appointed by and responsible to the Security Council of the United Nations.

In Trieste itself, communal trouble had continued throughout this period. On the day peace treaty discussions began, 11 September 1945, 80,000 pro-Tito Slovenes demonstrated outside Trieste, and 1,600 telegrams were sent to the four-power Council of Foreign Ministers reminding them that Slovene fighters had liberated the region. On 25 September a two-day industrial strike had 200,000 workers parading in the city organised by Pro-Yugoslav Communists. Major pro-Italy demonstrations also took place. During the visit of the commission of experts in March 1946 two people were killed and over 20 injured in clashes in the city, followed by a claimed 250,000 attendance at the funeral procession for the victims. A few days later over 100,000 paraded to demands Trieste's reunification with Italy. Violence returned again while the Council of Foreign Ministers was debating its decisions in Paris. Large pro-Italy and pro-Yugoslavia groups clashed with each other. Slovene businesses and Communist premises were attacked. The Titoists organised a two-week strike in June 1946. Both sides were affronted – the Italians because it was becoming increasingly clear that Italy was to lose most of the Julian region, and the Slovenes because Trieste was continuing under an AMG which they felt, increasingly, was favouring Italy (Novak:253–7).

The situation on the ground then calmed, but the implementation of the Peace Treaty on 15 September 1947 saw renewed conflict. The Italians were incensed at both the loss of most of the region to Yugoslavia and the separation of Trieste from Italy. Five were killed and hundreds reported wounded in clashes following rival demonstrations. The situation worsened as the appointment of a Governor of the FTT continued to be delayed, due to great power disagreement. All proposed candidates were vetoed by one side or the other. This was an early indication that the FTT, which never in fact came into formal existence, would not work, since it was dependent on a Security Council which was hamstrung by East-West disagreement.

Italy was happy to delay, as it did not want to see the FTT succeed. It still hoped to regain Trieste, while its worst fear if the FTT did get off the ground would be the spread of Communism from Zone B into Zone A. Yugoslavia sought to appear more co-operative towards the appointment of a Governor, but in fact it delayed as well, and still hoped that the FTT might become a part of the Yugoslav federation (Novak:277–9).

No progress was therefore made with bringing the FTT into existence, and on 20 March 1948 the three western powers issued a Tripartite Proposal, which promised to return the entire FTT to Italy, and declared that 'Trieste, which has an overwhelmingly Italian population, must remain at Italian city'. This surprise move did not mean much in practice, because it would have required Soviet agreement to become operational. The Proposal was issued just a month after the Communist take-over in Czechoslovakia and, even more crucially, a month before the Italian general election, at which it was feared by the western powers that the Communists might do well. But although the proposal's main importance was as a cold war manoeuvre, it did have considerable influence on the AMG's administration of Zone A. The Zone effectively became a part of the Italian economy through a series of measures and agreements with Italy during 1948–49, while pro-Italian influence also increased in the civil administration of Zone A.

Representatives of pro-Italian parties were appointed to key positions, supporters of Triestine independence were kept in a small minority, while Communist and Slovene representatives were excluded from Trieste's communal board altogether. Italian refugees from the former large Zone B were far more likely to be granted permanent residence status in Trieste than non-Communist Slovenes and Croats coming from the same territory. During 1948 new identity cards were issued, in Italian only for the city of Trieste, which indicated the citizenship the holder had held prior to the creation of the FTT. From September 1949 the Italian language was declared to be the official language of Zone A, with Slovenian being granted the status of a second language in the rural Slovene communes only. In due course the post of Slovenian schools adviser was abolished (Novak:283–98). Notwithstanding the stipulations of the 1947 Italian Peace Treaty, which made Italian, Slovene and even Croatian if necessary, official languages in Trieste, AMG officials recommended that bilingualism should be discouraged, on the grounds that it would have made Slovene official, which 'immediately brings in the national aspect'. Proposals for a new

Slovene cultural building to be erected by the AMG in 1954[20] were quashed when it was reported that the site chosen, in a formerly Slovene rural area, 'has in fact become largely an Italian residential district. Furthermore, the building is located on the main road from Italy into Trieste, which would make it unsuitably conspicuous for use as a Slovene centre' (Sluga 1994:297–9).

On 28 June 1948 a new external factor came to play upon the Trieste problem. The Yugoslavian Communist Party was expelled from the Cominform, and while for a time Stalin probably anticipated that Tito would be toppled from power, the outcome was in fact that Yugoslavia left the Soviet block and at the same time became liable to approaches from the Western powers. Immediately the Communist party in Trieste split into Titoist and Cominformist factions: each side retained both Italian and Slovene supporters. It was not until late 1949, however, that the West publicly acknowledged that Tito's break with the USSR was genuine, and that his authority within Yugoslavia remained firm. Thus the Western powers quietly sidelined their Tripartite declaration. Recognising Yugoslavia as a potential friend, they encouraged bilateral Italo-Yugoslav talks on the FTT. Yugoslavia, meanwhile, set aside its support for the formally-correct Soviet view that the FTT should be implemented as a neutral, demilitarised territory with a UN-appointed governor in accordance with the 1947 Italian peace treaty. From the summer of 1949 Yugoslavia demanded instead the dismemberment and partition of the FTT between itself and Italy, which in practice meant abandoning its claim to the city itself. Factors influencing this change included the very poor showing of the Titoists relative to the pro-Cominform Communists in the 1949 FTT elections, discussed below, and the success of the pro-Italy parties. This convinced Tito that Communists stood no chance of winning democratic control of the FTT at any future stage. Even if they did they would be Moscow Communists, hostile to Yugoslavia. Additionally there was a Yugoslav fear that the Soviet Union, out of spite, might withdraw its opposition to the West's Tripartite Proposal of 1948, which would have delivered the entire FTT to Italy (Novak:299–301, 316–17; Sluga 2001:146–55).

In the summer of 1949 the Yugoslav dinar currency was introduced into Zone B, thus beginning the merger of Zone B into the Yugoslav economy in the same way as the AMG in Zone A had already done regarding Italy. When Tito spoke on Trieste for the first time in a year,

---

[20] As a form of compensation to local Slovenes following the reassignment of Trieste to Italy, to replace the *Narodni Dom* which had been destroyed in 1920.

on 10 July 1949, he did not repeat earlier demands for the implementation of the FTT. In December 1949 Yugoslavia privately sounded out Dean Acheson about the possibility of partitioning the FTT. At this stage Yugoslavia's aim was to take over the whole of the FTT except the city of Trieste, which it hoped to trade for the ethnically-mixed city of Gorizia (pop. c.40,000), that had become part of Italy under the 1947 Peace Treaty. Italy was anxious about the implications of Tito's break with the Soviet block, and sought to remind the Western powers of their promise to return the entire FTT to Italy (Sluga 1994:319–20, 331). The pro-Italian faction in Trieste began to grow uneasy (Sluga 1994:335). Elections in Zone B in April 1950 led to some cases of harsh treatment of the local Italian minority, and to attacks on visiting journalists from Italy. Protests ensued in Italy and in Trieste, and in the winter of 1950–51 there was an outbreak of terrorist bombing aimed at Yugoslav and AMG buildings in Trieste, and a foiled attempt to smuggle weapons to Italian irredentists in Zone B.

How did the population of Trieste respond to these changing circumstances? There had been no meaningful census since the Italian count of 1921, which was regarded on the Slovene side as being a less fair measure than the revised version of the census of 1910. There had been nothing approaching fair elections since the first Fascist elections of 1924. A census was undertaken in Zone A of the FTT in 1949, but it was decided by the AMG, with the agreement of local Slovene groups, that to include an ethnic question would be to provoke civil strife. Local elections were at last held on Zone A in June 1949, and give us some indication of the balance of forces in the commune of Trieste (Table 3.3). It was alleged that the result was biased in favour of pro-Italian parties by (a) using Italian employees in the municipal office to prepare the electoral rolls, (b) 16,132 people not receiving voting certificates, as the seventh AMG Report recognised and (c) moving the

Table 3.3   Free Territory of Trieste: elections in Zone A, 1949

	Commune of Trieste 168,108 voters	Rural Communes 13,712 voters
Pro-Italy Parties	65%	25%
Trieste Independence	10%	–
Cominformists	21%	51%
Titoists	2%	10%
Slovene Democrats	2%	13%

Source: calculated from Novak:306–7

base date of residence in the FTT from the year 1940 – as agreed in the Peace Treaty – to 1947, which gave the franchise to Italian refugees who had fled Yugoslav Istria in the summer of 1946, variously estimated at between 24,000 and 35,000 people.

Of voters in Trieste commune, the electoral lists show that 50 per cent of the electorate had been born in Zone A of the FTT, 24 per cent in Zone B of the FTT or in that part of Yugoslavia formerly within Zone B, 21 per cent in Italy and 5 per cent in other states. The percentage born outside the city is quite high for a mid-twentieth century western industrial city which had experienced very little net population growth for 40 years. This factor was probably quite strongly favourable to the pro-Italy parties. Against this must be set the probability of some level of migration into Trieste by Slovene refugees from that part of Zone A transferred to Italy in 1946–47 and by anti-Communist Slovenes and Croats from Zone B at the same time.

The level of excitement was high, with a turn-out of over 94 per cent of the registered electorate. The results are interesting, had some considerable political impact, and probably give a reasonably accurate reflection of the true position, bearing in mind the deficiencies in electoral procedure outlined above. There is a striking difference between the patterns of voting in the city and the more thinly-populated rural communes of Zone A. It is estimated that the Slovene proportions of the electorate may have been about 13 per cent in the city and about 55 per cent in the rural areas (Sluga 2001:308–9). The most striking outcome was the large majority in the city in favour of unification with Italy. Seven parties had campaigned on a pro-Italy ticket, of whom the Christian Democrats were by far the largest. Most of these parties received considerable financial and speaker support from parent parties in Italy as did the main Cominformist party, while the Titoists received help from Yugoslavia. The Slovenian Democrats and the parties supporting Triestine independence probably received little help from abroad. The vote in favour of Italy was less that the 75 per cent which AMG sources had forecast, but it was still strong, and was hailed as a great triumph by the Italian press in Trieste and in Italy. The election was also an important test for the rival Communist parties, and here the outcome for Tito's supporters was very disappointing. This result, indicating as it did the relatively strong role likely to be played by Cominformists in an independent Trieste, probably played an important part in Belgrade's gradual switch from demanding the implementation of the FTT to a policy of partition. It also gave further encouragement to those in the AMG and in western governments who had come to regard the FTT as an unsuccessful (and increasingly costly) experiment which should be wound up as soon as diplomatic circumstances permitted. The British General Airey, administrative head of Zone A, who did not conceal his pro-Italian views, was very pleased with the election result, and dismissed the votes for independence as coming from 'those elements in the population who are personally interested in the continuance of AMG and who have been led to confuse existing conditions with those which would obtain in a free territory deprived of Italian economic support and protection' (Sluga 2001:312).

By late 1949 the Western Powers were convinced that the future of Yugoslavia outside the Soviet camp was secure. The cold war was no longer perceived as beginning just five miles south of Trieste at the Zone B border. The question of the FTT area therefore reverted to the status of a conventional boundary dispute. The Western powers had only limited interest in the details of the final boundary, provided that the city of Trieste went to Italy. The problem therefore became a matter of getting Italy and Yugoslavia to agree to bring the FTT to an end. That this took five years to achieve was mainly because a succession of precarious Italian governments were reluctant to take responsibility for the final surrender of the Istrian coastal towns to Yugoslavia.

Britain was anxious to achieve a settlement, for financial reasons. The Yugoslavs felt secure in their tenure of Zone B, and had given up hope of winning the city of Trieste. For them the only area for negotiation was really the rural part of Zone A: thus they were confident that they could not lose territory, and might win some. For the same reason Italy was less keen to come to the table. The United States took the view that procrastination was therefore the safest policy, for fear that any positive action might 'revive certain difficulties now dormant'. The Soviet Union on the other hand, strongly supported by the FTT Communist Party, demanded that the FTT be fully implemented as soon as possible. In 1951 Britain and the US told Italy privately that they would not honour the Tripartite Proposal of 1948 to give Italy the whole of Zone B. It had, in the words of US Secretary of State Dean Acheson, 'been overtaken by events'. The truth was that the West did not want to damage Tito's position by taking territory from him, whereas the domestic political challenge in Italy now came from the right rather than the Communist left, so that its stability in the cold war context had become a matter of less urgent concern to the western powers (Rabel:133–8).

It was left to local developments in Trieste to intensify pressure for action. A more even-handed approach by the AMG in Zone A stirred Italian irredentist feeling, including rioting and a general strike in March 1952. An Italian government representative was therefore added to the British and American political group which advised the Zone commander, and some parts of civil government in Zone A were transferred to the Italian government. These small changes provoked the increased integration of Zone B into Yugoslavia. Although relationships between the parties were by no means good at this stage, the reality was that the options available for a formal settlement were being increasingly narrowed in the direction of a partition of the FTT along existing boundaries. The United States, sensitive to Italy's domestic considerations and to Italian-American opinion, sought unsuccessfully to persuade Tito to concede one or two of the small Italian towns on the coast of Zone B. But by September 1952, British Foreign Secretary Eden was convinced that 'the cost and trouble of maintaining the Allied occupation of Zone A could not be endured indefinitely'. He thought Western pressure would be essential for a settlement to be achieved (Rabel:142–7).

The final stage in the drama revolved around the formidable personality of Clare Boothe Luce, the new American government's appointment to the Rome ambassadorship in 1953. Her role was crucial in bringing the FTT issue to the top of the agenda. She argued, in an overstated but effective way, that the continuation of the issue could bring down the Italian government and endanger its position in NATO, 'all for the want of a two-penny town' (Rabel:149). The US and Britain decided to take unilateral action to 'equalise' Italy's position in Zone A with that of Yugoslavia in Zone B. On 8 October 1953 they announced the withdrawal of Anglo-American troops from Zone A and a handover to Italy. Privately they notified Tito that they would not oppose Yugoslav annexation of Zone B. Tito's first response was a threat to invade Zone A, but he then backed off and proposed a four-way conference.

Pro-Italy riots in Trieste in November 1953 resulted in several civilian deaths, but in January 1954 a nine-month process of talks began: first between the two western powers and Yugoslavia; then between the western powers and Italy; and finally directly between Italy and Yugoslavia with western mediation. The US State Department was advised by its own negotiators that the reclamation by Italy of a 10-mile coastal strip in north-west Istria, which included three mainly-Italian towns, was not achievable and that the British formula of a partition based on the existing Zone line was the best bet. The Yugoslavs, long reconciled to the loss of Trieste itself, were offered $22 million aid for port improvements in Zone B (Rabel:156). Minority rights would be guaranteed by both Italy and Yugoslavia. A final hiccup was a late Italian demand for the reassignment to Italy of Punta Sottile, a small promontory of high ground immediately to the south of Trieste, the loss of which would have been intolerable 'from the psychological and political point of view ... because it meant Yugoslavia would always be at the point where they would be looking into the Trieste port'. This piece of Italian face-saving cost the United States further financial aid to Yugoslavia and a large dose of emergency wheat aid in view of a failed harvest. The agreement was signed in London in October 1954, and the Italian flag was raised over Trieste's Piazza Unitá. The USSR, by then in the post-Stalin era, and looking to patch up its relations with Yugoslavia, made no protest. The London Settlement was therefore accepted by all sides. It was not registered as a formal revision of the Italian Peace Treaty, for this would have required the consent of all the signatories to that Treaty. Technically it remained provisional until a brief flare up of the issue in 1974 caused Italy and Yugoslavia to formally confirm the settlement in the Osimo Accords of 10 November 1975, which were registered with the UN (Rabel:160–1).

Short-term military initiatives in March and April 1945, followed by Anglo-American political intervention in May and June 'saved' Trieste for Italy. That this had to take the form of direct confrontation with Slovene forces backed by Tito on the streets of Trieste was the outcome of Allied, especially American, reluctance to permit firm decisions about postwar boundaries policy before the war had ended. Churchill's famous 'per centages' agreement with Stalin was effectively the basis on which the Trieste intervention was ultimately made. The deadlock between the great powers was, after 1947, also responsible for the initial failure of the FTT. From the end of 1949 however the non-alignment of Yugoslavia created a situation in which the ultimate solution was never very difficult for outsiders to envisage, however difficult it was for the two states which were directly involved to bring their followers to the point of submerging their differences in an enduring compromise.

The Statute following the London Agreement of 1954 appeared to strengthen linguistic rights for Slovenes in public employment and several other areas. But in practice restrictions and suspicions continued – the use of Slovene forenames was not permitted in birth registrations until 1966, while problems concerning the qualification and recognition of service of Slovene teachers continued. By the mid-1960s the extreme bitterness of the inter-war and early postwar periods was beginning to ease. The large Slovene exodus to Australia during the 1950s, coupled with Italian in-migration from Croatian Istria, altered the ethnic balance of the region. In the city itself, the declared Slovene share of the population stabilised at around 5 per cent. Slovene fear of direct oppression withered away, to be replaced by anxiety about assimilation, especially through mixed marriage, which we shall encounter on a larger scale in the cases of Brussels and Montreal. There was always some level of Italo-Slovene inter-marriage, but during the two decades following the Second World War such unions were discouraged, or constrained within a strict cultural framework which was normally Italian. Since the 1960s the proportion of children of such marriages who have been sent to Slovene rather than Italian schools has risen from below 10 per cent to around 30 per cent. On the other hand a survey conducted in the Province of Trieste in 1984 found that more than half of the children of Slovene-educated parents were enrolled in Italian-language schools. Equally, although Slovene culture receives support from public funds and almost a quarter of Trieste's cultural institutions are Slovene, the culture of the minority has no visibility in the city centre or outside its own community generally. The Slovene demand during the past two decades has therefore been for bilingualism, by which has been meant a higher profile, a higher degree of public recognition for their language. To Trieste Italians, however, bilingualism has been taken to mean the linguistic imposition by a small minority – all of whom in practice can speak the local dialect or Italian – on the majority (Stranj:18, 41–42, 50, 96–7, 150, 160–1, 167).

Most academic authorities agree that in political and diplomatic terms the Trieste issue is 'settled'. After 1954 the issue at last shifted from being an insoluble conflict about territorial claims to problems of minority rights and individual dispossessions. Essentially those Istrian Italians deemed locally to have been 'Fascists' left Yugoslavia, while those that remained were, or quickly said that they were, Communists. The bilateral Osimo Accords of 1975 sought to finalise the 1954 agreement, confirming the borders, renouncing all other claims, and making provision for economic co-operation. By 1990 there were only an estimated 52,000 Slovenes remaining in Italy, and 18,000 Italians in Istria, mainly in Croatia. It is claimed that between 100,000 and 200,000 Italians left Istria under Tito, many being resettled in newly-created villages, or former Slovene villages, around Trieste (Ballinger; Gardner; Minority Rights Group). By 1971 Italian-speakers comprised 64 per cent of the population of the narrow corridor which links Trieste to the rest of Italy at Monfalcone, where 20 years earlier there had been a Slovene majority of 75 per cent (Stranj:41).

This creation of these facts on the ground, coupled with what they see as an enforced invisibility in the city of Trieste, is still capable of arousing a certain amount of Slovene resentment. More volatile, perhaps, as Dr Ballinger suggests, is the vestigial irredentism of local Italians regarding the loss of the Istrian coast. The latter issue could reignite in the future if the level of regional instability rose high enough. In 1978, for instance a local Italian party, the *Lista per Trieste*, took votes away from the national Italian parties which had signed the Osimo Accords. Italians currently receive more favourable minority recognition in Slovenia than they do it Croatia, where their claims tend to be perceived as 'Italian imperialism', and become embroiled with similar claims by Krajinan Serbs and others (Mazzolini:19–22, 44). But in Trieste itself there has been remarkably little serious discord since 1954. Paradoxically, one potential problem may lie in the ending of the cold war and of Yugoslav communism. For instance, the Slovene minority at Trieste's local university grew from 200 in 1991 to 680 in 1994, due to student migration from former Yugoslavia. Most staff at Trieste University come from elsewhere in Italy, and the number of Slovene staff is very small. Slovene teachers trained in Ljubljana are not qualified to teach in Slovenian language schools in Italy unless they have taken two additional semesters at the University of Trieste. This policy was justified by the territorial governor in 1980, on the grounds that to do otherwise 'would result in almost all Italian Slovene students going to Yugoslav universities', who would 'return to Italy well-drilled in nationalism and Marxist ideology' (Gardner). Such attitudes suggest that old animosities may be buried rather than dead. The current situation is not grave. But the neo-Fascist MSI Party has done relatively well in Trieste, basing its campaigns on emotions surrounding the capture of Italian Istria in 1919 and its loss in 1945, and calling for a review of the Osimo Accords. Its leader, Gianfranco Fini, went to Belgrade in 1991 to discuss with Serbia, fruitlessly as it turned out, a carve-up of the Croatian littoral between Serbia and Italy (Ballinger:52). It is quite possible to see how the Trieste dispute might have been brought to life once again during the recent Balkans conflagration. The fact that this did not happen is an encouraging sign.

What does the future hold for the Slovene community and for ethnic relations in Trieste? The most likely scenario is a further development of minority language protection within the framework of the European Union. Whether this succeeds or not may depend on the operation of other factors. The Slovene cultural activist Bojan Brezigar, former mayor of Duino-Aurisina (a group of villages on the coastal strip between Trieste and Monfalcone) is President of the European Bureau of Lesser-Used Languages, an EU-sponsored body. Under the auspices of the Bureau a group of minority language advocates from various other EU states undertook a study visit to Trieste and Italy's Slovene districts in October 2001 (ww2.ebul.org). They found that the lack of bilingual signs and visible Slovene symbols in Trieste continues to keep the community invisible to visitors. The younger generation seemed to them to be more italianised, more likely than their elders to support Italy at soccer and more likely to marry out. Furthermore, any expansion of the Italian population in the Trieste district would intensify the erosion by urban commuters of the remaining Slovene villages. The ambivalent attitude of the Italian state has been a further problem: notwithstanding the 1954 Statute followed by state legislation in 1961 and 1973, further major state and regional legislation was needed in 2001 to secure Slovene rights in education and the public sector. As in Belgium prior to the 1960s, the question remains as to whether new language laws will be effectively implemented.

On the other side of the balance sheet, Slovene-speakers have until now shown considerable resilence and determination. The Habsburg inheritance provided a tradition of schooling in Slovenian which the Fascist era was unable to eradicate. Building on this, the community was able to develop and sustain a string of remarkably strong cultural and sporting associations, variously supported by the Catholic Church, Communist Yugoslavia and the region's Slovene co-operative bank, *Zadruzna Kraska Banka*. The fact that these associations have remained divided – in the past, often bitterly – between Catholic 'white' organisations and Communist 'red' seems to have provided a stimulus to activity rather than the converse. State support, provided that it does not bring with it the poisoned chalice of dependency, now promises more than in the past, supplying 12 hours a day of Slovene radio and two hours of television, while Slovene institutions in Italy have an annual budget of 7 million euros, provided equally by the region of Friuli-Venezia Giulia and by the government of Slovenia. No Slovene community in Italy is more than about 10 miles from the Slovenian border. As both sides of the border prepare for Slovenia's entry into the

European Union, it is hard to predict whether local Slovene communities in Trieste and its region will be strengthened or weakened by the change. What seems increasingly unlikely, given the apparent restabilisation of most of the South Slav region, is that any kind of foreseeable international development will bring the same deterioration of ethnic relations to the city as it experienced for much of the twentieth century.

4

Peaceful Reconquest: Montreal

In Montreal the French outnumber the English three to one.
In the province we outnumber them more than seven to one.
And yet, the English own everything! ...The English in
Montreal, they own nearly the whole of Canada. And yet once
upon a time the whole of Canada belonged to the French.

Hugh MacLennan, *The Two Solitudes* (1945), p. 145

His first job had been as a copy clerk in the Snowdon
branch.... the whole suburb was English. A little later he had
been made a collection clerk in an East End branch...But the
East End reeked of gasoline...

Gabrielle Roy, *Alexandre Chenevert* (1954), p. 34

In 1945 the Canadian novelist Hugh MacLennan published what
became the classic novel of Montreal's language divide. He called it *The
Two Solitudes*.[21] The phrase has become the standard shorthand
description of the peculiar social arrangements that existed in a city of
over a million French- and English-speakers where, two centuries after
the fall of New France in 1760, only a quarter of the city's inhabitants
could speak the language of the other side (Levine 1990:16). Like every
major city in north America, Montreal has received an endless stream
of migrants from a variety of ethno-linguistic backgrounds. What

---

[21] The origin of the expression was a poem by R.M. Rilke 'Love consists in
this/that two solitudes protect,/and touch, and greet each other'
(MacLennan:title page). Coincidentally, Rilke himself had associations with
Trieste.

Map 4.1   Montreal, Quebec and Canada

makes it different is the way that this has taken place against a back-
drop of older rivalry between Anglophones and Francophones, often
described – with scant regard for the inhabitants who preceded
Christopher Columbus and Jacques Cartier – as 'the founding nations'.
The competition between these two communities has been managed in
a relatively civilised way. But unlike most ethnic competition in north
American history it has not been simply rivalry between groups to get
ahead, to get the best possible slice of the pie. It has resembled much
more closely a competition for supremacy between two cultures,
typical of the contested cities of Europe. This chapter traces the history
of the two solitudes and shows how they have coped with, and more
recently been transformed by, interaction with incoming groups.

   Montreal was founded as a fur-trading and military centre at the
western edge of New France in 1642. It was built on, but now extends
beyond, an island in the St Lawrence River 25 miles long by 7 miles
wide. It is more than 500 miles from the sea, located at the furthest
point up river to which ocean-going ships could penetrate. A popula-

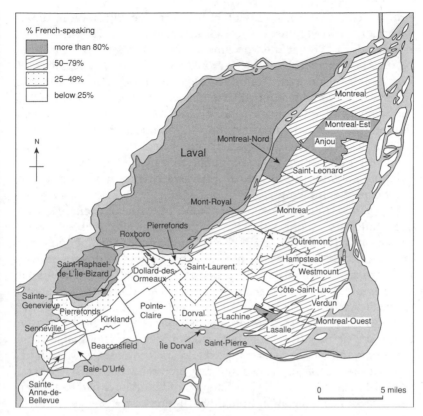

Map 4.2 Language Use on the Island of Montreal, 1971
The map does not show the level of linguistic segregation that exists within the core city of Montreal itself. The eastern part of Montreal, including its municipal acquisitions at the north-eastern end of the island, is very predominantly French-speaking. The neighbouring metropolitan city of Laval, on Île Jesus, is also shown.
Source: map from M. V. Levine, *The Reconquest of Montreal* (Philadelphia Temple University Press, 1990), p. xviii; data from A. Sancton, *Governing the Island of Montreal* (Berkeley: University of California Press, 1985) p. 140

tion of about 1500 in the 1670s had reached almost 9,000 by 1760 (Prévost:112; Levine 1990:8). During the nineteenth century the city's population grew to more than 300,000 as large-scale industry and a transport hub were added to its economic base. During the course of the twentieth century it diversified into a metropolitan and multicultural urban area of more than three million people, just over half of whom lived on Montreal Island, including about a million in the city proper (see Table 4.1). This is a familiar narrative, but in terms of ethnicity and power Montreal's story is more unusual. A French colonial outpost until 1760, it then became a French-speaking city in British North America. Avoiding state-imposed anglicisation in the late eighteenth century and anglicisation by weight of immigration in the early nineteenth, it nonetheless had to settle, between about 1860 and 1960, for being a city where Francophone demographic and electoral domination was subjugated to Anglophone economic and cultural domination. Since the 1960s this pattern has been dramatically reversed. Montreal now seems to have stabilised as a French city with an Anglophone minority which, while relatively comfortably off, is constrained and contracting.

Montreal's ethnic history poses a number of special problems. How was the ethnic survival of the tiny Francophone community of New France secured after 1760, in the context of an increasingly Anglophone British North America? How was the subsequent erosion of its position by economic forces prevented and, in particular, why did Montreal not fulfil its implicit role as an urban machine for the anglicisation of the province of Quebec? What have been the roles of central, regional and local tiers of government in these developments? How has the binary tension of the late eighteenth century between Catholic French-Canadians and Protestant Anglo-Canadians managed to retain centre-stage two hundred years later when one of the two founding groups has been largely without replenishment from outside the country, and both have had to adjust to very large-scale immigration from other cultures?

Conquest to confederation, 1760–1867

The fall of New France is symbolised by the British capture of Quebec City, 170 miles to the north, in 1760. Montreal surrendered without a

Table 4.1   Montreal: Population and language, 1871–1981

Year	Montreal Island population	Language of paternal ancestry %			
		French	English	Other	Multiple ethnicity
1871	144,000	60.3	38.1	1.6	n/a
1901	361,000	63.9	33.7	2.4	n/a
1931	1,004,000	60.2	26.3	13.5	n/a
1951	1,320,000	63.8	22.2	14.0	n/a
1981	1,738,000	56.9	13.3	26.4	3.5

Sources: Sancton:15

struggle. What was the British Government to do with its new inheritance of 65,000 orphaned French-speaking colonials? The first response was similar to that which had been attempted in Ireland 70 years earlier. The Royal Proclamation Act of 1763 was intended to remove the legal privileges of the Catholic Church, eliminate the seigneurial system of landholding, and establish common law in place of French civil law. But as the crisis in the American colonies developed, London's policy changed. The Quebec Act of 1774 reversed all the above measures, and the Constitution Act of 1791 set up representative institutions, dividing the colony into Lower and Upper Canada (the basis of the future Quebec and Ontario respectively), thereby giving territorial recognition to the Francophone community (McRoberts 1997:2–5; Levine 1990:8; Germain & Rose:17).

The population and economies of both the Canadas grew, but relations between the two groups did not improve. In his report on the rebellions of 1837, Lord Durham reported to the British government that 'I expected to find a contest between a government and a people; I found two nations warring in the bosom of a single state'. Believing that it would be possible to assimilate the French Canadians in the same way that the Louisiana French had been assimilated into the USA, he recommended a merger of the two Canadas. Accordingly, the United Canadas came into existence in 1840, with English as the only official language of government. Because the predominantly Francophone 'Canada East' still had a majority, each of the formerly separate colonies was granted equal political representation. The colonial administration soon accepted the special position of the Catholic Church, and French language and law, in Canada East. The curious practice of dual prime ministers was established, and the capital alternated, first between Quebec City and Toronto and then between Montreal and Kingston, before settling in Ottawa. In 1848 the legislature became officially bilingual. By 1851 the population of Canada West had overtaken that of its predominantly Francophone partner, thus rendering unnecessary from its point of view a continuation of the electoral compromise of 1840. A vociferous demand for 'representation by population' developed in Canada West, which ended crosscutting alliances with Francophone politicians in Canada East. London intervened again and, somewhat to Francophone alarm, the British North America Act of 1867 swept all British-ruled territories into a new, all-Canadian confederation. The official dualism of 1791 and the unofficial dualism of 1840 had gone (McRoberts 1997:7–9; Germain & Rose:21–3).

Between 1760 and 1867 the population of Quebec grew from 65,000 to one million, the Anglophone proportion rising from one per cent to 25 per cent (Rudin:28). It was still a predominantly rural society. Montreal overtook Quebec City to become the largest city in British North America, but at around 60,000 it still accounted for only 6 per cent of Quebec's population. In three important ways, however, Montreal was developing differently from the rest of Quebec. First, it was developing as a metropolis for Canada as a whole, rather than for Quebec in particular. This arose partly from its location and its economic function, but it was also related to a second difference. A French town of less than 10,000 people at the time of the Conquest had by 1820 grown to a town of some 20,000 in which the economic elite was almost entirely Anglophone. By 1831 half the population were English-speakers, rising in 1851 to a high point of 55 per cent (Levine 1990:8). This in turn helped to create a third difference: Montreal was coming to be perceived by the rest of Quebec as in it but not of it. Anglophone demographic and economic power in the city reinforced the growing tendency of French Quebec to identify its values with those of rural society. We do not know the extent to which English Montreal in these early years succeeded in anglicising Francophones, but influential forces in Francophone society, most notably the clergy, came to regard Montreal as something apart (Levine 1990:8; Germain & Rose:12; Rudin:82).

French migrants into Montreal nonetheless came, almost exclusively, from rural Quebec. Some Anglophone migrants also came from English-speaking pockets in rural Quebec: the Eastern Townships, the Gaspé peninsula and the Ottawa valley. But many more came across the Atlantic. They included English, Scots, Protestant Irish and, increasingly, Catholic Irish. Scottish entrepreneurs took over the formerly French-dominated fur trade, and later exported timber to Britain. Many of the craftsmen who made Montreal a canal and railway hub were recruited from Britain. Others were labourers in building, the docks and timber processing.

Both the massive population increase in Ireland from the late eighteenth century onwards, and its brutal reversal in the great famine of 1845–49, stimulated the overseas migration of Irish Catholic unskilled workers. Quebec City, for instance, which began as the entirely Francophone capital of New France, and which in the twentieth century reverted to 97 per cent French-speaking, was 40 per cent Anglophone in 1861, of whom about three-fifths were Irish Catholics. In Montreal in 1871 the Anglophone population was reported to be

25 per cent English in origin, 25 per cent Scottish, and 50 per cent Irish, about three-quarters of the latter being Catholics (Rudin:116). The emergence of an English-speaking Catholic community brought an additional ethnic dimension to Quebec society, posing new questions for Quebec Catholicism and Catholic education. Anglophone Catholics experienced higher levels of contact with the Francophone community than did Protestants, but Irish and French Catholics were often in conflict over employment, sometimes to the point of Belfast-style workplace riots. As in Glasgow and other British centres the Irish were lobbying as early as the 1840s for Irish priests, which meant an English-language Catholic church. This was bitterly resisted in Montreal by the local bishop, and although such a church was opened in 1847, it took papal intervention in 1873 before it achieved parish status. English-language Catholicism, and the associated demand for English-language Catholic education, were regarded as serious threats to the French-Catholic ethos of Quebec. It was resisted in the pre-Confederation period, and corralled thereafter. In practice Irish Catholics did not become a third ethnic force in Montreal: they were regarded by Francophones, and largely regarded themselves, as an addition to the Anglophone community (Rudin:110–14).

Demographic versus economic power: an uneasy balance, 1867–1960

A century after the Conquest, Confederation brought constitutional stability to Canada's ethnic divide. On the one hand Quebec lay firmly within an Anglophone Canada. On the other hand the BNA Act confirmed that French would continue to be the working language of provincial and local government in the province. Quebec comprised about one-third of the new Canada, while French-speakers comprises four-fifths of the population of Quebec (Rudin:153). A century after the Conquest it was clear that the linguistic assimilation of French-speaking Quebec into Anglophone Canada was very unlikely to happen. The one area of uncertainty was the city of Montreal. For whereas the other areas of Anglophone settlement in Quebec experienced steady decline throughout this period,[22] the English-speaking population of Montreal grew with the city. In fact, though the Anglophone majority of 1861 fell to 38 per cent in 1871 and 22 per

---

[22] The one exception was the Ottawa Valley along the Ontario border, with 35,669 Anglophones in 1871, rising to 50,525 a century later (Rudin:179).

cent in 1951, the absolute number of English-speakers in the city rose from 66,062 in 1871 to 587,095 in 1971. In 1871 Montreal was home to only 23 per cent of Quebec's Anglophones, but by 1961 this figure was 74 per cent. Montreal's share of the province's Francophones, by contrast, rose from only 9 per cent to 39 per cent across the same period (Levine 1990:10). Thus French Quebec's 'English problem' narrowed to its 'Montreal problem'. On the one hand, by the time of Confederation Francophones had, thanks to one of the highest birthrates in the western world, regained their majority in the city's population (Sancton:16). On the other hand the firm continuation of economic power in Anglophone hands, and Montreal's continuing role into the mid-twentieth century as a national rather than a regional economic centre, ensured that the face and ethos of Montreal continued to be that of an English city which happened to have a majority of French-speakers.

Population growth, and the development of Canada's natural resources, aided the economic advance of Montreal in the mid-nineteenth century. Manufacturing was added to commerce as a source of its wealth, and its Anglophone business elite developed a powerful lobby in nearby Ottawa, the federal capital. Anglophone Canada sponsored Anglophone Montreal. In 1870 it was awarded the Canadian Pacific Railway contract, with a large federal subsidy. The Bank of Montreal became the federal government's bankers. There was large-scale British investment in manufacturing. Montreal became the hub of the shipping and the rail networks. In 1900 it handled 46 per cent of Canada's imports and 36 per cent of its exports. Residents of its 'Golden Square Mile' neighbourhood were said to own 70 per cent of Canada's wealth (Rudin:203–5; Lewis 2000:*passim*).

All this began to change after 1918 as the main source of inward investment shifted from the UK to the USA. Montreal had been best placed to link Canada with Europe, but Toronto was closer to both western Canada and to the expanding middle-American market. Often said to be the most American of Canada's cities, it had surpassed Montreal in manufacturing output by 1918, and by 1930 its stock exchange had also achieved greater volume (Germain & Rose:29–31; Rudin:213). In 1931 Montreal still housed a majority of Canada's corporate headquarters, but by 1961 it was barely equal with Toronto at 32 per cent (Levine 1990:42). By the mid-twentieth century Montreal business had to face the fact that a city which for more 150 years had turned its face from Quebec to the wider Canada would in future need to explore its potential as a *regional* city.

A good city to get rich in, Montreal offered relatively poor prospects to the majority of its citizens in the late nineteenth and early twentieth centuries. The city's death rate in 1884 was 33 per thousand against Toronto's 20; in 1893 its rate exceeded that of London and was double that of New York (Jenkins:422,435; Copp:26). For although the heavy engineering industries provided relatively well-paid skilled jobs, a large fraction of Montreal's economy was in unskilled work supporting these activities, in seasonal work in the docks – which were closed by ice for up to five winter months – and in labour-intensive consumer industries. Cheap labour, provided initially by large numbers of Irish and rural French immigrants, attracted such industries (Germain & Rose:26). In 1900, 70 per cent of households were headed by manual workers, of whom well over half were unskilled (Lewis, 2000:93–4). Montreal acquired a reputation for low wages and poverty, which it did not shake off until after 1945. These conditions are described movingly in the social commentary of Herbert Ames in his *City Below the Hill* (1897) and, for the Second World War era, in Gabrielle Roy's novel *Bonheur d'occasion* (1945).

Montreal in the second half of the nineteenth century contained three major ethnic groups: British Protestants (who may be subdivided into English on the one side and Scots and Irish Protestants on the other); Irish Catholics; and French-Canadians. There was a French-speaking middle class of small business people and professionals serving the Francophone community, but more broadly it was recognised that English was the language required for economic success. As late as 1961, the average earnings of a Montreal English-speaker were 50 per cent higher than those of a French-speaker. In 1931 30 per cent of Anglophone males in the non-agricultural workforce of Quebec province were in non-manual jobs, as against 12 per cent of Francophone males (Rudin:202, 209). Irish immigrants also had a distinct profile, mainly due to their concentration and to the pace and volume at which they had arrived during the 1840s and 1850s. In 1871 a quarter of the city claimed Irish descent. By the later nineteenth century there was some ethnic clustering in employment. The Irish tended to dominate in day-labouring; the French in construction, carting and shoemaking; British Protestants were over-represented in employment in the railway yards and various areas of metal working (Bradbury:39–43). As specialised districts of employment began to emerge in the 1850s, ethnic concentration in particular industries and plants became an important factor in the growth of ethnic residential segregation (Lewis 1991:146). By 1860, at a time when the city's overall balance was divided approximately equally between

English- and French-speakers, the eastern wards of the city were 69 per cent French, the central wards 51 per cent French, and the western wards only 32 per cent French (Levine 1990:11). This trend intensified considerably during the later nineteenth century (Bradbury:40,255; Lewis 2000:93).

Unlike in Belfast, where it was sustained by fear and violence, the extensive residential segregation in Montreal happened through labour market concentration and cultural preference. In Saint Jacques ward, for instance, on the eastern fringes of the city centre, about a quarter of the population in 1861 was still Protestant and English-speaking, mainly business and professional people. These people stayed, but as the ward expanded eastwards the new arrivals were almost entirely French. Well before the end of the nineteenth century the pattern was firmly established of a 'French east' and an 'English west' of the city. The Boulevard St Laurent ('the Main'), running north-west from the city centre, became recognised as a language line. The only major exception to this was the Sainte Anne ward in the south-west. This was Herbert Ames's 'city below the hill', where physical location, especially once the Lachine Canal was cut in 1825, determined that it would be an industrial neighbourhood. Here French-speaking labourers steadily replaced the Irish in the last decades of the nineteenth century. Within this, micro-level segregation appears to have been quite strong, with the newcomers penetrating certain streets and 'forming French-speaking ribbons and pockets along the once Irish-dominated streets' (Bradbury:43). The growing Francophone majority in the city was boosted by the pattern of municipal development. From about the 1870s a large number of separate municipalities established themselves in what were in effect suburban neighbourhoods of Montreal. Many of these small municipalities sooner or later over-reached themselves, not infrequently due to overambitious investment in infrastructure by land developers at the taxpayers' expense. Municipal bankruptcy in fact became the main means through which the City of Montreal was able to annexe its parasitical neighbours. Twenty-three such suburbs were so annexed between 1883 and 1918. These were mainly in the Francophone east of the city. At the same time more and more of the better-off Anglophones were leaving the city for the financially-buoyant west island suburbs. By 1931 one third of Montreal Anglophones lived outside the city, but only one-tenth of Francophones. Francophones comprised 63 per cent of the city population but only 47 per cent of the suburbs (Levine 1990:11–15; Sancton:26).

Ethnic barriers were not absolute. Improved census evidence in 1931 revealed, for instance, that 15 per cent of all Quebecers of Irish origin reported French as their mother tongue (Rudin:110). A common Catholic faith gave some encouragement to marriages across the linguistic divide. Surname analysis also indicates that the number of Anglo-French names was not insignificant. But, whatever the volume of ethnic intermarriage, in practice two distinct ethnic communities continued to exist. Census statistics on language use bring this out clearly. Firstly a measure of the net volume of language transfers[23] was heavily in the direction of English: 74 per cent of all transfers in 1941, rising to 90 per cent in 1961. Most of these were allophone[24] immigrants switching to English: probably only about 10,000 Montrealers of French origin had, at any given date, shifted to English, with practically no traffic in the opposite direction. Secondly, the rate of bilingualism remained remarkably low for a city in which two ethnic entities had coexisted for so long. Between 1931 and 1961 the proportion of bilinguals among British-origin Montrealers rose from 23 per cent to 27 per cent, while that of Francophones declined from 31 per cent to 24 per cent (Levine 1990:16–17). Montreal during the century following Confederation may have worked effectively to preserve Anglophone economic supremacy in Quebec, but as a machine for the assimilation of French Quebec to Anglophone Canada, it notably failed.

An important part of the explanation is that neither Anglophone nor Francophone elites wanted it. From the English point of view the divide was not threatening: it was manageable, it was not violent or unstable, it did not challenge the economic status quo and it was not perceived as an impediment to further economic development. On the French side there has been ongoing debate about whether or not the conservative Catholic character of *québecois* culture impeded economic development. Certainly the Catholic clergy, a key element in the French elite through the 1950s, tended to regard economic development as a force for Anglicisation which, in turn, would lead to de-Catholicisation. *La survivance*, survival through maintaining separation and distance, was the policy. The values of French Canada's Catholic church were conservative and rural. But because the lack of Francophone economic power, in Montreal in particular, had restricted the growth of a lay elite, clerical leadership survived for longer than

---

[23] Calculated by subtracting the number of British- or French-origin populations from the number of declared English or French mother-tongue speakers.
[24] 'Allophone' = native speaker of another language (other than English and French in this context).

might otherwise have been the case. Writing of the working-class Montreal parish of St Henri, the novelist Gabrielle Roy noted its 'tranquil durability. School, church, convent: a close-knit, centuries-old alliance, *as strong in the heart of the urban jungle as in the Laurentian valleys ...*' (Roy, 1945:34. My italics.).

Further evidence that neither elite wanted change is their mutual acceptance of a curiously pre-democratic schools system: until 1964 the Province of Quebec had no public department of education. The City of Montreal and the suburban municipalities continued to operate denominationally-based school boards. There was a multiplicity of them until 1925, when the various Protestant boards federated, finally stabilising as the Protestant School Board of Greater Montreal (PSBGM) in 1945. This body, which provided teaching through the medium of English, received public funds and managed primary and secondary education for Protestants, while the Commission des écoles catholiques de Montréal (CECM) performed a similar role for Catholics. Because the system was, at least notionally, based on religious denomination rather than linguistic affiliation, a potential problem arose early on with the onset of large-scale Irish Catholic immigration. But the strategy of *la survivance* dictated that the best protection for French-Canadian culture was distance and aloofness. Thus the arrival, in strength, of Irish Catholics who saw no reason to identify with the British Empire was perceived by French Catholicism as a threat rather than as an opportunity for counter-assimilation. These incomers were not encouraged to enter Francophone education, but were insulated from it by CECM's provision of a large and growing Anglophone Catholic sector. By 1945 this had a curriculum very similar to that of the PSBGM (Levine 1990:32; Sancton 42–50). The Francophone response to the growth of the Italian Catholic community in Montreal in the 1960s was to be very different, but for a century an increasingly creaky denominational system was propped up by the English and French elites in the interests of stability.

Ethnic relations in Montreal during this period did indeed remain relatively stable. Violent conflict occurred only rarely. But its occasional recurrence was enough to highlight the deep vein of differences regarding major public issues which ran between the two communities. Montreal was not greatly involved in the rebellions of 1837–38 but when, 12 years later, the Rebellion Losses Act compensated French victims of over-reaction by the army, English rioters burned down the Canadian parliament building, resulting in the permanent removal of the capital from Montreal (Levine 1990:28–9). Half a century later, the execution of Franco-Indian leader Louis Riel again divided the communities. Riel, who had been educated at a Montreal seminary, stirred a number of minor uprisings along the western US–Canada border between bouts of treatment in mental hospitals, and he was hanged for treason in Saskatchewan in 1885. There had been little previous sign of support for Riel in Montreal, but his execution quickly sparked French-Canadian anger and a winter of agitation in the city (Jenkins:415–18; McRoberts 1997:27).[25]

Of broader significance were attitudes to matters of military recruitment and conscription. Editorials in Montreal's French and English newspapers took diametrically opposed views on the Boer War. After the relief of Ladysmith an English mob attacked public buildings in Montreal which were not flying the Union Jack, and there were fights between students from McGill and Laval-Montréal universities. Again it was a minor episode, but it helped to create the platform from which modern Quebec nationalism was launched. Henri Bourassa (1868–1952) broke with the Quebec Liberal Party over its support for the Boer War, and from 1910 his newspaper *Le Devoir* provided a new and articulate voice for nationalism. During the First World War recruiting rallies were attacked, and rioting greeted the passage of the Military Conscription Bill in 1917 (Jenkins:429–33, 452–5).[26] During the 1930s French students sided with Franco while Anglophones supported the Spanish Republic. In a referendum on wartime military conscription in 1942 all Canada's other provinces voted around 80 per cent 'yes', but in Quebec only 28 per cent did so. In Montreal the western Anglophone districts all voted 'yes' and the others voted 'no' (Jenkins:486–96; Sancton:17). Once again conscription was never actually introduced, but a fundamental difference of national identity between French Quebec and the rest of Canada had been underlined, with Montreal as its interface.

We now turn to the style of politics generated by this ethnic divide. We shall need to examine both provincial and municipal politics. On the one hand ethnicity was central to political life. On the other hand it would not be accurate to say that the parties divided along ethnic lines. In effect, the unspoken agreement at provincial level was that

---

[25] Even today the Riel case continues to resonate in Canadian public life, being the subject of a recent TV drama and debate. In a related on-line poll, 87 per cent of the 10,000 who voted said that Riel should not have been hanged (*Ottawa Citizen*, 24 Oct. 2002).

[26] As in Ireland, the measure was enacted but never implemented.

the French would run the political system. Francophone provincial governments would safeguard Catholic religion and education, and French law, but the public status of the English language in provincial government and in Montreal would not be challenged. Anglophone business would continue its dominant position in the economy of the city and beyond, and any disputes would be solved by 'back-channel communication' between the political and economic elites, or by political influence directed through Ottawa. Until 1944 the key post of provincial treasurer almost always went to an Anglophone, whose department would correspond only in English. But the majority of provincial ministers were always French-speaking, and after 1920 Anglophone cabinet representation was reduced to two. Through the 1950s Quebec governments might project a Quebec nationalist image at election times, but they did not challenge Anglophone business and indeed received subventions from it (McRoberts 1997:27;Levine 1990:30–2). The state, as an institution, kept a low profile in Quebec, partly because of the association of 'government' with Anglophone Canada and partly because a weak state suited both the French Catholic clergy and Anglophone big business (Heintzman:9–10).

The party political culture which supported this system did not fracture along the ethnic divide, partly because of Anglophone demographic weakness. The main reason, however, was that only after 1960 did language rivalry become the stuff of politics. Until then communal defence worked through Anglophone business leadership and the traditional clerical and rural Francophone elite. All of the 33 Quebec premiers since 1867 have been native French speakers.[27] The Conservatives ran Quebec with few breaks until 1897, but in the previous year the Quebec-based Liberal Wilfrid Laurier had become federal prime minister, receiving massive support from his home province despite the opposition of Catholic church leaders. The Liberals then held office in Quebec for almost 40 years, government by 'les rouges' not proving as alarming in practice as the Catholic hierarchy had feared. Even a burgeoning reputation for corruption scarcely weakened

---

[27] All except five of the premiers had French names. The exceptions were in fact all French-educated sons of Francophone mothers, while four of them also had Irish Catholic antecedents. John Jones Ross (1884–87) and Edmund James Flynn (1896–97) were Conservative premiers; Daniel Johnson *père* (1966–68) led *L'Union nationale*; Daniel Johnson *fils* (1994) led the Liberals, while his brother Pierre-Marc Johnson (1985) even more briefly headed a *Parti québecois* administration. Flynn and Johnson *pére* had Irish Catholic fathers (www.assnat.qc.ca).

the Quebec Liberals, because the new 'imperial' image which the federal Conservative party came to acquire (including its military conscription policy during the First World War) made it unelectable in Quebec, where it never achieved more than a quarter of the vote in provincial elections after 1900.

Attempts to develop an alternative to the Liberals took many years to coalesce. Henri Bourassa was unable to translate his articulation of French-Canadian nationalism into party politics. The Liberal hegemony was not challenged until the provincial Conservative leader Maurice Duplessis (1890–1959) formed an alliance with some Liberal dissidents to create *Union nationale*, a new province-only party which won power in 1936 and held it for 23 of the following 34 years. The breakaway Liberals claimed to have made their move out of disenchantment with Liberal corruption, but in fact Duplessis and his new party were themselves to become an absolute byword for patronage and clientelism. His electoral strength lay in rural Quebec, in close links with the Catholic Church and in his appeal to French ethnic sentiment. Duplessis never won the political support of Anglophone Montreal, but he never took any action which threatened the position either of Anglophone big business or of English-language interests in the city. Most analysts have portrayed his regime as 'the last of the old', and it is true that he made no attempt to alter delicate and long-established ethnic relationships. His regime was based on patronage, most especially with regard to jobbery related to the liberal professions which, together with the priesthood, continued to represent the main avenues for Francophone upward mobility. Quebec politicians were said to be 'besieged' in this era by people seeking jobs or preferment (Heintzman:12–13). In this sense, perhaps, we may regard the Duplessis era as being in part 'the first of the new': the very patronage which had for so long characterised Quebec politics and which reached new heights under his leadership, was in fact a symptom of the growing pressures for upward mobility which were to burst out into a new style of politics after 1960. It is perhaps symptomatic that when opposition to the strongly ethnic *Union nationale* did finally build up in the late 1950s it came not from English-Canadian business but from French-Canadian intellectuals (Sancton:18).

The same patterns of patronage, elite accommodation and, for the most part, avoidance of the politics of language characterised Montreal city politics. Here, of course, the ethnic demography was rather different. Until the 1870s wealth and status were the dominant elements in local politics, and about 60 per cent of the city council was English.

Demographic change, and the introduction of the secret ballot in 1889 hastened changes, and by 1900 French-speakers held about 70 per cent of council seats. By custom, the mayoralty had alternated annually between French- and English-speaking councillors. This came to an end abruptly in 1914 with the election of the populist Méderic Martin (1869–1946). Martin may have been the first modern Quebec politician to mobilise the language issue in politics. He coined the slogan 'no more English mayors here' (Sancton:23–30; Levine 1990:35). Martin's regime was too shamelessly corrupt even for the provincial government in Quebec City, and many of his powers had to be taken into commission. He used ethnic appeal to counter the efforts of municipal reform movements in the classic 'boss' manner (Jenkins:446). Martin was finally toppled after 12 years by another political boss of working-class origins, Camilien Houde (1889–1958). Houde managed to exceed Martin in both populist style and political longevity. His four terms in office, totalling 18 years, were interrupted by a spell of four years military internment, 1940–44, after he had called on young men to refuse to register for military service. He also rivalled Martin for corruption. Houde refused to co-operate with a judicial inquiry into his regime, but managed to retire without penalty (Sancton:31–3). He was replaced in 1954 by one of the investigating lawyers in the inquiry, Jean Drapeau (1916–99) who was to run the city for almost 30 years. Like his predecessors Drapeau made nationalist gestures, such as replacing the Queen's portrait in the mayor's office with a crucifix, and like them he received virtually no Anglophone votes. Unlike them, as we shall see in the next section, he was able to take advantage of changed times to implement substantive changes in ethnic relations as well as simply using the rhetoric for electoral advantage. Like Houde, he was opposed by Duplessis's provincial government, whose concept of ethnic politics and relationships with Anglophone Quebec was a rather different one. A local party sponsored by Duplessis turned Drapeau briefly out of office in 1957, so the ethnic situation in city and province appeared to be little changed from the end of the previous century. But whether society and politics could continue to be insulated from the economic changes manifesting themselves in the 1950s was a question which was soon to be put to the test.

Reconquest? 1960–2000

The two decades following 1960 saw dramatic changes in the pattern of ethnic relations in Montreal. Provincial state action, stimulating and stimulated by social, economic and municipal change, appears to have accomplished a French 'reconquest' of the city. It began with a series of legislative reforms by the provincial Liberal government of 1960–66, which became known as the Quiet Revolution. By 1968 things had become less quiet however, as the collapsing *Union nationale* government and, after 1970, the returning Liberals struggled to appease the rising tide of Francophone expectations. In 1967 Quebec nationalism found in the *Parti québecois* a unified political voice for the first time, based on the language issue. In 1976 the *PQ* won control of the provincial government, holding it for 17 of the next 27 years. Dramatic legislative changes were introduced relating to education and other areas, while important local government reforms – involving activity by both municipal and provincial politicians – altered the balance of power between Anglophones and Francophones in many areas of economy and society. Except for a brief period in 1968–70, these were accomplished without violence or major disturbances.

In 1900 'Montreal' meant a city and dependent suburbs occupying no more than one-third of Montreal Island. By the end of the century it had come to mean the entire island together with extensive north- and south-shore suburbs. While French industrial suburbs in the east of the island were being annexed to the city, many affluent Anglophones were moving out to more viable municipalities in the west. In 1931 32 per cent of Anglophones lived outside the city proper, but only 12 per cent of Francophones. By 1971 only 30 per cent of Montreal's Anglophones lived in the city, and 45 per cent of Francophones (Levine 1990:12–13). This pattern of dispersed municipal development has been fairly typical of modern cities, especially in north America. But it is also related to Montreal's particular ethnic characteristics. As we have seen, the dominant figure in city politics during the second half of the twentieth century was Jean Drapeau, a flamboyant and controversial politician, an expansionary and ambitious city leader, and a strong French-Canadian nationalist. He brought to Montreal a subway system, a baseball team and two grand international events of global stature – Expo '67 and the 1976 Olympics. Blame for the vast debt incurred by the Olympics was laid by an inquiry at his door, to which he is said to have responded that 'Pericles, too, was criticised for building the Acropolis'. He made effective efforts to move the city centre eastwards by means of new buildings such as the Radio Canada Tower and the Olympic Stadium. His pressure for the relocation of a planned concert hall from the west to the east of the city was resisted, and it was never built. Meanwhile the old 'Golden Square Mile' in the west of the city centre, symbol of Anglophone financial power, suffered increasingly from demolition. But as well as pursuing major projects vigorously and with a hint of ethnic bias, as many city bosses have done, Drapeau also pursued structural reforms in the organisation of local government. By the 1950s the municipal administration of greater Montreal was creaking. Much-needed reforms were not being made because of the reluctance of key players to disturb the ethnic equilibrium. The provincial government was not anxious for reform, for the greater Montreal area contained more than a third of Quebec's population, and rising. A new tier of metropolitan government for an entity of such size alarmed the provincial politicians in Quebec City. The Liberals, though a predominantly Francophone party in Quebec, were wary of alienating Anglophone support. Thus the linked language and education questions took precedence over municipal reform in the minds of the provincial parties (Sancton:107–8).

A scheme of metropolitan government for the Montreal area had been advocated as early as 1910. In practice annexations took place only when a suburb was facing financial collapse. As Map 4.2 illustrates, the city expanded massively through the east island, sweeping in many former suburbs, but in the west the independent suburbs remained until 2002. The main part of the reason for this was, as Méderic Martin characteristically put it, because 'these gentlemen are English', although in fact several prosperous Francophone suburbs were also located in the west island, and were also in no hurry to sign up for the city's higher tax levels (Sancton:29). In 1959 provincial Premier Duplessis bowed to suburban pressure and brought it a weak scheme which denied the City of Montreal overall control within the conurbation. Duplessis was an enigmatic leader who had some sympathy with suburban resistance to 'big government'. His party also received financial support from the leaders of Anglophone big business, most of whom lived in the west island suburbs. Mayor Drapeau refused to have anything to do with this token metropolitan body, and it petered out by the end of the 1960s. In contrast, the relative ease with which the 14 suburban municipalities on the exclusively-Francophone neighbouring island of *Ile-Jesus* were brought together as the City of Laval in 1965 is an indication of the influence of linguistic and ethic rivalries on Montreal's struggle for metropolitan government (Sancton:38–40, 104).

Another approach, which was explored and rejected, was municipal partition. This would have created a Francophone city in the centre and east of the island, and a predominantly Anglophone city in the west. It was proposed by *Union nationale* from the opposition benches in 1964, but quietly dropped when they came to power in 1966. A similar proposal came forward from the West Island Fusion Committee of mayors of the outer west suburbs in 1971. They proposed that all the suburbs to the west of Dorval Airport be joined in a single West Island City. The Liberal government backed off when it became clear that the scheme was opposed not only by the City of Montreal but also by the Francophone western suburbs (which accounted for 25 per cent of the population of the proposed new city) and by the Anglophones of the inner western suburbs, who would have been on the wrong side of any boundary (Sancton:105,141).

At last, in 1969, Drapeau was able to take advantage of ethnic disorder to get some action from the provincial government. The city's police force, resentful that their pay was significantly lower that that of the Toronto force, and having sustained two deaths and 250 injuries during 1968–69, went on strike. The city council argued that the city's police force constituted a shield on which the whole island depended, and that the stubborn history of suburban independence was the reason why the cost of law enforcement had become unsustainable. The *Union nationale* government quickly passed legislation to create a Montreal Urban Community (MUC) for the territory of the island, to comprise seven members of the city council executive together with five suburban mayors. Its immediate task would be to gather funds, and little was said about the management of services. Even this limited step in the direction of metropolitan government had been greatly delayed by anxieties over the language issue, and no mention was made of language in the legislation. Paradoxically, it was the political crisis generated by the language divide which at last created the conditions for the MUC's implementation (Sancton:111–19).

The MUC's subsequent record was not stunning. It provided the degree of financial control which the city had demanded, but as so often happens where ethnic rivalries are concerned, demographic changes proved to be a destabilising influence. Continued population movement from Montreal city to its suburbs during the 1970s weakened the City's authority over the MUC. It was becoming proportionately smaller within the conurbation. In an effort to redress the balance, Drapeau annexed a bankrupt Francophone suburb in 1982. But the *PQ*, with a strong election victory just behind it, intervened to introduce parity between city and suburbs in metropolitan government. At the same time it boosted its ethnic credentials by weakening the power of the smallest suburbs, most of which were English. The onward march of metropolitan government came to a halt at this point. Greater Montreal still had far more municipalities – 28 in 1985 – than any of Canada's other big cities (Sancton:142–8). An unholy alliance between Anglophone and prosperous Francophone suburbs made a formidable opponent. Not until January 2002, after several unsuccessful experiments, was full metropolitan government at last implemented in Montreal. *La Nouvelle Ville de Montréal* now embraces 1.8 million of a greater Montreal population of 3.4 million. For 54 per cent of the population of the new city French is the mother tongue (including immigrants from Francophone countries), while 19 per cent are native English-speakers. Fifty-three per cent of the population were reported to be bilingual in French and English, more than double the proportion of half a century previously (http://www2.ville.montreal.qc.ca).

The language issue therefore underlay resistance to municipal change. It is now time to examine other aspects of this fundamental conflict. Prior to 1960 an informal and unequal consociationalism had been the basis of language relations. Social and economic change began the sequence of events which overturned this. The power of the city's Anglophone elite was weakened by the shift in leadership from British to American capital and by the general westward shift of Canada's centre of gravity. This was compounded in 1959 by the opening of the St Lawrence Seaway, which enabled ocean-going vessels to by-pass Montreal. Rather than the pivotal link between Canada and the rest of the world, Montreal was beginning to look more like the regional centre of a French-speaking province. The energy and expense which went into international spectaculars like Expo and the Olympics was in part a compensatory activity. The link between Montreal and the rest of Quebec was also strengthened by continued rural–urban migration, so that by 1961 the Montreal area accounted for 40 per cent of Quebec's French-speakers. A Francophone society insulated from the rest of north America by a policy of *la survivance* was no longer a realistic strategy. The Francophone middle class, which had in the past been led mainly by clergy, free professionals and small-town business, expanded rapidly in Montreal in the 1950s and 1960s, with the growth of public services and the developing need for Montreal business to improve its trading links with the rest of the province. At the heart of the Quiet Revolution was an expansion of public sector employment. Thirty two thousand state employees in 1959 became 70,000 in 1970; the province's energy sector, previously 80 per cent private, was taken into public control in 1962; and a ministry of education was at last established in 1964, which soon accounted for 25 per cent of the provincial budget (Levine 1990:46–7).

By the early 1960s these socio-economic changes were beginning to manifest themselves in linguistic demands, and the language issue became of central political importance for the first time in Quebec's history. The Societé St Jean Baptiste de Montréal mounted *'operation visage français'*, a campaign 'to make Montreal the metropolis of French Canadians, a city of the French language and culture', while a more militant group, *Le Rassemblement pour l'independence nationale (RIN)* began the call for unilingual French with its pamphlet *Le bilingualisme qui nous tue* (Levine 1990:51–3). These attempts to introduce radical cultural demands into what had been a programme for social and economic modernisation were problematic for the cross-cultural Liberal regime which had implemented the Quiet Revolution. But the issue which brought language reform to a head was the anglicisation of immigrant children in Montreal's schools.

In an earlier era their common Catholicism had resulted in a certain amount of French-Irish intermarriage, to the demographic advantage of the Francophone community. But, as we have seen, the Catholic schools system showed little interest in reaching out beyond the established French-speaking community, so that the English-language sector of Montreal's Catholic schools system had been permitted to expand on autonomous lines. The acculturation of allophones to Francophone society was not a conscious aspiration prior to the 1960s. In 1900, all but 16,000 of the population of Montreal island had been of British, Irish or French background. But the picture was beginning to change, and the pace accelerated after 1945. During the 1960s alone, more than 150,000 allophones settled in the city, bringing the overall total to half a million, or 23 per cent of the metropolitan population. Italians became the largest immigrant group. In 1935 allophones in the Catholic schools system had divided about equally in their choice of English or French schools. But by the late 1960s, 92 per cent of all allophone children in Montreal were choosing to study through the medium of English, and three-quarters of the children in Anglophone Catholic schools were now allophones. Thus, by 1970, whereas less than 23 per cent of Montreal's population were native-speakers of English, almost 38 per cent of the school population were enrolled in Anglophone schools. With suburbanisation and lower birth-rates causing falling rolls in city schools, rolls in the Francophone sector were declining at more than twice the rate of the two Anglophone sectors. It was projected that, within another decade, the majority of

Montreal's new school entrants would be in the Anglophone sector (Levine 1990:55–61).

French concern at this trend developed quite suddenly. It was mobilised by events in the new suburban municipality of St Leonard in 1967. This community had grown from almost nothing to over 50,000 in 10 years, a lower-middle-class neighbourhood which was about 60 per cent French and 30 per cent Italian. In 1963 the local Catholic school board decided to meet allophone parental demand by providing bilingual as well as French-only primary schools. Demand was much greater than had been anticipated, and by 1967 over 85 per cent of these children were going on to Anglophone secondary schools. Alarmed at this, the St Leonard school board decided to phase out provision in English. Allophone protest was matched by Francophone counter-protest, which soon spread more widely. The annual *Fête Saint-Jean Baptiste* in Montreal on 24 June 1968 turned into a riot, 'the Monday of the truncheon', with 135 injured, 300 arrested, and federal prime minister Trudeau's car stoned. A local issue had become a stalking horse for something much bigger, which school boards could not be expected to handle. Many Francophones now came to agree with *PQ* leader René Levesque that 'maintaining the *status quo* ... undermines French' (Levine 1990:75). The provincial government could no longer avoid addressing the issue of language education.

Quebec had never had very much in the way of language laws. The Lavergne law of 1910 required public utilities to present bills, signs, tickets and contracts in both English and French. This had been directed against previously 'English-only' practices by some concerns in the Montreal area (Levine 1990:34). In the late 1960s and early 1970s both *Union nationale* and Liberal governments in Quebec floundered in their attempts improve on this. In 1968 the Gendron Inquiry into the position of the French language in the province was set up but, although it was to become an important document, it did not appear until 1972. In 1969 a bill requiring all Quebec schoolchildren to acquire a working knowledge of French was watered down under Anglophone pressure, so that schooling would still have to be given in English to the child of any parent who requested it. As the historian of the city's language struggle wrote: 'this was the last gasp of the old order: an urban linguistic regime in which elites from both major linguistic communities conceptualised Montreal as a dualistic, bilingual city ... rather than a primarily French city with a large English-speaking minority ...' (Levine 1990:84).

Francophone pressure groups continued to campaign for French to be declared Quebec's only official language, and for an end to the anglicisation of allophones through the school system. The rapid collapse of *Union nationale* and the slow rise of the *Parti québecois* (founded 1967) allowed the Quebec Liberals, under their new young leader Robert Bourassa (1933–96), to dominate politics for a while, but it did not make their path an easy one.[28] Firstly, the party was a coalition of diverse interests: the Anglophone community, which made up about 25 per cent of its support; most of Quebec's allophones; and those Francophones who remained loyal to the idea of a federal Canada. On the other hand the emerging *PQ* performed particularly strongly in the French areas of Montreal island (Levine 1990:98). A nervous Liberal government tried a string of half-hearted and unsuccessful measures. The number of school boards on the island was reduced, but the confessional structure was retained. The all-island council was given only limited powers. The Gendron Commission recommended delay before any further action was taken on the language of instruction. Francophone activists denounced the report as 'cowardly' and 'a trojan horse', and shortly afterwards Gendron personally changed his mind and recommended early action to ensure that immigrant children attended French schools (Levine 1990:97).

The greatest failure of the Bourassa government of 1970–76 was Bill 22 of 1974, intended to be the cornerstone of the province's new language regime. Although declaring that French was the official and working language of Quebec, behind the rhetoric a strong element of bilingualism was retained and there was little compulsion. Anglophones disliked the bill's emphasis on collective rather than individual rights, allophones were anxious lest their children failed the language test for entry to Anglophone schools, while many Francophones thought that the language tests had no teeth. Bourassa's Liberals had looked for the middle ground, but it no longer existed. In the provincial election of 1976 Francophones deserted Bourassa in droves for the *PQ*, while Anglophones gave their votes to minor parties. The number of Liberal assembly members fell from 102 to 26 and for the first time in Quebec's history a party committed to national independence took power.

The *PQ* leadership was divided as to priorities. Its experienced leader René Levesque, a former Liberal cabinet minister, saw the attainment

---

[28] The Liberals won 72 out of 108 seats in the Quebec National Assembly in 1970 and 102 out of 110 in 1973.

of sovereignty as the essential measure from which resolution of cultural and economic problems would then flow. But east Montreal's strongly *PQ* neighbourhoods wanted, above all, to see a prompt reversal of the pattern of linguistic domination. Measures which Levesque had discouraged as humiliating 'legislative crutches' were seen by his zealous colleague Camille Laurin as 'the collective psychotherapy' which the Francophone community needed to overcome its history of subjugation. Laurin's viewpoint predominated and by August 1977 Bill 101 had transformed the language balance in Quebec. Montreal was to have a *visage français*, with all signage other than for very small businesses to be in French; all Quebecers would have the right to conduct all their dealings in French; and public bodies could communicate in another language alongside French only where a majority of their clientele was non-Francophone. Most important of all was the effective circumscription of Anglophone schooling: English-language education would in future only be available to children who had at least one parent educated in English, and who was domiciled in Quebec at the time of the new law's implementation. Freedom of choice in language of instruction was at an end. English was reduced to the status of a protected language for an existing minority (Levine 1990:112–18).

The impact of Bill 101 on Anglophone Montreal was considerable. While the decade up to 1976 had seen a net loss of 68,000 Anglophones to other provinces, the absolute number of English-speakers had increased through international immigration. In the 10 years from 1976, by contrast, there was an absolute fall of 99,000 in the number of Montreal Anglophones. One-sixth of the entire community departed. The proportion of residents of the west island suburbs whose mother-tongue was English fell from 63 per cent in 1971 to 49 per cent in 1986. Major north American cities have always had much higher rates of geographical mobility than European cities. But surveys show that almost three-quarters of those who left cited the language laws as a reason for their departure, more than a quarter saying it was the main reason. Young, well-educated people and middle-income groups predominated in the exodus (Levine 1990:120–2; Rudin:163). Within 12 years of the passage of Bill 101, the proportion of Montreal's schoolchildren who were educated through the medium of English fell from 41 per cent to 29 per cent, and the proportion of allophones studying through the medium of French increased from 22 per cent to 66 per cent. The number of pupils in Montreal's Anglophone schools fell from 148,000 in 1970 to 61,000 in 1987. Over 50 schools closed down or became Francophone, and the number of Anglophone schoolteachers fell by 35 per cent. In Gabrielle Roy's 1954 novel *Alexandre Chenevert*, a bilingual bus conductor shouting instructions on a crowded city bus was 'instinctively more polite when he spoke English' (p. 195). After Bill 101 this sort of deference declined. French-speakers lost the habit of switching automatically to English when an Anglophone joined a conversation. Federal civil servants continued to speak English in Ottawa, but in Montreal customarily used French. Nonetheless, life in Montreal for many of the remaining Anglophones was still economically and socially buoyant, with access to autonomous schools and services. In 1987, 60 per cent of respondents reported that it was still possible 'to live completely English in Montreal' (Levine 1990:139–40,146–7; McRoberts 1997:84).

In 1983, even Mayor Drapeau, French-Canadian nationalist that he was, told a parliamentary hearing that Bill 101 had damaged the city's economy and international image and that his city should have a special status exemption from some parts of the law. The *PQ* response was that, far from having a case for exemption, Montreal was at the heart of what Bill 101 was all about, and the city should 'find glory as a French, not a bilingual city'. But the bill was modified in 1984 to eliminate some of the provisions which had proved harsh or even ridiculous. Anglophone municipalities were no longer required to conduct their internal business and their communications with other Anglophone authorities in French, while Anglophone hospitals could be 'institutionally' bilingual rather than just personally so (Levine 1990:129–30). Meanwhile the *PQ* government, thrown off course by the defeat of its independence motion in the provincial referendum of 1980 and by subsequent policy splits, was badly beaten by the Liberals in the 1985 and 1989 general elections. Thus when higher courts ruled Bill 101's proscription of bilingual signs to be unconstitutional, *PQ* activists in Montreal made frantic efforts to revive the language issue through zealous and sometime fanatical campaigning against non-French signs.[29] But while the issue served a purpose in re-galvanising *PQ* activists, it was negative and divisive, and was not widely regarded as a matter of substance. Whereas polls showed that 70 per cent of Montreal Francophones had supported Bill 101's line on schooling,

---

[29] The Anglo-Jewish Montreal writer Mordecai Richler (1931–2001), in a brilliant satirical commentary on language bigotry, describes 'a solemn middle-aged man' gathering evidence by taking photographs of a pub lunch notice which read 'Today's Special: Ploughman's Lunch'. This external display in English was a blatant violation of Bill 178 (Richler:1).

over 60 per cent of the population were happy with bilingual signs (Levine 1990:137).

Through all this turmoil the archaic, confessionally-based management structure of Montreal's schools lived on. An alliance of Anglophone business interests with the Protestant and Catholic school establishments continued to resist change. In 1983–85 the *PQ* failed to establish linguistically-based schools commissions on Montreal island responsible to the provincial department of education. Not until 1988 did a Liberal compromise establish secular linguistic school boards alongside the existing confessional boards. The confessional schools would in future only be available for families of that religion. At that time only 45 per cent of pupils in the PSBGM system were even nominal Protestants, so that the reform looked set to reduce its enrolments by more than half (Levine 1990:223–5).

The raising of Francophone economic status between the Quiet Revolution and Bill 101 was considerable. The ethnic income gap for males narrowed considerably from 1961, when the average Anglophone earned 51 per cent more than his French counterpart, to a much narrower advantage of 14 per cent in 1980. French private-sector business moved into symbolically large office buildings in the formerly English western side of the city centre, as well as developing in the east. In the language of work, the control of capital, the distribution of incomes and the external face of business there was a remarkable transformation. Far more people were able to work exclusively in French, and fewer exclusively in English. There were still significant differences between categories of work, but these were more related to customer and other circumstances than directly to status, as had previously been the case. Bilingualism was still needed for many senior business positions, but this now had more to do with the nature of markets in north America than with local power structures. These developments arose from the emergence of a powerful French business sector after 1960 – strongly state-initiated – rather than from any changes, other than contraction and exodus, in the practice of Anglophone companies. Thus in 1986 a survey showed that almost all the decision-making staff were Francophone in companies such as Bombardier, Provigo, La Laurentienne and *Banque nationale*, but there were fewer than 10 per cent in Canadian Pacific, the Royal Bank, Molson and the Bank of Montreal (Levine 1990:193).

There is some debate over the extent to which these economic changes were the outcome of the linguistic reforms. Did the practical and psychological encouragement given to Francophones by the legal implementation of *francisation* make the difference, or was change underway already through market forces: the growth of a Francophone consumer market, improvements in Francophone education after 1945, and Montreal's enforced switch of role from national and international economic centre to regional one? Clearly these developments are intertwined. We saw earlier that social and economic change prompted the Quiet Revolution as well as developing from it. A shift in the balance from manufacturing employment to the service sector made language in the workplace a more important issue. These changes helped to create the new pressure groups and political forces. On the other hand the provincial state's language legislation and public-sector business investment were the vehicles through which this was achieved. It is hard to believe that the changes which have taken place in Montreal since the 1960s would have happened without politics and the active role played by the state, even though this in turn could not have happened without the social changes that brought the new politics about.

What has happened is that the ability of Anglophone society to ignore 'the French fact' has ended. An Anglophone social world still exists in west island Montreal, with perhaps a third of young Anglophones still unilingual in 1981. Many Anglophones still do not have close contact with Francophones. But power balances and the character of the workplace have changed. Previous linguistic trends appear to have been reversed, securing Montreal as a French-speaking city. But, as a city in the western hemisphere, its demography is more volatile than that of most European cities. Rates of immigration and geographical mobility are higher than in Europe. The linguistic contest in Montreal is a struggle between Anglophones and Francophones of course, but the object is not the conversion of one by the other: both communities are wrestling for the linguistic soul of the allophones. The language laws have ensured that the children of most allophones do indeed study through the medium of French; the provincial government has done all it can to influence the sources of immigration so that as large a proportion as possible comes from Francophone countries, in the Caribbean, in Asia and in Africa. The remaining danger to French is that the global attraction of Anglophone north American culture, reinforced massively in Montreal by the proximity of the Anglophone economies of Canada and the USA, as well as the presence of Anglophone Montreal itself, will override the linguistic impact of the education reforms. Children of new immigrants will study in French, but will it become their main language of use? Only 25 per cent of computer users in Quebec work with French-language software, and it was estimated in 1985 that almost half of the television watched by Montreal Francophones was on English language channels. In 1986, after almost a decade of Bill 101, the census revealed that the net percentage of linguistic transfers to English was more than twice the percentage of transfers to French. Over 100,000 more Montrealers reported using English at home than were of English mother-tongue. The significance of this is highlighted by the contrasting evidence from Quebec's overwhelmingly Francophone cities: in Quebec City, Chicoutimi and Trois-Rivières, the net transfers are heavily in favour, not of English but of French (Levine 1990:212,225–6). So although Anglophones are a minority in Montreal it may be that their large absolute numbers, underpinned by the proximity of Anglophone north America, will hold firm or better.

'Third party' immigration was not new to Montreal. We have seen that the arrival of large numbers of Irish Catholics in the mid-nineteenth century was accommodated within the existing bilateral structure. Large-scale Jewish immigration from eastern Europe at the end of the century was assimilated in the same general way. There was considerable anti-semitism on the French-Canadian side, while the Protestant school boards resented having to fund school places for Jews. The 1903 decision of the provincial assembly that Jews should be treated as Protestants for educational purposes was formally overruled in 1928 by the Judicial Committee of the Privy Council in London, but in practice Jews retained the legal right to attend Protestant schools, and the Jewish School Board remained a shadow organisation. Between 1931 and 1972 Jews were required to pay taxes to the Protestant board, but were not eligible to become board members (Sancton:45–7). This was plainly inequitable, but the great majority of Jews became thoroughly anglicised through the Protestant school system and, by and large, lived and worked through the medium of English. Symbolically, the first Jewish neighbourhoods developed around the north-south line which divided the English west from the French east of Montreal, and later spread northwards along the same axis. By 1951 Jews comprised 5 per cent of the city's population, but people of British, French and Irish background still made up 86 per cent.

By 1986 this figure had fallen to less than 70 per cent, as first Italians and later other southern European groups, followed by migrants from Africa, Asia and the Caribbean, arrived in large numbers (Levine 1990:217–18). All western societies have had some difficulty in coming to terms with such immigration but through the 1960s, for *les québe-*

cois, it went against the entire ethos of *la survivance*. It was probably
not the case that Quebec's Francophone community was any more
racist than other western receiving communities but rather that the
usual kind of unease or outright hostility to non-white immigrants,
which mainstream political movements in other western countries
have resisted responding to, slotted more readily into a Quebec nationalism which had been geared to the discouragement of alien newcomers for two centuries. The schools crisis in St Leonard in 1967–69
illustrated this, when the line between resistance to immigrant
demand (mainly Italian at that time) for local schooling in English and
resistance to immigrants as such was a narrow one (Levine 1990:78). A
black Haitian social worker, a French native-speaker resident in
Montreal for 20 years, told the television presenter Michael Ignatieff in
1993 that 'the independence of Quebec terrifies me because there
won't be any room for us any more. I believe that if Quebec succeeds
in becoming independent it will be all over for ethnic minorities (*Blood
& Belonging*, BBC TV,1993).[30] If such anxieties are widespread then the
opposition of immigrant Francophones may cause any future referendum on independence to fail, and all the efforts of PQ governments to
broaden the base of *la francophonie* will have been of little avail in their
drive for independence.

This account of Montreal's divide has not yet considered the
response of the Canadian federal government to the emergence of lan-
guage as a dominant issue. Although Quebec is suspicious of the
federal government, that government has is fact been headed by a
Quebecer (Trudeau, Mulroney, Chrétien) for 33 of the last 35 years.
The federal Conservative Party has been weak in Quebec for more than
a century, but Liberal Canadian prime ministers have frequently been
Quebec Francophones, including Wilfrid Laurier (1896–1911), Louis
St Laurent (1948–57), Pierre Trudeau (1968–79, 1980–84) and Jean
Chrétien (1993–).[31] The expansion of the role of the federal state after
1945 inevitably increased the importance of Ottawa, and was a further
factor which helped to bring the Quebec situation to a head. Both
St Laurent and Trudeau saw the language issue as a matter of individual rights. Trudeau was firmly opposed to Quebec separatism or special
status for the province, which he regarded as 'ghettoisation'. In his

---

[30] Surprisingly, the televised interview is not included in the companion book
to the television series (Ignatieff:1993).
[31] Both St Laurent and Trudeau were of mixed parentage and entirely bicultural
in outlook.

view the core of the problem was the absence of equal status for Francophones across Canada: the federal state effectively functioned in English only. He set out to change all of this with the Official Languages Act of 1969 and subsequent measures. English and French were both declared to be official languages throughout Canada, and the external face of Canada became that of a bilingual country (McRoberts 1997:xiv–xv, 21, 29).

In the federal civil service the proportion of Francophone employees rose from a low of 13 per cent in 1946 to 27 per cent in 1980, a proportion which in fact exceeded their share of the population (McRoberts,1997:80; Levine 1990:92). But in other ways the reforms have been less successful. The development of a federal policy based on the assumption that French-Canadian concerns could be met by addressing individual rights in an all-Canada context did not reflect the group outlook of the 80 per cent of Canadian Francophones who live in Quebec. From about 1960 the political and intellectual leaders of French Canada increasingly referred to their nation as 'Quebec'. Their demand was not equal rights for the French minority in a Canadian nation, but effective control of the language and culture of the territory of Quebec. Bilingualism throughout English Canada in fact implied bilingualism in Quebec, which they regarded with some justification as having in the past had a corrosive effect on the use of French. The Quebec National Assembly was not prepared to institutionalise the long-standing and – in its view – damaging practice of bilingualism in the Montreal area in order to secure bilingual status for French minorities in new Brunswick (31 per cent French in 1971), and the other provinces, all of which were below 5 per cent French-speaking. By 1971 French was declining everywhere in Canada outside Quebec. Trudeau effectively backed off this issue when he later accepted that the language issue would have to be resolved at provincial rather than federal level (McRoberts 1997:31,86–7,111; Levine 1990:92–3).

What will happen at the federal level in the future is uncertain. Since 1993 Quebec has effectively broken with Canada's party political culture by voting for a regional party at Ottawa, the *Bloc québecois*, which won 54 of Quebec's 75 federal parliamentary seats in 1993. Because of the fragmentation of the opposition parties the *Bloc* became for a while Canada's second largest party. Its number of seats fell to 44 in 1997 but it is such a large group in the Canadian legislature that the outcome, should it manage to gain the balance of power in a future parliament, is not easy to predict. In provincial politics the *PQ*'s loss of the 1995 sovereignty referendum, narrow though it was, took some of the steam out of its boiler. Montreal had a clear majority against sovereignty. In 1998 the Canadian supreme court decided that a unilateral declaration of independence by Quebec would be illegal. In the same year the *PQ* was re-elected in Quebec with a comfortable majority, but it won 40,000 fewer votes than the Liberals, whose support translated less well into seats because of its degree of concentration among English-speakers and immigrants in Montreal and western Quebec. More recently, the heavy defeat of the *PQ* government by the Quebec Liberals in the provincial elections of April 2003 appears to have postponed indefinitely the prospect of any further sovereignty referendum.

A slightly surprising feature of the ethnic division in Montreal is the relative lack of violent conflict, notwithstanding the national origins of the division, the persistent pattern of economic inequality, and the intensity of feeling on the language question over the past 40 years. The reasons for this are several. Most important has been the long acceptance of the linguistic hierarchy: until half a century ago many Francophones accepted, implicitly, that big business and industry were Anglophone activities, and that the Francophone spheres were politics and patronage, the law and professional and other services to their own community. For the few with broader aspirations, the opportunity of language transfer has been at least potentially available, as it had been to the Francophone farmer's son Wilfrid Laurier (1841–1919) who, after a French elementary school education, was sent to a nearby town to learn English. A century later another Francophone prime minister Pierre Elliott Trudeau, son of a rich Montreal businessman, undertook his higher education consecutively at the Université de Montréal, Harvard, the Ecole des sciences politiques, Paris and the London School of Economics.

Disorder in Montreal's community relations has been the exception rather than the rule, but there is a history of direct conflict. Down to the 1960s, politicians at all levels were skilful is managing conflict and avoiding party-political polarisation along ethnic lines. It seemed by the end of the 1960s that the new linguistic tensions might alter this. *L'operation McGill français* in 1969, a protest at the English character of the city's most prestigious university, was tame in comparison to what was happening in American universities at the same time: the opening of a second French-language university in the city quickly defused the situation. But the schools crisis in St Leonard and elsewhere was more serious, and brought aggressive demonstrations into local neighbourhoods. Although seeking to influence the linguistic policy of the regional state, the Francophone demonstrators were also expressing direct animosity towards Italians and other immigrants. On 10 September 1969 one hundred were injured when a Francophone march through an Italian neighbourhood provoked a violent response.

Rhetoric was violent in the provincial election of April 1970, and was soon followed by real violence as the *Front de Libération du Québec* (*FLQ*), which had been responsible for various violent incidents since 1963, stepped up its campaign of bombings in the Montreal area, attacking both public buildings and private homes associated with the Anglophone business elite. In October 1970 the *FLQ* kidnapped James Cross, the UK Trade Commissioner, and a Francophone member of the Quebec cabinet, Pierre Laporte. Cross was finally released, but Laporte was murdered. Supported by Bourassa's liberal government in Quebec, and by Mayor Drapeau (whose home had been the object of a previous bomb attack), the federal government intervened on a massive scale, declaring Montreal to be in a state of 'apprehended insurrection'. The War Measures Act was invoked to suspend civil liberties and round up almost 500 suspected FLQ sympathisers. The FLQ proved to be a small group, which was quickly eliminated by the police. The War Measures Act was draconian, but polls suggested that an overwhelming majority of Quebecers believed that the measures were justified. The legislative reform programme of the 1970s drew the teeth of Francophone anger and frustration. Later protests were relatively peaceful. As the language reforms worked their way through it was the turn of many Anglophones to be angry and frustrated. In this case it is probably correct to say that the existence of an Anglo-American safety valve, in the form of ample opportunities – at least for people with youth and education on their side – to move outside Quebec may have helped avoid more violent confrontations in Montreal in the decade following the passage of Bill 101.

The Anglo-French struggle for Montreal was ignited in war, but the long-standing resentments which that inevitably engendered did not find an effective voice for two centuries. The levels of ethnic residential and workplace/occupational segregation were relatively high, as was the income gap between rich and poor, and yet the level of ethnic conflict for the most part remained low. There has now been a dramatic reversal in the relative power of the two communities, but a slight question mark remains over the final outcome. This doubt arises from the pervasive presence of Anglo-American culture. *Les Québecois* may be immune to it but new immigrants, Francophone or not, are considerably less so. Thus, although we may regard Montreal as a contested city where there has been no international intervention since 1760, we must note that the contemporary American cultural challenge, added to long-term transatlantic immigration and the economic influence of the United States in shifting Canada's centre of gravity from Montreal to Toronto, are international factors of a different sort. The role of government has also been important. Central government, in both pre- and post-1867 forms, played a discreet but important role in sustaining Anglophone Montreal, thanks mainly to the powerful influence which the latter had within that government. In the twentieth century the economic strength of Anglophone Montreal declined, while the growth of Toronto and western Canada further reduced its influence. Perhaps most important of all has been the role of regional government, first in preserving the status quo down to the mid-twentieth century, and then in overturning it thereafter. This is turn reflected social change, as one of the two solitudes which had for so long acquiesced in an improbable equilibrium decided that it was no longer prepared to do so on the same terms. Montreal appears to have achieved a new equilibrium during the past decade, but it is too soon to predict the long-term outcome with any certainty. It seems likely that what happens to ethno-linguistic relations in Montreal, especially among the immigrant communities, is likely to determine the ultimate outcome of the wider question of Quebec sovereignty.

5
Peaceful Contest: Brussels

> Brussels is probably the only capital city in the world where there is so much disdain for the language spoken by the majority of the country's population.

> Dirk Wilmars, *Diagnose Brussel* (1971, transl. Deprez & Vos:232)

> For the Flemings...territorial limitation of Brussels is essential....it stops the frenchification of Flanders, and in particular the Brussels 'oil stain'.

> Wouter Pas:18

> The clear purpose of creating these federations of communes was to better imprison Brussels in the iron collar of its [existing] nineteen communes.

> Paul Debongnie[32]

> If I were king, I would send all the Flemings to Wallonia and all the Walloons to Flanders for six months. Like military service ...

> Jacques Brel

Brussels, unlike Trieste, did experience a reversal of its linguistic balance during the nineteenth and twentieth centuries. This did not happen suddenly or as a result of violence, as it did in Gdańsk. But it

---

[32] Paul Debongnie (1923–2002), director of the Front Democratique de Francophones (www.fdf.be/infodoc).

Map 5.1 The Provinces of Belgium
Source: B. C. Donaldson, *Dutch: a Linguistic History of Holland and Belgium* (Leiden: Martinus Nijhoff, 1983) p. 32

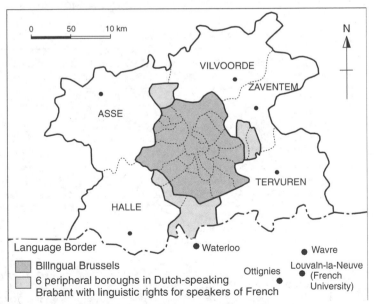

Map 5.2 Brussels and its Periphery since 1970
Source: as for Fig. 5.1

was a change which ran counter to the prevailing trend in the city's hinterland – unlike the case of Montreal – and, for that reason, it remains contested. Belgium is unique in Europe as a state where the everyday language of most of the population of the capital city differs from that of the majority in the country as a whole. Throughout much of its long history Brussels was a city where the Flemish majority spoke the local Brabant dialect of Dutch. French was also long established in the city, having been the language of the court and government since the fifteenth century. But as late as 1788 a Dutch dialect was still the main language of at least 85 per cent of the population. By 1846 that proportion had had fallen 67 per cent and, a century later to 24 per cent (Table 5.1). Since 1947 the Flemish voice in Belgian politics has ruled out any further official language census, but estimates based on surveys and on voting behaviour suggest that the proportion of the Brussels population which speaks mainly Dutch may now be as low as 15 per cent.[33] Articulate elements of the Flemish population, with considerable support in Flanders, would like to reverse this trend, while the contemporary situation is complicated by the large and growing number of non-Belgian residents, which includes both elite Europeans employed by the European Union and immigrant workers from north African countries and elsewhere. The language situation in Brussels is

Table 5.1   **Brussels: Population and language, 1846–1947**

Year	Greater Brussels*	French only %	Dutch only %	French & Dutch %	French only or mainly %	Dutch only or mainly %
1846	212,000	–	–	–	32.0	66.7
1866	309,000	19.3	46.2	31.7	–	–
1900	626,000	22.3	25.5	42.8	–	–
1910	762,000	27.1	23.2	40.8	48.7	45.5
1920	806,000	31.6	16.4	46.7	58.7	37.8
1947	956,000	37.0	9.5	43.9	70.6	24.2
Post 1947	Census question discontinued. Survey estimates of Dutch community/identity of 18% (1969) and 24 % (1972)					

Source: McRae 1986):295ff.
*Dutch monolinguals within the city boundary were around 6% less than in the overall metropolitan area until 1930, since when the difference has eroded. Small German minority excluded.

---

[33] But a high level of daily commuting into Brussels from across the Flanders border means that the proportion of the Brussels workforce which speaks mainly Dutch is considerably higher than the proportion of residents in the capital.

not stable therefore, although it is unlikely to undergo any drastic or violent change in the foreseeable future.

The language divide itself is not clear-cut. Because the top layer of Flanders-Brabant society was French-speaking for several centuries, and the region was politically cut off from the Netherlands, the Flemish dialects spoken in Flanders, northern Brabant and Brussels itself differ quite considerably from standard Dutch or ABN.[34] The Brabant dialect spoken in Brussels is *brusseleir*, a mixed dialect with a Dutch rather than French base, but lacking in social, cultural or literary prestige (Hasquin:37). The traditional working-class Flemings of Brussels tended to regard ABN as pretentious, snobbish, artificial and associated with Antwerp and Flemish extremism. French was for so long accepted as the language of high culture in Brussels that upwardly-mobile Flemings have tended to make that particular language shift, rather than adopting the less-familiar ABN. Only since 1945, with the migration to Brussels of large numbers of educated people from Flanders, have Flemish attitudes begun to change. Not until 1973 did the Flemish movement officially adopt ABN as the standard language, leading to a belated agreement between Belgium and the Netherlands in 1980 to establish a Dutch Language Union with a brief to implement and maintain the standardisation of the language (Deprez & Vos:16; Donaldson:33; McRae 1986:300-1). The Walloon dialects of southern Belgium were scarcely any closer to formal French but, as the country's ruling language, standard French was able to win recognition and acceptance more easily. There is also a small German-language group, concentrated in the eastern border region of Belgium, which today has its own institutions. It is not a significant feature of the Brussels situation however, and will not be discussed here.

Capital of the southern Netherlands to 1830

Brussels has existed since Gallo-Roman times. Its name is believed to derive from '*broekzelle*', a Dutch word meaning 'village of the marsh'. By the twelfth century it was a centre for trade and crafts. In 1430 it became part of the Duchy of Burgundy before passing by marriage to the Habsburg family in 1477. In 1530 it became capital of the Habsburg Netherlands and went to the Spanish wing of the family when the dynasty's territories were divided in 1555. As the new

---

[34] Standard Dutch is normally referred to by linguisticians as ABN or *Algemeen Beschaafd Nederlands* (general cultured Dutch). See Donaldson 1983:17.

Counter-Reformation rulers sought to roll back Calvinism the Netherlands was torn apart by a long and bitter war, which began in 1568 and dragged on into the seventeenth century. Brussels was held briefly by the Protestant rebels, but recaptured by Habsburg forces in 1585. Within a few years the future boundaries of the region were established. The Netherlands was effectively partitioned into an independent republic in the north with a new capital of Amsterdam, and a continuing Spanish Netherlands in the south, with its capital at Brussels. Catholicism was consolidated in the Spanish territories but the seven northern 'United Provinces', though having a Calvinist majority, also included a sizeable minority which remained Catholic. Conversely, while the northern population spoke exclusively Dutch dialects (soon to be developed into standard Dutch by the new state), the Habsburg south was made up of four provinces speaking dialects of Dutch ('Flemish dialects') and four provinces in the far south speaking dialects of French ('Walloon dialects').[35] Thus each of the two new states was united in either language or religion, but neither was united in both. The distinguished Walloon historian Henri Pirenne, writing in 1911, argued that the Flemish and Walloon peoples of the economically-advanced southern Netherlands, even before the sixteenth century, had more in common with one another than with their then more backward Dutch neighbours to the north. These arguments were effectively refuted by the Dutch historian Pieter Geyl, who demonstrated that the frontier established *de facto* by the 1580s, and finalised at the Treaty of Westphalia in 1648, was in fact determined not by cultural factors or popular wishes but by military and strategic considerations: the complex of river deltas which divided the Netherlands gave a measure of protection to the northern rebels which their southern colleagues lacked, and it was this physical factor which determined the new and lasting frontier.[36]

Through much of recorded history the region has been of particular interest to the great powers. In the early modern period it was a meeting point for Anglo-French-Habsburg rivalries. British policy in particular was to insist on the continued closure of the Scheldt estuary, to the detriment of the city of Antwerp and the Flanders economy, and

---

[35] The ninth Belgian province of Brabant was mixed in language but, like a microcosm of the bigger picture, it was divided into a southern French-speaking sector and a northern Dutch-speaking sector which included Brussels.

[36] H. Pirenne, *Histoire de Belgique* (vol iv, 1911); P. Geyl, *The Revolt of the Netherlands* (1932). Their arguments are summarised in Zolberg (1974), pp.228–30.

to resist the further advance of France towards her 'natural frontiers' on the lower Rhine. In this spirit the Treaty of Utrecht of 1713 transferred the southern Netherlands from Spain, which had become a dynastic ally of France, to Austrian rule. The linguistic impact of all this on Brussels was probably quite minimal. For three centuries down to 1790 the working language of the Burgundian court, and later of the Spanish and Austrian Habsburgs, was French (Hasquin:33; McRae 1986:294; De Lannoy:198). There was nothing unusual about this, for French was then the language of court and government in several major European states. The great majority of the population of the city continued to speak Flemish dialects of Dutch: Brussels was probably less than ten per cent French-speaking in 1760, rising to no more than 15 per cent by 1780 (Hasquin:34). The language line between Dutch and French dialects moved steadily northwards in the coastal region, where part of historic Flanders had been incorporated into France in the seventeenth century. But further inland, within Belgium, its ran east–west about 10 miles south of Brussels, where it has remained fairly static for some centuries except for a small elite in Brussels and Flanders, which became Frenchified during the course of the eighteenth century. This was not a matter of Walloons advancing over Flemings, but of standard French establishing itself as the language of high culture in the region at a time when the Flemish dialects were not being standardised, and were in some cases 'mutually incomprehensible' (Lorwin:387–8). The predominantly Calvinist ethos of the Netherlands meant that during the period of upheaval and state reformation in the period from 1789–1848 there was little propensity among the Flemish elite to adopt standard Dutch as their language of high culture. In Brussels the choice for educated people therefore lay between a local, non-standardised Flemish dialect with little or no literary culture, and a standardised French (Donaldson:24). J.B. Verlooy (1746–97), a leading Brussels lawyer and would-be revolutionary, published a angry pamphlet on the neglect of Dutch ('the language of freedom') by the bourgeoisie in favour of French ('the language of absolutism'), but he was not heeded (Hermans:3). 'French in the parlour, Flemish in the kitchen' is an oft-quoted summary of linguistic practice in Brussels during this period and through much of the following century.

Brussels in the late eighteenth century was still largely contained within its fourteenth-century city walls. Its population of around 70,000 was a small fraction of Paris's 500,000 or London's 900,000 (Hasquin:34). Having experienced Habsburg family rule for three centuries Brussels then underwent three major changes of regime within 40 years. Between 1789 and 1793 Austria was ejected by a combination of nobles and others who were opposed to the enlightened absolutism of Joseph II (who conducted their activities in French), lawyers and other petty bourgeois democrats who sought independence without anticlericalism or outside intervention (and who conducted their activities in Dutch), and Francophile Jacobins who lacked the power-base of their compatriots in Paris, but who exercised considerable influence once the French took control of the country after 1793 (Polansky:89–104). Thus, between 1793 and 1815 the former Austrian Netherlands became a part of the French Empire, and *verfransing* (*francisation* or Frenchification) of its capital proceeded rapidly. Thus when, in 1815, the victorious allies decided to turn everything on its head by putting the entire country under Dutch rule as part of an expanded 'United Netherlands', it proved to be a disaster. After a mere 15 years under the Dutch crown, with associated attempts at Dutchification, Walloons and Flemings came together to eject Dutch rule from a country where the majority of the population spoke dialects of Dutch, and replace it with a new state of 'Belgium' whose major institutions, for more than half a century, were to conduct their business exclusively in the language of the French minority.

How did this happen? First, the growth of bureaucracies stimulated by the absolutist reforms of the late Austrian period was promoted through the medium of French. Revolutionary and Napoleonic France regarded the languages and dialects of Belgium, like those of Brittany or Provence, as obstacles to national unity. After 1815 the Dutch state endeavoured to reverse this linguistic policy, but French was by then firmly established as the language of upward mobility. Dutch policy was soon limited to hesitant interventions in the Flemish areas, including Brussels, with a view to providing advanced education in Dutch. In 1830, in the wake of the revolution in France, a 'union of oppositions' in Belgium, composed of an alliance of Catholics and Liberals, came together to overthrow Netherlands rule in Belgium. After some reluctance the European powers agreed to sanction this unilateral rejection of their previous diplomatic efforts, and Belgium was recognised as a neutral state.

The Dutchification policy had been strongly opposed by French-speakers. This was especially true in Brussels, where *verfransing* had received a further boost from a colony of Bonapartist exiles, who made up almost 7 per cent of the city's population by 1842 (Van Velthoven:27; De Metsenaere:135). But there were other, cross-cutting issues at this stage. The Belgian revolution of 1830 was not initially a victory of Walloons over Flemings. The Catholic Church in both communities had opposed the Protestant and Masonic establishment of the Northern Netherlands during the years of Dutch rule. At the opposite extreme many of the secular industrial and commercial bourgeoisie of Wallonia, some of whom were masons or Bonapartists themselves, saw the United Netherlands, at least initially after 1815, as an economic opportunity and a way of continuing religious liberalism. There is also good evidence of the existence of Belgian patriotism in 1830. It was strongest in Brussels, where the revolution started, and amongst the urban upper strata generally and in the Walloon centres, but it also spread to the Flemish provinces. Opponents of an independent Belgium in the Flemish areas were virtually all 'Orangists' (i.e. wished to continue with the United Netherlands), but in the Walloon areas there was much more of a mixture of those who favoured reunion with France and those who wanted to remain part of the Netherlands for fear of either economic dislocation and/or of the over-powerful Catholic Church which they thought would thrive in a separate Belgian state (Zolberg:186–91).

Thus, after a half-century of upheaval the Belgian state in 1830 assumed its modern form. But another kind of revolution was also well under way in the country. During the eighteenth century the Austrian Netherlands had been regarded by some as 'the garden of Europe'. Agricultural revolution led to industrial revolution, and by 1830 Belgium was well-established as 'the second industrial nation' (Polansky:11,18). The impact of this on the development of Brussels as a commercial and financial centre was considerable. The population of the city proper grew from about 70,000 in the late eighteenth century to 100,000 in 1831.[37] The French-speaking population of the capital rose from around 5 per cent to around 30 per cent. This was as much a measure of Frenchification of the upwardly mobile elements in the city's Flemish population as it was of Walloon urban migration, for Wallonia's coal mines and heavy industries were acting as a centre for economic growth and a magnet for population within Belgium. The early centres of economic advance had included the agriculture and the rural linen industry of Flanders, boosted by the growth of Antwerp's trade following the re-opening of the Scheldt Estuary during the period of French rule. But by the 1830s Britain had secured the re-closure of the Scheldt, while the Flanders economy was approaching collapse.

---

[37] The population of Greater Brussels by 1831 was about 140,000.

Capital of Belgium, 1830–1914: French unchallenged

Belgium thus became an independent state for the first time in 1830. It was economically advanced and relatively liberal, with free speech and no political censorship. But as language, nation and state in western Europe came, or were forced, more and more into harmony, Belgium began to look odd. Although it had a Flemish majority over Walloons of about 60 per cent to 40 per cent and it was laid down in the constitution that 'the use of language is free', in practice Belgium came into existence as a Francophone state. French was to be the only language of government and administration for more than half a century, and it remained the only language of a predominantly Flemish army until well into the twentieth century. Brussels, the designated capital of this Francophone state, was still more than two-thirds Dutch-speaking. In the other Flemish cities of Belgium and in rural Flanders, the small minority of elite Francophones tended to dwindle as the nineteenth century progressed. In 1790 Antwerp and Ghent, like Brussels, each had Francophone minorities of about 5 per cent. As early as 1846, Ghent remained steady at 5 per cent while Antwerp had fallen to 2 per cent, but Brussels had become more than one-third French. The role of Brussels as a capital, and the associated social forces, thus provided the further contrary twist that Brussels became more Francophone as Flanders became more Flemish (Van Velthoven:21).

By this time the city was linguistically segregated in a way that reflected the class basis of the language divide. French-speakers and bilinguals tended to live in the upper part of the city, while monolingual Dutch-speakers lived in the poorer areas below. Until the economic collapse of Flanders in the 1840s more urban migrants came from Wallonia than from Flanders. But it is also clear that the assimilation of Flemings into the French community was proceeding apace: whereas Dutch-speaking streets were occupied almost exclusively by people born in Brussels or in Flanders, French-speaking streets also included a large minority of people from Dutch-speaking areas. By the 1850s, as Frenchification progressed and the city as whole assumed a French public face in its shops and street signs, segregation took the form of a French city containing Flemish enclaves, which were found mainly in the industrial suburbs (De Vriendt:201; De Metsenaere:131–3). French quickly became accepted as the language of opportunity and advancement, and many thousands of native-Dutch speakers switched to it. The French poet Baudelaire hinted at this in 1866 after a two-year stay in the city: 'People [i.e. the educated circles in which he moved] do not know French; *nobody* knows it, but everyone *pretends* not to know Flemish. This is the fashion, but the proof that they know it very well is that they tell off their servants in Flemish' (McRae 1986:294).

The higher social status attached to French was powerfully reinforced by economic developments. In Flanders the collapse of the domestic system of linen production in face of mechanised competition from the United Kingdom in the 1840s was compounded by the destruction of rural communities as a result of the same potato blight that afflicted Ireland. By 1850 'poor Flanders' had reached an economic nadir. High food prices combined with mass unemployment provoked what one economic historian has described as 'a complete disintegration of the Flemish rural economy' (Buyst:35). The heavy industries of Wallonia meanwhile entered their heyday, based on coal-mining, the iron industry and machine-building, and supported by large-scale investment channelled through Brussels. The capital city grew in size and wealth in step with the country's strongest industries. Thus the economy gave a further boost to the French language in the capital, where Brussels Dutch was ever more easily dismissed as a local dialect associated with poverty and backwardness (Van Velthoven:17). During the last decades of the nineteenth century the regional economic balance began to alter again, although the pace of change was slow, and the cultural-linguistic impact was even slower. Wallonia's coal resources began to wane, and the need to import coal favoured Flanders' ports. The Flanders textile industry at last attracted capital which enabled it to mechanise, while Antwerp achieved economic take-off as a successful port and centre for a range of modern manufactures. Industrial Wallonia had been through the demographic transition several generations before Flanders, so that by 1900 its weak demographic base was impeding the growth of the labour market (Saey:171). Between 1892 and 1910 the four entirely Flemish provinces of Belgium increased their share of Belgium's manufacturing employment from 26 per cent to 32 per cent, while the share of the four exclusively Walloon provinces fell from 57 per cent to 51 per cent (Buyst:36–7).[38] But Flanders was still some way off achieving economic parity with Wallonia, and it would be some generations yet before this second reversal of ethnic economic fortunes would have an impact on ethno-linguistic stereotypes in the capital.

---

[38] The ninth province, Brabant (which included Brussels) had its own internal language line between Flemings and Walloons. Its share of manufacturing employment remained unchanged over this period at 17 per cent.

The Catholic Church was dominant in Belgium to an extent almost unparalleled in Europe. It played an important part in the development of the language question throughout the nineteenth century and the first half of the twentieth. Belgium had more school children in the Catholic schools system than in the state system. The Church owned Louvain, the country's leading university. The Catholic Party was one of the major forces in national politics. And its heartland was in Dutch-speaking Flanders, rather than anticlerical, liberal, industrial Wallonia. Catholicity was a central component in the ethnicity of rural Flemings, who regarded godless Wallonia in very much the same light as they regarded apostate Holland. The lower clergy played an important role in the early development of Flemish national consciousness. It would, nonetheless, be a mistake to think of the Catholic Church in general as an institutional support for the Dutch language in this period. The bishops and senior clergy were integrated into French intellectual life. They operated in French and, pragmatically, would have regarded any shift towards Dutch as an added handicap in their struggle against anticlericalism in Wallonia. In Brussels, specifically, the Church became increasingly favourable to French as the nineteenth century progressed, and in fact made a significant contribution to the *verfransing* of the city. Sermons in Dutch tended to be confined to the early services, the so-called 'servants' masses'. The main explanation for this seems to have been class-related. Whereas the rural poor of Flanders were pious, the urban poor of Brussels were more likely to be associated with anticlericalism and, later, with socialism. To the extent that religious observance in the nineteenth-century city was associated with upward mobility, with the artisanate and with the middle and upper classes it came – in Brussels – to be associated with French (Van Velthoven:30; Witte 1992:24–5).

There is debate about precisely how the linguistic transition in Brussels came about. Variations in the questions which the census asked, and the interpretation given to bilingual declarations, are certainly factors. The census did not set out to do any favours for Dutch. Equally, it is clear that for very many families – as Baudelaire's comment implies – linguistic designation was not a straightforward matter. While the majority of marriages took place within linguistic communities, marriages across the linguistic divide were quite common – by no means the rare occurrences that they have been in cities with sharp religious differences such as Belfast and Jerusalem. In the Dutch-speaking neighbourhoods there were not many mixed-marriage households, but in predominantly French-speaking neighbourhoods an estimated 18 per cent of men married to French-speaking women had been born in Dutch-speaking areas, while 10 per cent of Francophone men in such areas were married to Dutch-speaking wives (Witte 1992:18; De Metsenaere:141). The experience of an American researcher in Brussels in the early 1970s indicates the complexity of linguistic relationships. His landlady spoke French to her husband and son; her parents, living in the same building spoke French to her and her son, but Dutch to one another; her husband, who commuted to Antwerp to work for a Dutch-language newspaper, spoke French to his wife and son, but Dutch to his in-laws (Obler:404). In a context such as this one can see that language can be viewed by many people simply as a tool of communication rather than an ethnic identifier.

Linguistic developments in the other cities and towns of Flanders took a very different turn. There the different balance of numbers meant that Francophones remained a very small elite, and Flemings were able to achieve upward mobility and prosperity without making the language shift. This was most pronounced in the province of East Flanders, which was better able to resist the economic crisis of the mid-nineteenth century than the other Flemish provinces. Here the years of Dutch rule had alerted the small, urban intelligentsia of Flanders to the existence of a modern literary culture in a language close to their own. After about 1840, this stratum was to form the basis of the Flamingant cultural nationalist movement, its main strength being among teachers and free professionals. It was by no means a powerful movement in the nineteenth century. Political alignments developed along class and religious axes rather than linguistic ones, there was little unity between the various Flemish dialect regions, and the failure of the United Netherlands project removed for a considerable period the prospect of ABN acting as a unifier. But this middle-class stratum in the Flanders towns carried the standard of Flamingantism, and the movement grew as the stratum expanded. There is no evidence that Flamingantism in the nineteenth century aroused the passions of the depressed peasantry or the urban working class. It did not make any particular impact in areas close to the language border with Wallonia, but it began to build a base in the urban Flemish heartlands (Hroch:113–14, 164–5, 172).

In this context it is not surprising that Flemish linguistic and national consciousness scarcely appeared on the radar screen of nine-teenth-century Brussels. The social forces that produced Flamingantism in Flanders produced in Brussels a move in the opposite direction, towards bilingualism and upward mobility through French. It is often said that the Flemish working class carried the torch for Dutch in the capital. This is true in a pragmatic sense, but it was not a dynamic or nationally-conscious group. Political development, when it came, was towards socialism rather than linguistic nationalism. Such Flamingantism as existed in Brussels in the nineteenth and early twentieth centuries was an immigrant import via the Flanders intelligentsia. Thus the language question was not the major issue in nineteenth-century Brussels that one might have expected it to be. This is true both of the pre-1880 period, when the Belgian state still tended to act as if Belgium was simply a Francophone country, and also of the period 1880–1960, during which the vision of a unitary state with two national languages was steadily developed. Of course a growing number of Flemings were exercised by the low social status and legal standing of their language, which is why the original Francophone conception of the state became unsustainable. But language did not become a central organising feature of politics before the 1960s. The party political system which evolved after 1830 on a limited franchise, and which continued after the implementation of universal male suffrage in 1894 and the extension of the vote to women in 1919, remained organised around issues of religion, civil liberties and class. Linguistically-based parties existed, but were not of great importance.

Much of the early Flamingant movement was drawn into the Belgian Catholic Party, with a minority going to the Liberals. The main exception to this was in the Dutch-speaking city of Antwerp, where the *Meeting-partij* held power for 10 years from 1862 and succeeded in institutionalising Dutch as the administrative language of the city and its province. This group was also influential in securing the first language laws for Flanders, whereby Dutch was permitted in the courts (1873), the administration (1878) and the state secondary schools (1883). Although Brussels still had a Dutch-speaking majority at this time, it was not included in the legislation (Vos:84–5). The Flemish movement in Brussels, though culturally active, had little political support. By the 1890s there was a 'Flemings Forward' association in the city. It had a coherent programme of demands, but attempts to create a unified Flemish party in Brussels failed, because of the attractions of other cross-cutting issues. Middle-class Brussels Flemings were divided between the Catholic and Liberal parties, while the extension of the previously very narrow franchise to all adult males in 1894 resulted in the commitment of the Flemish working class to the Socialist Party (Witte,1992:28). All three major party groupings were historically Francophone in ethos, but the pattern of the period from the 1890s onwards was of growing Flemish organisation and influence within each of the three main parties.

Capital of Belgium, 1914–60: French challenged

As elsewhere in Europe, the First World War gave a new intensity to questions of state loyalty and identity in Belgium. The initial patriotic response in both communities – that the country should unite in opposition to the German occupation – was eroded by German *flamenpolitik* on the one hand, and ethnic grievances in the Belgian army on the other. In the past Germany had shown far less interest in supporting Dutch culture in Belgium than France has displayed in Wallonia and Brussels. But now the occupiers agreed to grant the long-standing Flemish demand for the University of Ghent, which was the main university in Flanders, to become the first institute of higher education in the country to teach through the medium of Dutch. Likewise, in the sphere of government, a Council of Flanders was established and in April 1917 an administrative separation of Flanders (including Brussels) and Wallonia was announced, with parallel ministries. But the number of 'activists' – the arch-collaborators with Germany who wanted an independent Flanders – was small, and after the war all these arrangements were promptly reversed.

In the long run a more important stimulus to the Flemish movement was the situation in the army, traditionally an entirely Francophone institution, although 70 per cent of the infantry were Dutch-speakers. The language law of 1913, which gave a measure of recognition to Dutch for the first time, was not effectively implemented. It is still said in Flanders that many Flemish troops died unnecessarily in the First World War because they could not understand orders. The war greatly increased the number of educated Flemings in the army, and a 'Front movement' was formed in the unoccupied part of Belgium. It called for Dutch language rights, literacy provision and Catholic morality for Flemish troops, and for separate regiments for Flemings and Walloons. It was quickly driven underground and, like the activists in occupied Belgium, was discredited and dismissed in the immediate postwar era (Witte:1999; Buyst:37). But the expectations of Flemish nationalism had been raised, and its base had broadened. Its confidence had been increased by the economic recovery of Flanders, and its voting power was strengthened by the extension of the franchise to women in 1919. A 'maximalist' group, the small Flemish nationalist party, campaigned for a full federal partition of Belgium, while the larger 'minimalist' group sought to apply internal pressure on all three major political parties. 'Minimalist' demands were in fact quite radical. They wanted the total Dutchification of Flanders, with bilingualism for Brussels and Brabant. In 1921 a language law on administration appeared to accept the territorial principle that the regional language should be the language of public communication. Since it was to apply throughout the country however, it was hedged with various provisions covering circumstances in which minorities could obtain concessions to bilingualism. In 1923 the University of Ghent became bilingual, and in 1928 monolingualism was permitted in the army up to a certain level, so that separate Flemish and Walloon battalions could be recruited (Witte,1999:121,128–33).

A bilingual approach permeated these reforms of the 1920s. They did not satisfy Flemings who, because of the unequal power and status of the two languages, continued to regard bilingualism as an essentially transitional arrangement which could only result in the continued advance of French. Change in the parliamentary balance of power, however, together with the changing climate of Walloon opinion, permitted a more radical approach in the language reforms of 1930–32. After the earlier attempt to make Belgium a fully Francophone state had failed, Wallonia had been happy to accept the principles of bilingualism in Flanders and monolingualism in Wallonia. But once the Flemings began to demand bilingualism across the state and its institutions, including as a requirement for posts in the civil service, this line could no longer be held. Flemish Catholic organisations began to encourage the Flemish minority in Wallonia to hold on to its national and religious character, and to demand Dutch-language Catholic schools (Witte, 1999: 145). Rather than admit bilingualism into Wallonia as well as Flanders, Walloon opinion retreated to a more defensive position. It came to accept that the price of maintaining French monolingualism in Wallonia was the granting of Dutch monolingualism in Flanders (Detant:45). Thus in 1932 the University of Ghent became entirely Dutch-speaking, education in state and free Catholic schools in Flanders was to be entirely in Dutch, as was the language of administration. In the Belgian Parliament the introduction of simultaneous translation in 1936 led to an increase in the proportion of speeches delivered in Dutch from 22 per cent in 1930 to 48 per cent in 1940. But while bilingualism became required of civil servants in principle, the details of a complex scheme left considerable scope for flexibility, so that in a country with a clear Dutch-speaking majority at the national level, 90 per cent of the highest grade of civil servants were still French speakers in 1963 (Witte,1999:141,143). Effective implementation of these laws, and the equal treatment of language minorities in the two halves of the country, remained an issue for another generation, but a pattern for the future had been established.

Conflict now focused more sharply on Brussels and the mixed areas along the language border. While Flanders was becoming more securely Flemish, the national capital continued in its transition from a predominantly Dutch-speaking to a predominantly Francophone city. Under the reforms of 1932 the principle of parental choice of the language of children's education – *la liberté du père de famille* – continued to apply throughout the Brussels area. The municipalities on the language border including, crucially, the Brussels suburbs were given 'floating status' (Witte, 1999:139–42). This meant that the obligation of the local authority to provide schooling and other services in the local minority language would be decided by measuring proportionate numbers in the local community. In districts close to a growing city these proportions were of course highly susceptible to change. In practice, therefore, the decennial language census became a regular referendum on future language policy in each of these districts – an indication of how communal stability and individual democratic rights can be at odds with one another.

The 1932 language laws, deficient and over-flexible though they were, nudged Flanders and Wallonia along the road to mutual monolingualism. From the Flemish point of view the application of these laws in the Brussels area left a lot to be desired. But the unresolved position of the capital now also came to be a matter of concern for Francophones. Once the principle of national bilingualism was replaced by that of monolingualism for Flanders and Wallonia and bilingualism for Brussels, the interests of the Walloons and the Brussels Francophones diverged. The latter began to set up their own associations and defence groups, most especially to protect the position of Brussels-based French speakers in the civil service and in the local administrations of the Brussels boroughs. Francophones called for the extension of the Brussels conurbation into the new suburbs as the city expanded into the Dutch-speaking countryside, whereas Flemings took the view that Brussels should be recognised as a constituent part of Flanders, albeit temporarily aberrant in its linguistic practice (Witte, 1999:146–9).

During the Second World War the German occupiers again sought to implement a *flamenpolitik*, but the situation differed in some respects from that of 1914–18. Although many perfectly respectable Flemish nationalist political, cultural and commercial bodies had flourished in the inter-war period, some elements of the Flemish movement in the 1930s had taken up the corporatist ideology and paramilitary style of fascism. As elsewhere, fascism was fuelled by high unemployment. The Flemish National Union (VNV), founded in 1933, though strongly Catholic in ethos, in practice sought to challenge the Catholic hierarchy of Belgium for the leadership of Flemish Catholics. Ideological bonds which had not been present in 1914–18 meant that the VNV collaborated actively with the Nazis throughout the 1940–44 occupation. The *flamenpolitik* ensured that the 1932 language laws were implemented more fully. The linguistic reconquest of Brussels by Flanders was encouraged, although Germanisation of the city was the long-term goal. After the Liberation the VNV and the Flemish movement in general were much more strongly tarred with the collaborationist brush than had been the case in 1919. For Francophones the movement was now linked not just to peasant backwardness, but also to fascism and treason (Witte, 1999: 161–5). Not until the late 1950s was the Flemish movement again able to reassert itself in Belgian public life to any great effect. Even as late as 1977, in his bitterly critical song 'Les F…', the internationally-renowned Belgian cabaret artist Jacques Brel characterised *Les Flamingants* (Flemish activists) as 'Nazis during wars and Catholics between them', and called on them not to 'oblige our children, who have done nothing to you, to bark in Flemish'.[39]

The language census of 1947 – in the event the last such census to be conducted in Belgium – showed that the position of Dutch-speakers in the capital had fallen to a new low. The results were potentially so inflammatory that the government kept them concealed until 1954; before the next census in 1961 Flemish politicians had secured the banning of any language question from future censuses (Hasquin:38). During these years, as urbanisation intensified once more, the question not just of the *verfransing* of the city but of the spread of Brussels beyond its boundaries came to be a central concern for the Flemish movement. The image of Brussels as an 'oil stain', spreading French into the Flanders countryside, began to be used by Flemings, just as Brussels Francophones later railed against the 'iron collar' of legislation which constrained the growth of Francophone Brussels.

A third region? The emergence of Brussels-Capital

By 1960 the previously low level of linguistic conflict had intensified to the point where it was bringing demonstrations and riots to the streets of Brussels and threatening to undermine the long-established ethnic equilibrium of Belgium's main political parties. By 1980 Belgium was a federal state, with control of most of its domestic policy devolved to Flanders and Wallonia, and by 1993 Brussels-Capital had been confirmed as a region in its own right. What prompted such dramatic changes? The explanation must begin with economics. The desperate condition of 'poor Flanders' in the mid-nineteenth century had been specifically related to the circumstances of the industrial revolution era. It had not been characteristic of the early modern period, and it was beginning to recover by 1900. From the mid-1950s the Flanders revival gathered pace. The income gap between Flanders and Wallonia narrowed to parity in 1965, since when it has opened up steadily in the opposite direction. Wallonia's coal mines contracted considerably, while the relatively cheap labour and good port facilities of Flanders attracted multinational industries. The international oil crisis of the mid-1970s damaged Wallonia as it did other 'rustbelt' regions of the world. Unemployment in the region's industrial centres rose to

---

[39] Jacques Brel (1929–78) was born in Brussels of French-speaking parents from the landed gentry class of West Flanders. Although he performed some songs in Dutch, and many more displayed a strong sentimental attachment to 'mijn platte [flat] land, mijn Vlaanderenland' (Marieke, 1961), Brel was often accused of being anti-Flemish. 'Les F ...', one of his last songs, certainly supports such a view, although his defenders stress that it is an indictment of Flemish national-ism rather than of the Flemish people. It continues:

> Nazis durant les guerres
> Et catholiques entre elles
> Vous oscillez sans cesse
> Du fusil au missel
> Vos regards sont lointains
> Votre humour est exsangue
> Bien qu'y aient de rues à Gand
> Qui pissent dans les deux langues
> Tu vois quand j'pense á vous
> J'aime que rien ne se merde
> Messieurs les Flamingants
> Je vous emmerde
>
> Vous salissez la Flandre
> Mais la Flandre vous juge... .

This song is not to be confused with 'Les Flamands' (1959), a more gentle satire on what Brel saw as the conservative/Catholic and comfortable bourgeois image of Flanders: 'The Flemings dance without saying anything ... dance without smiling ...' (http://www.paroles.net/chansons/14781.htm and 15144.htm).

25 per cent at one point, and it was estimated than 10 per cent of Flanders' social security contributions were being spent in Wallonia (Buyst:41–5).

Meanwhile Brussels, traditionally regarded as the most prosperous area of Belgium, had in fact become relatively poorer. Its metropolitan population declined by 12 per cent between 1971 and 1994 and its share of national income decreased from 12 per cent in 1980 to 10 per cent in 1990. An important factor in this decline was the lack of coherent economic planning arising from the delay in creating stable governmental structures for the metropolis. Although the European Union and other international institutions were estimated to bring BF32.5 billion p.a. (1991 figure) into the city, social costs such as high rents and the prioritisation of office space over housing reduced the popularity of these bodies with Brusselers. But from the Flemish point of view, a downturn in the city's growth during the past 20 years has had the beneficial effect of slowing down demographic pressure on the city boundary and easing the problem of the *verfransing* of the suburbs (Govaert:235, 238; Favell:18; McRae 1986:318; De Lannoy:193).

From around 1960, therefore, Flanders was able to add a new-found economic clout to its long-established demographic superiority. As memories of Nazi collaboration began to fade, and with Flemish demonstrations increasingly vociferous on the streets of Brussels, Flemish politicians pressed for a general review of the inter-war language legislation. Their demands included the confirmation of monolingualism in Flanders and Wallonia, the securing of Dutch in the bilingual provisions for the Brussels conurbation, the stabilisation of the language border to protect it from the vagaries of population movement, and better implementation of equal opportunities for Dutch-speakers in public employment.

Since 1947 there has been no official record taken of language use in Belgium or its capital. We do not know the proportions of Dutch- and French-speakers in Brussels today. One Francophone writer, in a piece not generally characterised by extreme partisan views, describes this situation as 'outrageous' (Hasquin:39).[40] Given the high level of workplace bilingualism, the social status of French, and the mixed ethnicity of so many people, ethno-linguistic identity is to some extent a subjective matter. There are few direct data on levels of intermarriage in Brussels, but a survey 20 years ago of the municipalities along the

---

[40] Former academic Hervé Hasquin is also President of the French Community Commission in Brussels.

language border produced an estimate as high as 19 per cent of all marriages. In a remarkable piece of statistical symmetry, the same survey found that in the case of all-Dutch marriages 81 per cent of children were educated primarily through Dutch, whereas in the case of mixed marriages this was so only for 19 per cent of children. It is not surprising, in this context, that estimates of the relative size of the two language groups in the city should vary considerably. Seven studies made by various researchers between 1963 and 1969 estimated proportions of Dutch-speakers in the Brussels conurbation as follows (in chronological order of publication): 20 per cent, 22–27 per cent, 27–32 per cent, 18 per cent, 13 per cent, 24 per cent, 22 per cent. In 1985 a French-language Brussels newspaper, *Le Soir*, put the proportion at 14 per cent (Louckx:76–7, 81, 117–18; McRae 1986:300, 304).

Since 1989, with the introduction of separate language lists for elections to the Brussels Metropolitan Council, a better measure of linguistic self-identification has been available. With turnouts of around 82 per cent, the percentage of voters choosing Dutch-language parties in the three elections to date – 1989, 1995 and 1999 – has been 15 per cent, 13 per cent and 14 per cent respectively (www.vub.ac.be/POLI/ elections). The French- and Dutch-speaking representatives at an international conference in 1994 agreed in estimating the Dutch proportion at around 15 per cent (Hasquin:39; Detant:49). Equally significant in the long run is probably the dramatic growth in the number of non-Belgians resident in Brussels over the past 30 years. In 1966 this proportion was still below 10 per cent. By 1983 it was 24 per cent, and by 1994 almost 30 per cent. Between 1971 and 1990 the number of Belgian citizens resident in metropolitan Brussels declined by 24 per cent, while the number of foreigners increased by 58 per cent (Louckx:78; Detant:49; Govaert:234). This third ethnic component of the population includes economic migrants from North and Central Africa and elsewhere, most of whom are native or near-native French-speakers, and also elite workers employed in the institutions of the European Union, the great majority of whom adopt French rather than Dutch as their second language. Thus, as in Montreal, the impact of large-scale immigration in the second half of the twentieth century was to favour the dominant language. Many thousands more Dutch-speakers cross the language border every day to work in Brussels, but because they are not residents of the capital they do not show up in population or electoral statistics.

Ethnic consciousness in Flanders and Wallonia was well-established, at least among some social groups, by 1900. A Brussels consciousness, albeit rather a negative one in origin, began to develop in the 1960s within both communities, as both Flanders and Wallonia developed a new hostility towards the capital. For Flemings it began with the campaign to halt and thereby contain the Brussels 'oil stain'. At the same time the Walloon industrial economy was in deep trouble, for which it blamed the policies of the government in Brussels. Thus, more or less by default, Brussels politicians of both traditions began to build Brussels identities which were distinct from those of Flanders and Wallonia. A new and entirely local grouping, the *Front Democratique de Francophones (FDF)*, became the city's largest party between 1974 and 1985, and in 1981 it terminated its alliance with *Rassemblement Wallon*, the main linguistic party in Wallonia. By 1975 party politics in the city had completed a shift from parties which sought votes in both communities to a system which was entirely polarised on linguistic lines (Obler:419–20). In 1993, the Dutch-language *TV Brussel* was started because of the widespread feeling among Brussels Flemings that their city received inadequate coverage from the Flanders television stations. By the late 1990s it was clear that for all parties except the extremist *Vlaamsblok* on the one hand and the *Front National* on the other, the appeal to a distinct French or Dutch 'Brussels identity' had become a persuasive one (Govaert:230–5).

The cultural identity of *les bruxellois* was well-established. For Flemish activists, on the other hand, the challenge was to persuade immigrants from Flanders and all classes of Flemings already resident in the city that they should assert the right to operate in Dutch. In the 1950s Flemish associational life in the city had consisted of a few nostalgia-based migrant societies linked to the various Flanders provinces. By the 1960s middle-class and professional Flemings, themselves mainly first-generation migrants from Flanders, began to organise on a broader basis. In 1966 a major cultural centre was opened and by 1971 there were an estimated 805 Flemish cultural associations in the city providing for (in descending order of numbers) youth, parents, sports, theatre, music, film and social work. Of the many other categories of activity folklore was, interestingly, bottom of the list (Louckx:105–7).

The preponderant *visage* of Brussels is French: a 1977 survey, for instance, found that almost two-thirds of the large billboards in metropolitan Brussels were solely in French, with less than a quarter solely in Dutch. Their distribution was related to some extent to the ethnic balance of particular municipalities, but there are no sharply defined linguistic borders in the city. The residential segregation of foreign immigrants is considerably more pronounced than that of French- and

Dutch-speakers (Louckx:80–1; De Lannoy:192). The relatively high level of intermarriage is therefore matched by a visible but low level of residential segregation. Analysis of voting behaviour confirms this (Map 5:3). In the eight cantons which now make up the region of Brussels-Capital the percentage of electors voting for parties in the Flemish list in 1999 ranged between 7.6 per cent and 21.4 per cent. This broad measure confirms that there are no large areas where Flemings are in the majority. But there are significantly higher concentrations of Flemings in the north-western sections of metropolitan Brussels than in the south-eastern districts. A 1981 survey of the distribution of Dutch-speakers across the city's 19 municipalities, based on mailing lists, found a similar geographical pattern, with 35 per cent and 4 per cent Dutch-speakers being the extremes of distribution. The same survey found that the breakdown of Belgian immigrants to Brussels from Flanders and Wallonia was in the ratio 52:48 (De Lannoy:180–1). It may be that, in the future, Brussels will develop into a city with more clearly-defined French and Dutch sectors and a re-expanded Flemish population driven by higher in-migration, more linguistic consciousness-raising, and the buoyancy of the neighbouring Flanders region. On balance, though, it seems more likely that the established status of French in the city and the established expectation that mixed marriages will be French marriages, supported by the presence of the EU and NATO and by the continued preponderance of French-speakers among foreign immigrants, will maintain the balance at or around its present level.

How does the ethnic division relate to patterns of employment in the modern city? More than three-quarters of Brussels workers are

Map 5.3 Elections to the Brussels Regional Council, 1999
Percentage of electors who voted in the Flemish list, by canton.

employed in the service sector, with clerical workers in public sector employment being the largest group. This is also a major element in the private sector as well, for since the growth of the EU, Belgium and Brussels have become magnets for multi-national companies (Louckx:81–2). In 1950, 60 per cent of senior civil servants were Francophones. A 1979 study of comparable grades in five major government departments suggested that the Francophone share, at 49 per cent, had fallen to numerical parity. The main factor influencing these changes was the language law of 1963, although educational and other social changes also played a part. In municipal government in metropolitan Brussels, linguistic patterns until recently reflected local population balances rather than national ones. At the level of departmental supervisor, the proportion of Dutch-speakers rose from 11 per cent in 1963 to 28 per cent in 1970 to 49 per cent in 1979. Taking all of the 12,356 municipal employees into account, the Dutch proportion in 1979 was 41 per cent (Louckx:83–9). Whether this should be regarded as a low level to find in the nation's capital, given the substantial majority of Flemings in the national population, or whether it should be regarded as a high level relative to the proportion of Flemings in the metropolitan population, is ultimately a matter of political opinion. The great majority of opinion in Flanders regards it as essential that the state's linguistic majority should have linguistic and cultural parity in the capital, however small its numbers locally. This is seen as a fair exchange for the parity at national level which has been accorded to the Walloon minority, now less than 33 per cent of the national population. The decision of the Flanders regional government in 1980 to make Brussels its centre, even though Brussels is outside its region, has boosted Flemish white-collar employment, although many of these workers are daily commuters from Flanders.[41]

There are few data available on the private sector in Brussels employment. Banking is a partial exception, with surveys of two major Brussels banks having been undertaken in 1976–77. In one bank 22 per cent of the workforce was Dutch speaking, but when broken down by grade considerable variance emerged: Dutch-speakers comprised 13 per cent of managers, 18 per cent of supervisors, 23 per cent of clerks and 44 per cent of manual workers. In the second bank studied there was considerably less variance, but the overall proportion of Dutch-speakers was low at 14 per cent. In the labour market in general it is

---

[41] In the mid-1990s, only 4 per cent of Belgium's Flemings lived in Brussels, but 10 per cent worked there (Detant:49).

clear that reform has been easier in the public sector than the private and that, in the former, major changes have been achieved since the early 1960s (Louckx:89–95). In the past 20 years the cumulative impact of relative improvement of the economy of the Flanders region has created in Brussels both stronger labour market pressure from Flemings to be recognised and pressure from Flemish consumers to be dealt with in Dutch. There was, until recently, a degree of linguistic imbalance in employment, but it fell well short of a full cultural division of labour.

The provision of public services has also been an area of linguistic tension in Brussels. There have been few problems over Dutch-language primary schools, and in secondary education an historically low level of Dutch-language provision was brought up to par and maintained after about 1960. The implementation of cultural autonomy since the reforms of 1970 has helped to stabilise the position, and during the 1980s it was accepted that the overall volume of educational provision for Flemings was satisfactory. At the level of the individual municipality the picture differed somewhat: in 1979 seven of the nineteen Brussels municipalities offered no Dutch-language education at all, a factor calculated to increase linguistic segregation and/or further encourage the *verfransing* of mixed marriages. The declining birth-rate posed a special problem for Dutch-language schools, inasmuch as the impact on Francophone schools has been relatively cushioned by the growing number of immigrant children over the previous generation.[42] In 1967 only four out of thirty-four hospitals in Brussels had a bilingual staff of doctors (although the position regarding other categories of hospital employment was better balanced), and it was estimated in 1978 that only one in ten doctors was competent to deal with patients through the medium of Dutch (Witte 1987:96–101; McRae 1986:316–17; Louckx:101–4).

By the 1960s, therefore, Flanders' demographic ascendancy in Belgium as a whole had been given new weight by is economic development, but the group position of Flemings in the national capital was continuing to decline. The drive to change this came less from the established Flemish community in Brussels than from Flanders activists, many of whom were new migrants to Brussels. A newly-educated and culturally-self confident class of incoming Flemish professionals and white-collar workers deliberately set out to reverse the language shift in the city, with crucial support from commuters and

---

[42] By the early 1980s one in every four children in Brussels was of non-Belgian origin.

day-tripping demonstrators from nearby Flanders, as well as from Flanders politicians who were obliged to pay ever-increasing attention to the language issue. Parades and demonstrations in Brussels were a factor in bringing about change, but only for a short period of time, and the level of violence was low. Between 1961 and the early 1970s, the period of highest excitement, one death and about 50 injuries were reported in the press. Community relations were tense in Brussels during these years and, in the words of an American scholar who did fieldwork at that time, 'occasionally unpleasant; but rarely have such contacts led to personal violence or wider collective riots'. More important than direct action itself, though deriving energy and urgency from it, was the response of the political parties. The Flemish nationalist *Volksunie* emerged in the late 1950s, its vote in national elections rising from 6 per cent in 1961 to 19 per cent in 1971. This in turn encouraged the Flemish branches of what were then the three main national parties – the Catholics, Liberals and Socialists – to adopt a harder line on linguistic issues. In Brussels itself, linguistic parties had never achieved even 2 per cent of the vote between 1946 and 1961, but by 1974 they had 46 per cent (Obler:401, 414).

The era of reform was so protracted because each step along the road was the outcome of shifting parliamentary negotiations and coalitions, not infrequently derailed by changes of government.[43] The first outcome was the cluster of language laws of 1962–63. This included more determined measures to increase Dutch-language employment and service provision in the public sector, and a positive effort to encourage the use of Dutch in Brussels. The former, though not greatly liked by Francophones, were largely effective. The latter, with its emphasis on group rather than individual rights was a more controversial measure. In effect it shifted the decision as to the language in which Brussels children should be educated from the parents to the local authority. This law required that children living in Brussels must be educated in the language normally spoken in the family home, the *langue maternelle ou usuelle*, which might not necessarily be the language of the parents' choice. Before a child could be enrolled in school, a linguistic declaration from the head of the family was required, certified by an inspector from each community (Obler:415). This measure was reversed as part of a wider compromise in 1970, and the principle of *la liberté du père de famille* was restored. The measure was always more

---

[43] Between 1961 and 1981 the average lifespan of a Belgian government was two years.

symbolic than it was effective, but it provoked great hostility among Brussels Francophones.

Equally controversial, and always likely to be vulnerable to socio-demographic change, were the attempts to resolve disputes about the language border between Flanders and Wallonia, and between Flanders and Brussels. Francophones thought it normal and reasonable that the border should be a changing one, responding to natural processes of population movement and linguistic preference. Flemings on the other hand regarded this as a blank cheque for French to expand into Flanders as the suburbs of metropolitan Brussels spread across municipal boundaries. This was to them the feared 'oil-stain', threatening large areas of monolingual Flanders, for under the 1930s legislation any borough in which the self-defined Francophone population reached 30 per cent would be added to the bilingual region. Flemings therefore called for the establishment of a legally-fixed and unchanging language border, and this became law in 1962. A concession was made whereby, in six specified boroughs adjacent to the language borders, 'language facilities' would be granted where sizeable linguistic minorities existed. But officially these boroughs would be monolingual, and every effort was made by the Flemings to distinguish the provision of 'facilities' from what they regarded as the corrosive bilingual approach of 1932.

In 1963 it was envisaged by Flemings that these 'facilities' would be transitional arrangements in the drive towards monolingualism, while Francophones continued to press for the 'iron collar' to be broken and more territory added to the metropolitan bilingual area. In 1980 the boundary of metropolitan Brussels was confirmed at its existing borders. Initially this was simply by default, as a by-product of the finalisation of the Flanders and Wallonia borders. But in the later reforms of 1990 these boundaries were written into the Constitution, to the satisfaction of the Flemings, while the 'language facilities' in the six adjacent Flanders boroughs were also written in as a consolation to Francophones. It is probable that the close proximity of Wallonia to the southern fringe of Brussels – separated only by one 7km municipality with language facilities – has helped to ease both political tensions and demographic pressures on the iron collar. Comparing a five-year period in the late 1960s with another a decade later, it was shown that whereas migration from metropolitan Brussels to Halle-Vilvoorde[44] increased by only 20 per cent that from Brussels to Nivelles, just across

---

[44] Halle-Vilvoorde is the area of Flanders immediately surrounding Brussels.

the language boundary in Wallonia, increased by 123 per cent (Detant:47; Witte, 1999:183–5; Falter:183–7).

In 1970 the focus of reform shifted from language laws as such to constitutional reform. The Eyskens government of 1970, despairing of being able to resolve the intractable Brussels problem, decided to postpone it and go for a resolution of the wider Flanders/Wallonia issue. It laid the foundation for a complex but innovative scheme with the introduction of both Regions and Communities for the two groups. Communities are non-territorial bodies which took over control of certain cultural matters from the central state (including education) on behalf of the three (including the German) linguistic communities, while Regions are territorial bodies with economic powers devolved to them. The former was designed mainly to meet the cultural-linguistic concerns of Flemings, the latter to meet the economic concerns of Walloons. In practice the Eyskens government was unable to do more on the Regions than write the intention to create them (Flanders, Wallonia and Brussels) into the revised 1970 Constitution. But Eyskens made more progress with the non-territorial Community structures, which soon took responsibility for providing educational and cultural services for their own linguistic groups, in Brussels as elsewhere (Falter:181–3). This body of reforms was in effect imposed on Brussels by Flanders and Wallonia, for only one-third of Brussels parliamentarians voted for the legislation. In local politics the government's intention was to bring in a measure of parity for the minority Flemings in the city, matching the parity of the minority Walloons in Belgium as a whole. This required 'compulsory cultural separation for electoral purposes' (McRae 1986:311). All Council candidates had to be identified as, and nominated by, members of one or other of the linguistic communities. In 1971 the disaffected Francophone parties managed to sabotage the first operation of the scheme by finding several hundred renegade Flemings to sign nomination papers (McRae 1986:311–12; Obler:421).

Not until 1980 was a parliamentary coalition strong enough to bring the regions of Flanders and Wallonia into operation.[45] For Flanders to be fully designated it was necessary to encircle and define Brussels, which thus became a region by default. No parliamentary agreement

---

[45] Provision for the small and concentrated German-speaking community of eastern Belgium, with a population of 68,000 members, was a less contentious matter, and this was in fact the only group for whom matters were sufficiently resolved to permit the immediate creation of a working Community parliament.

could be achieved as to how a Brussels Region might work, so it remained under the direct control of central government. Its borders, still officially regarded as provisional, encompassed only the long-recognised territory of metropolitan Brussels, which consisted of the central city itself and the 18 neighbouring boroughs. As for the two working regions, the Flemish Community and the Flanders Region voted immediately to merge. This was an easy decision, because only the 4 per cent of Flemings who lived in Brussels were not constituents of both bodies. On the other side the Francophone Community and the Wallonia Region decided to remained separate, for the Brussels element comprised 18.5 per cent of the total French-speaking population. We have also seen how the interests of Francophone Brussels – bilingual, liberal in politics, and feeling under increasing threat from the attempted Flemish revival – had come to diverge quite sharply from those of Wallonia, which was monolingual, socialist in politics, and increasingly secure culturally, if not economically, behind its language border. This aspect of the problem was not resolved until 1993, when the two elements of the Francophone Community agreed to go their own ways, their community budget divided by the state into one for Wallonia and one for a Brussels-French community commission operating within the Francophone membership of the Brussels parliament (Falter:191).

Thus by 1980 the two regions were fully established, with their own administrations, share of national taxes and marginal tax-raising powers of their own. A unique feature of the Belgian federal scheme is that it is not hierarchical, in the sense that the decisions of its devolved bodies may not be overruled by the higher tier of government. Because Walloons regarded central government powers as potentially dangerous in a country with a clear Flemish majority, the revised Constitution laid down *legal* arbitration procedures to resolve disputes (Falter:183–5). Wrangling continued over language facilities in the border communes, and not until 1988 was a new federal government coalition strong enough to address the Brussels problem. The capital at last achieved full regional status in 1989, with its own government and a directly-elected parliament – the latter something which the other two regions had not yet achieved. This body had the authority to divide into separate community commissions to deal with educational, cultural and health matters for the two language groups. Although in three general elections to the Brussels parliament the Flemish list has never obtained more than 15 per cent of the vote it controls by law two of the five seats in the Brussels government, while parliamentary decisions require a majority in both language groups (Falter:186–8). The borders of the region were confirmed as those of 1980, i.e. the central city and its 18 neighbouring municipalities. Retention of the iron collar satisfied the Flemings. Permanent constitutional guarantees for language facilities in the six boroughs surrounding the new region gave security to local Francophones, while confirmation that the same boroughs were, with equal permanency, to be part of Flanders gave some reassurance to Flemings that the oil stain had been contained.

Major potential for future destabilisation remains. Belgium as a whole almost broke up in the crisis of 1991–92, when the Flemish left wing attempted to block a set of arms contracts to Saudi Arabia which were crucial to the future of several Walloon arms factories. Dissolution of the state was avoided by a fourth round of constitutional reform in 1993. This further strengthened the regional governments by creating directly-elected parliaments and increasing their powers in certain areas, including some aspects of foreign policy (Falter:189–91). Procedures have been put in place to resolve potential deadlocks, but any major crisis in the future could end in a Czechoslovak-style separation. Brussels is the main barrier to such a development. Were it to happen, Brussels would be left as a city state, a formation for which modern European precedents are not encouraging, although the presence of EU and NATO headquarters constitute special factors. Within Brussels itself, the structural reforms appear to have stabilised the position of the Flemish resident (as distinct from commuting) minority at around 15 per cent of the population. But with an immigrant and non-Belgian population of more than 30 per cent, very few of whom will assimilate to the Flemish community, it is likely that new issues will graft themselves on to this internal ethnic conflict in a way that is hard to predict. The success of the extreme right-wing *Vlaamsblok* in city politics appears to have aroused the ethnic consciousness of the Flemish working class for the first time, although the movement's growing popularity appears to have a lot more to do with its extreme right-wing policies towards immigrants than with its radical Flemish programme. [46]

---

[46] 2.1 per cent of votes for the Brussels regional parliament in 1989, 4.5 per cent in 1999, raising it from the fourth to the first party on the Flemish list. Support for the *Vlaamsblok* continues to creep upwards: in the national parliamentary constituency of Brussels-Halle-Vilvoorde (where the Flemish proportion of the population is rather larger than in Brussels itself) the party's vote increased from 8.7 per cent in 1999 to 10.3 per cent in 2003 (http://www.vub.ac.be/POLI/elections).

Belgium came into existence in 1830 because the great powers would not permit an expanded France, and the Netherlands had failed in its attempt to manage the region. Ironically, though it was of no concern to the powers, this coincided with the growth of Francophone economic strength and social status within the emerging state. It was these factors which brought about the language shift in the capital and established the predominantly French character of modern Brussels. Now that a big French city exists, it seems unlikely that the Flemish economic revival of the twentieth century will reverse this – although the *Vlaamsblok* demands the incorporation of Brussels into Flanders on precisely these grounds. Some Flemish nationalists on the other hand have argued in favour of letting Brussels go and acknowledging Antwerp as the real capital of the Flemish people, as it is already the cultural one. Others *fear* such an outcome if Flanders goes for full independence. The writer and one-time mayor of Antwerp, Lode Craeybeckx, probably got it right when he declared in the 1970s that 'Flanders won't let go of Brussels'.

Without Brussels it would not be at all clear that the relationship between Flanders and Wallonia is stable enough to resist the challenges which future events may bring. The Brussels Region itself presents the prospect, on the one hand, of increasingly determined efforts by Dutch-speakers to retain and strengthen their position in the city and, on the other hand, of the further strengthening of French through social change. Will the iron collar continue to contain Francophone demographic pressure on the narrow band of territory which separates it from the boundary with Wallonia? Or will the promotion of multi-culturalism, and of English as a 'neutral' language, undermine the predominant position of French in the capital in the way that the more pessimistic Francophones fear? (Favell:16) As in the Montreal case, it is by no means clear whether a generation of rather frantic legislative reforms will be followed by a long and calm period of consolidation or by a steady erosion of the new structures resulting from further social and cultural change. For students of ethnic conflict, however, and with particular regard to most of the case studies in this book, the surprising feature of the Brussels conflict is its low intensity. Notwithstanding Belgium's 400-year history as a battleground for the European powers, its legacy of division and collaboration in two world wars, and the remorseless progress of language change in the capital side-by-side with language preservation in the immediate hinterland, the conflict to date has been a remarkably peaceful one.

6
The Failure of Chronic Violence: Belfast

> ...but tell me truly, if it's possible,
> what holds the future for the citizens
> of my divided city? Is there one just man
> in it? Or are they all sectarians?

The Inferno of Dante Alighieri, transl. Ciaran Carson (London & New York: Granta Books, 2002, Canto VI, lines 60–3)

> The southern [Irish] nationalist speaks harshly and angrily about Belfast .... Belfast – it may almost be said Belfast alone – has stood between him and his hopes.

G.A. Birmingham, *An Irishman Looks at his World* (London: Hodder & Stoughton, 1919)

Belfast, in one respect, stands alone of the cities examined in this book. Nowhere else has the pattern of ethnic conflict and violence over the past two centuries been so unchanging and unremitting. It is a depressing thought that the ethnic warriors – Catholic and Protestant – who participated in Belfast's early-nineteenth century riots would in many ways have felt quite at home among their descendants at the end of the twentieth century. They would have had little difficulty in adapting to the rhetoric of the conflict or to the techniques of intimidation and provocation, and they would even have recognised some of the more long-established territorial interfaces, the flashpoints where the two sides have so often collided. Violence and the threat of it became almost normal at an early stage in the history of industrial Belfast. Throughout the past two centuries it has imposed a pattern on the urban terrain, shaping and bending the geography and the psychology of the city.

Map 6.1 Belfast and Ireland, showing the 1921 partition line and the three border counties.

This is all the more surprising given the scale of constitutional and economic change during the period. Founded by Protestant English and Scots settlers in 1613, the town was a small port and linen trading centre under a colonial parliament in Dublin until 1800. Until the last years of this period it remained a small and almost exclusively Protestant town.[47] Between 1801 and 1921 it underwent one of the more dramatic expansions in European industrial history. The population grew accordingly,

---

[47] Belfast was not formally designated as a city until 1888.

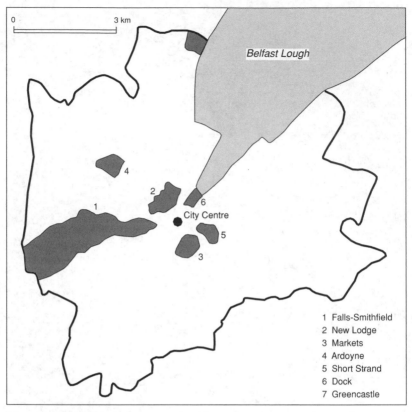

Map 6.2   The Catholic Districts of Belfast, 1901
Showing neighbourhoods more than 90 per cent Catholic. More than two-thirds of the city's Catholics lived in these neighbourhoods.
Source: A. C. Hepburn, in M. Engman *et al.*, *Ethnic Identity in Urban Europe* (Aldershot: Dartmouth Publishing, 1992) p. 69

and the Irish Catholic minority became demographically significant, expanding rapidly during the first half of the nineteenth century, but growing more slowly relative to the Protestant majority during the second half. In this era administrative government continued from Dublin, but political and legislative power shifted to London. In 1921 Belfast became a capital city itself as regional government for Northern Ireland was devolved from Westminster. A new border came into existence, creating an independent state in southern Ireland and leaving Northern Ireland's Catholics as a discontented irredentist minority. During these years the minority saw its political influence decline further, but its population experienced relative growth. Meanwhile the city shared most of the problems of economic decline known to many heavy industrial areas of the United Kingdom and elsewhere, which became more acute still in the 1970s and 1980s. Since 1972 Belfast has once more been governed directly from London, although some limited powers have been exercised, intermittently since 1998, by a new power-sharing regional government. Local government, in contrast, has been remarkably stable in its structure – though far from harmonious in its working – for most of these two centuries. It is surprising, in the midst of such drastic changes in these other spheres, that the character of the conflict has changed so little.

The ethnic division in the city reflects that of its Ulster hinterland. Ulster, or more precisely six of its nine counties, is the area of mixed religion in Ireland, where levels of local segregation are high but where both Catholics and Protestants are present in large numbers.[48] Belfast does, however, merit special study within its region. This is partly because of its relative size: it comprised less than a thirtieth of the region's population in 1821 but almost a third in 1911, while today almost half the population of the province lives within daily commuting distance of the city. Another reason for the city's discrete importance is the persistent intensity of its conflict and the particular problems of managing high levels of violence in a large city which has so many Catholic–Protestant interfaces. Belfast is thus a microcosm of the wider Ulster conflict, but the conflict there has also had special features of its own. Furthermore, the demonstrated potential of Belfast for uncontrollable outbreaks of mass violence, especially on the majority Protestant side, is the main factor which has for a century stood between governments and any form of imposed settlement.

At the heart of the ethnic divide is a conflict over national identity. On the one hand are people – the great majority of them Catholic by background – who perceive themselves as 'Irish' and regard this as incompatible with allegiance to Britain. On the other are people who regard themselves as either 'British' or 'British-Irish' or 'Ulster people' or simply 'Protestants'. There are individual Catholic Unionists and Protestant Nationalists, but their numbers have always been far too

---

[48] Counties Antrim and Down have large Protestant majorities, while Counties Armagh and Londonderry have small ones. Fermanagh and Tyrone have small Catholic majorities. These six counties, together with the cities of Belfast and Derry/Londonderry, have made up the province of Northern Ireland since 1921. The remaining Ulster counties of Cavan, Donegal and Monaghan have large Catholic majorities, and form part of the Irish Republic.

small to be of any political significance. In practice the labels 'Catholic' and 'Nationalist' are close to being interchangeable, as are 'Protestant' and 'Unionist'.[49] What then is the content of ethnicity in Belfast and its region? Religious denomination is without doubt the badge of nationality and the best predictor of ethnic identification. The great majority of Catholics regard themselves as members of an ethnic group as well as a confessional group. During the nineteenth century this Catholic ethnicity developed into an Irish nationalist ethnicity, while retaining a strong Catholic content. For Irish nationalism in general, the early decades of the twentieth century were characterised by a greater emphasis on Ireland's distinct history and distinct culture, symbolised by a growing if spasmodic interest in the revival of the Irish language. No doubt a proportion of the Catholic migrants who came from Ulster hill-districts into early nineteenth-century Belfast were native Irish-speakers but language difference has not been of much, if any, practical concern in the history of modern Belfast. Of more political significance has been the fact that since the second decade of the twentieth century, and with more vigour in Belfast since the 1970s, the Irish language – as manifested through street signs, posters and the introductory sentences of political speeches – has acquired great symbolic significance, even for that large majority of Catholic-nationalists who have little or no knowledge of the language.

Protestant or 'British-Irish' identity is also complicated. Protestants, by and large, regard themselves as the descendants of English or Scottish settlers of the seventeenth century. To the extent that this is a long-held belief, there is therefore an old-established 'Protestant' identity. On the other hand Ulster Protestantism is made up mainly of large Presbyterian and Anglican communities which, until the mid-nineteenth century at least, displayed elements of separate and distinct ethnic identities. There were differences in class and status profile and, especially, in political allegiance. The more salient elements of this difference evaporated during the second half of the nineteenth century, as 'Protestant unity' became the dominant political sentiment. The Orange Order, dedicated to resisting the advance of 'popery' and of Irish nationalism, which it characterised as 'Rome Rule', was able to add large numbers of Presbyterians to its Anglican base. Orange halls became community centres around which all 'Protestants' could

---

[49] Militants on the Catholic side tend to use the label 'republican' rather than the more generic 'nationalist', as their Protestant equivalents favour 'loyalist' rather than 'unionist'.

gather, just as the Catholic community tended to organise around the institutions of the Catholic Church.

Since the early nineteenth century, more than 85 per cent of Belfast's population has always come from the six counties which now make up Northern Ireland. Migration from the rest of Ireland or from Great Britain has seldom exceeded 5 per cent, while immigrants from further afield have never risen above 1 per cent. Unlike Montreal or Brussels, therefore, such groups have never been present in sufficient numbers to alter the character of the city's divide. They have, in fact, been assimilated into one or other of the existing groups. Jews and, more recently, south Asians, whether or not they maintained their religious practice, have tended to become part of the majority Protestant community in terms of residence, schooling and membership of voluntary associations. Catholic immigrants, on the other hand, most notably Italians, have tended to become part of the Catholic community.

1801–1921: rule from London

The European war of the 1790s had devastating side-effects for Ireland, as the Society of United Irishmen, inspired by events in France, endeavoured to bring about revolution at home. Young Presbyterians from Belfast were especially prominent in the leadership of this movement, although elsewhere in the country it had a more Catholic and rural flavour. The 1798 uprising was ruthlessly suppressed, and in 1801 Ireland was taken into the United Kingdom. It retained an administration based in Dublin, but legislative and executive authority was transferred to Westminster. The majority of Protestants in the still small town of Belfast were appalled at the bloody uprising and subsequent repression of 1798. Although Presbyterians and Anglicans continued to some extent to espouse Whig/Liberal and Tory/Conservative politics respectively for a further two generations, Presbyterian Belfast soon drew in its revolutionary horns, and the alternative strategy of 'Protestant unity' began to develop. Catholic–Protestant relations at the elite level remained cordial for a while longer, with many of the town's leading Protestants subscribing to the building fund for a large new Catholic church in 1815, but the ethnic fault line gradually came to dominate the character of the town.

Initially a small port and linen trading centre, Belfast began to develop from the 1780s as a centre of textile manufacturing, first with cotton and, after that failed in the 1820s, with linen. The workers in these mills were mainly migrants who brought with them the ethnic rivalries of the nearby countryside. These had originated in the seventeenth century, but had been reinvigorated during the fierce competition for land which had occurred in places like north Armagh in the late eighteenth century. Some of the rural ethnic-defence societies of these years outgrew their agrarian origins. The Ribbon Society for Catholics and, more important in the long run, the Orange Order for Protestants, migrated along with their members to Belfast, and further afield to the cities of Britain and North America. The occasion of Belfast's first recorded lethal riot, in 1813, was a battle between Orange marchers and a hostile crowd. Residentially-segregated industrial suburbs existed in the city by the 1820s if not earlier, separating Catholics and Protestants both from one another and from the town centre. Violent clashes on election days and on 12 July became commonplace.[50] From the 1850s these conflicts escalated into far more widespread battles, which came to set the tone for community relations in the growing town. Riots in 1857, 1864, 1872 and 1886, in particular spread around the town on a scale and at a pace which the authorities were unable to control for weeks or months on end. These riots established patterns of fear, aggression and ethnic defence which Frank Wright (1996) called 'deterrence relationships' and which to a great extent determined the ethnic character of social and economic development in the city.

There are two distinct narratives of the economic history of nineteenth century Belfast. One is the 'economic miracle' of the only industrial city in Ireland, the city which for the 60-year period 1841–1901 was the fastest growing major centre in the United Kingdom. Without convenient access to any natural resources, other than labour, the city achieved a remarkable economic take-off as textiles stimulated port infrastructure investment, which stimulated iron shipbuilding, which stimulated heavy engineering. In this sense it was a success story that came to an end only with the crisis of heavy industry throughout western Europe during the inter-war period. The other narrative is the way in which the trickle-down effects of this growth were not only slow and limited, as they were elsewhere in the nineteenth-century industrial world, but also ethnically one-sided. Catholics did not feature significantly in the better-paid sectors of the new industries at the skilled-worker, white-collar or

---

[50] The most important victory of the forces of William of Orange over the deposed Catholic monarch James II was the Battle of the Boyne, fought on 12 July 1690. Celebration of the occasion became the main focus for the activities of the Orange Order, founded in 1795.

entrepreneurial levels. Before about 1900 this fact alone did not greatly differentiate Belfast's Irish Catholics from the experience of their fellow-countrymen in British and north American cities. The differences were that, in Belfast, the differentials seemed to grow wider rather than narrower as the generations passed, while at the same time Belfast Catholics were naturally less inclined to adopt the immigrant's mantle of patience and deference to their 'hosts'. Another factor was that Belfast, like Ireland in general, had far more unskilled labour available throughout the industrial period than it could provide work for. Not only was the Catholic minority heavily over-represented in unskilled labour but the Protestant community, though relatively better-off, had in numerical terms an even larger unskilled working class. The presence of two such groups, living separately but in close proximity to one another, helped to exacerbate the more confrontational aspects of ethnic encounter.

How have two groups, seemingly so similar in physical appearance, dress, diet and language, sustained an urban conflict, at such a level of intensity, for so long? The wars of the seventeenth century – local, British and international – and the peasant conflicts of the later eighteenth century played their parts. Catholics and Protestants who came to Belfast to work in the mills, factories and docks were already well-aware of the practices of ethnic deterrence as a way of ordering their lives and addressing their problems. The more fortunate male Protestant workers were able to use an ethnically-controlled apprenticeship system to maintain the value of their labour. Workers without this advantage, both male and female, were more inclined to resort to deterrence relationships to consolidate their positions in the workplace. Thus Protestant women customarily worked in the cleaner and less unpleasant processes of the linen industry; Protestant men predominated in the cross-channel docks where work was relatively regular, while Catholics predominated in the more spasmodic work of the deep-sea docks. This came to be underpinned by factors which gave some content to the underlying ethnic rivalry. First, from the Protestant point of view the growing visibility and increased energy of Catholic Church organisation appeared to be a provocation. All denominations sought to take religion to the urban masses in the mid-nineteenth century, often in a competitive and sectarian way. Later in the century religious competition was reinforced by national conflict: communal Orangeism blended with political Unionism; Catholic ethnicity embraced Irish nationalism.

In the face of widespread and recurrent violence, the city could continue to function only by developing a very high level of residential segregation. The exceptions to this were the small number of professional and white-collar neighbourhoods and, at the other end of the spectrum, the twilight zones of transient population close to the city centre. But for the industrial working class, more-or-less exclusive residential segregation between Catholic and Protestant became the norm during the second half of the nineteenth century and through the twentieth. We know that the Pound and Sandy Row, adjacent mill districts in the south-west of the city, were associated with Catholic and Protestant ethnicity respectively as early as the 1830s, with summertime rioting frequent at the interfaces (Hirst, *passim*). During the first summer of protracted, uncontrolled rioting in 1857, a notable feature was the expulsion of obnoxious individuals and households by both sides. Micro-level ethnic cleansing continued to be a feature of later rioting, and was 'necessary' intimidation if the sharp lines which had been established were to resist erosion in the context of a competitive housing market. For those individuals foolhardy enough in periods of relative quiet to risk crossing the line, the standard landlords' practice of requiring potential tenants to produce a letter of reference from a clergyman provided a less threatening but equally effective mechanism. But once the imperative of segregated living was understood and accepted, individual 'adjustments' became less important than maintenance of neighbourhood boundaries and – most important in a rapidly-growing city – the securing of new neighbourhoods on greenfield sites where neither side had a historic claim.

Catholics, as the minority community, were more adversely affected by this informal system. Belfast developed a pattern of inner-city Catholic neighbourhoods which became encircled by Protestant territory as the city spread (Map 6.2). Only in the Falls, the south-west quarter, was there a breakout from this encirclement. Wright (1996:373–4) has documented an aspect of the 1872 riots, known as 'the battle for Leeson Street', which opened up this sector for Catholics. Because the two communities were similar in appearance, and in dress and diet, each could use the facilities of the developing city centre for certain activities. But as the century progressed and the Catholic community grew in size its public buildings, including the Cathedral and the main communal hall and clubs, developed either within Catholic neighbourhoods or in a complex of side streets around Smithfield market, in the city centre but not on the main thoroughfares. In quieter times a nationalist meeting might be permitted to use the city's main Ulster Hall, but on other occasions it would be barred to them. In 1912, when the Liberal cabinet minister Winston Churchill

(1874–1965) proposed to address a home rule meeting there, Unionists occupied the building ahead of time, and Churchill's meeting had to be transferred to a sports ground in Catholic territory, where it went off without difficulty. The pattern of residential and associational segregation was not, therefore, an equal one but one in which developments at odds with the values or wishes of the majority were confined to the territory of the minority.

Whereas in some of the cases studied in this book the implicit objective of the dominant community was to use the city as a machine for assimilation, in Belfast this was not the case to any significant extent. There were attempts at proselytism by Protestant churches in Ireland during the famine era of the 1840s.[51] A feature of the riots of 1857 in Belfast was aggressively anti-Catholic street preaching, but the whole tenor of its suggests that its purpose was not to convert Catholics but to arouse and inflame Protestants. The scale of intermarriage between Catholics and Protestants was effectively minimised and contained by the practices of both communities. From 1857 – if not earlier – working-class Protestant neighbourhoods would not tolerate the presence of a mixed-marriage family. Such marriages were tolerated within Catholic neighbourhoods, but as the century progressed the Catholic Church made it a condition of such marriages that the children be educated as Catholics, and that the Catholic partner endeavour to convert the other. Thus intermarriage was strongly discouraged by both sides and its outcome was contained within a single generation. We have seen in the cases of Brussels and Trieste that, where language was the ethnic indicator, language shift was a common occurrence associated with urbanisation and social mobility. An analogous religious shift was possible in Ireland, whereby individuals might remain Catholic in religious practice but effectively cease to be part of the Catholic 'community' or ethnic collectivity. Those who made such a shift tended to be labelled dismissively by their co-religionists as 'west Britons' or 'Castle Catholics'.[52] In effect such a shift was socially and residentially possible only for higher professionals, officials and senior members of large businesses whose markets were external. This constituted a group of some size in Dublin but in Belfast, where such Catholics were a very small fraction of a minority community, the numbers involved were insignificant. And of course the fact that

---

[51] Sometimes known as 'souperism' in reference to the 'soup' which missionaries would allegedly offer to the starving in return for conversion.

[52] Dublin Castle was the centre of British administration in Ireland.

Catholic religious practice continued to the next generation, even in these cases, meant that it was not a once-and-for-all change, as tended to be the case with language shift.

Belfast developed during the nineteenth century as an economic and social environment in which Catholics could survive, but they could only hope to flourish there within certain constraints. The linen industry was the largest employer of labour. As mechanisation took place, jobs required less skill, training and physical strength. Most of the workforce by 1870 was female and low-paid, while wages for those jobs which remained male compared unfavourably with other skilled trades. But, until the 1920s, the linen workforce remained very large indeed – 36 per cent of all employed females and 6 per cent of males in 1911, with both Catholics and Protestants finding employment in large numbers. Ethnic segregation in this industry occurred mainly *within* the workplace. We have seen that Protestants tending to be engaged in the less unpleasant processes of the industry such as weaving and finishing, rather than wet-spinning. In the shipbuilding and engineering trades, however, where the proportion of skilled workers, and the wages, were significantly higher, Protestants had an overwhelming predominance from the small beginnings of these industries in the 1850s to their period of greatest success around 1911, when they accounted for 15 per cent of the male workforce. In the skilled building trades too, which accounted for nearly 7 per cent of the male workforce, Protestants had a clear, if less pronounced, over-representation. Catholics were over-represented mainly in poorly paid, arduous or casual areas of employment such as dock work, carting and general labour, which made up almost a quarter of the male workforce in 1911, and in declining handcrafts. Catholic men and women were both over-represented in personal and domestic services. The only major non-manual areas in which Catholics were prominently employed were professional services and, especially, retail trading. This is explained partly by the classic minority route to mobility of providing services to the minority community: a small number of physicians, nurses, barristers and solicitors and a large number of neighbourhood shopkeepers, some of whom had quite flourishing concerns. Related to this is the special case of publicans. This trade came to be completely dominated by Catholics, the imbalance becoming more pronounced as time went by. By 1900 running a pub was the best route to upward mobility for a Catholic family. It is no coincidence that publicans predominated in the funding of Catholic churches and political movements, and on the boards of sports associations and newspapers. The absolute decline of Protestants in the *retail* side of Belfast's liquor trade during the last quarter of the nineteenth century was very dramatic, and can only be accounted for by the growing strength of the temperance movement in the evangelical churches. The outcome was to create a highly beneficial and much-needed ethnic niche for Catholics (Hepburn 1996:75–80).[53]

The pattern of Belfast's demographic development tends to reflect these economic trends. Table 6.1 illustrates how the town grew quite rapidly from the late eighteenth to the mid-nineteenth century. During this period the minority Catholic population grew at a more rapid rate than the population as a whole. There are no data on the religious demography between 1834 and 1861, so it is possible that the Catholic proportion rose even higher at some point between these dates. Certainly one might have expected the Famine to have contributed to an increase in the Catholic proportion, as the town's overall population increased by one-third in the famine decade of 1841–51. After 1861, however, although the city continued to grow rapidly, the trend of ethnic demography was reversed: whereas the 41,406 Catholics in 1861 represented 34 per cent of the population, the 93,243 Catholics of 1911 represented only 24 per cent of the population. Part of the reason for this reversal was no doubt the fact that

Table 6.1   **Belfast: Population and religion, 1784–1991***

Year	Total population (city proper)	Protestants (& others) %	Roman Catholics %
1784	13,650 est.	92.0	8.0
1808	25,000 est.	84.0	16.0
1834	61,000	67.7	32.3
1861	121,602	65.9	34.1
1881	208,122	71.2	28.8
1911	386,947	75.9	24.1
1951	443,671	74.1	25.9
1991	279,237	58.0 est.	42.0 est.

Sources: Budge & O'Leary:32; *Census of Ireland*, 1831–1911; *Census of NI*, 1951–91; Boal: 28
*Figures are for Belfast Co. Borough. By 1951 17% of the population of the urban area lived outside the city boundary, rising in 1991 to 41%. These neighbourhoods were 78% Protestant in 1991. People of non-Christian background never accounted for more than about 1% of the total. Since 1971 a proportion of the population has declined to answer the question on religious denomination.

---

[53] The manufacture and wholesaling of liquor in the north of Ireland remained a predominantly Protestant activity.

more opportunities and networks were opening up for Irish men and women in Britain, America and Australia. But the factors which made emigration from Ireland attractive to Catholics should have applied also to Protestants, other things being equal. It seems highly likely that the relative decline of Catholic migration to Belfast arose from a Catholic perception of reduced opportunities there. Fewer Catholics would therefore have chosen Belfast as their point of entry into the urban-industrial world, while of the families that did settle or remain in the city, the evidence of age:sex ratios by religion from 1901 suggests that there was a differential out-migration of young adult Catholics, especially males, as they encountered the relatively limited employment opportunities open to them in the city.

The role of international factors in the development of the Belfast conflict was a limited one, partly because of the city's remote location on the fringe of Europe, and partly because of Britain's great power in the Victorian era: third-party interventions were not possible. The growing influence of the Irish diaspora in America brought a slight international dimension to Irish nationalism in general, strengthening its finances and, on occasion, its resolve. More important was the enormous influence of Cardinal Paul Cullen (1803–78) on the organisation and character of Irish Catholicism in the generation after 1850, which ensured that Belfast Catholicism, like Irish Catholicism in general, would maximise its differences with the Protestant churches and stand very firmly against any fudging or erosion of its values and practices, especially in the areas of marriage and schooling. In a sense the Catholic church might be regarded as a quasi-state institution, but to the extent that Cullen's reforming movement arose from ultramontane Roman influences, acquired during his 20 years as a priest in Rome, there was also an international dimension to it.

The role of the state in the conflict requires more detailed examination. British governments opposed revolutionary Irish nationalism strongly, and until 1885 they also opposed the secessionist or devolutionist claims of parliamentary nationalist movements. After 1885 the Conservatives continued with this policy, whereas the Liberals endorsed, in principle at least, a policy which would have brought Belfast under the rule of a devolved Dublin parliament. Within this framework, the policy of pre-1914 British governments towards Belfast's ethnic divide was essentially a pragmatic one of attempted conflict management, moderated at times by the vestigial anti-Catholicism of the British establishment. Until the 1860s it was widely assumed in government circles that provocative Orange marching was a major source of ethnic conflict in the north of Ireland, and that it could be discouraged if not actually stopped. It was suppressed under temporary legislation in 1825, and the Grand Lodge of Ireland formally dissolved itself in 1836. But the Order survived at the local level, notwithstanding a formal legislative ban on public marching between 1850 and 1872. The ban was withdrawn because it became unenforceable. Mass defiance of it had been the cornerstone of William Johnston's 1868 election as an Orange radical MP for Belfast, when he defeated the sitting Conservatives. After this *bouleversement* the policy of successive British governments became 'equal marching rights' – that is, the acceptance of the right of both communities to conduct parades of an ethno-political nature – combined with an attempt to restrict them, by means of elite accommodation with local community leaders, to routes which either avoided direct provocation and dangerous interfaces, or which were capable of winning a degree of acceptance as 'traditional routes' (Wright 1996:284–332).

For much of the pre-1921 period the body responsible for administering these matters was the magistracy, most of whom were central government appointees via the administration in Dublin Castle. The police force also played a crucial role. The Royal Irish Constabulary was a paramilitary style police force founded in 1836, organised on a county basis under central government direction. Dublin had a separate metropolitan police force, again under central rather than local government control. Belfast's mid-nineteenth-century provision, a locally-raised police force, though closer to the English model in some respects, was therefore very unusual in the Irish context. Appointed by a city council which was almost exclusively Protestant for the first fifty years of its history, it is scarcely surprising that the Belfast Town Police was an unsuitable force where ethnic sensibilities were involved. It failed disastrously to maintain order during the riots of 1857 and 1864. The royal commission of inquiry into the events of 1864 found that the force of 160 men, all but five of whom were Protestants, had been incompetent if not highly partisan (Hepburn 1980:34–6). It was abolished by central government in the following year. From then until 1921 the city was policed by the RIC, a body still under the control of the British government through Dublin Castle. The RIC in Ireland as a whole was predominantly Catholic in membership, and this was often the case in Belfast as well.

Attempts to divert ethnic conflict by means of a cross-cutting party-political or organisational culture were not successful. In mid-nineteenth-century Belfast and Ulster politics the Whigs/Liberals and the Conservatives were identified mainly with particular family-based interest groups. There was a measure of association between the anglican Church of Ireland, the Orange Order and the Conservative party on the one hand, and between Presbyterianism, a conciliatory attitude towards Catholics, and the Liberal party on the other. But these distinctions were eroded quite rapidly from the 1830s onwards. As the right to vote was extended down the male social structure, Liberalism and Protestant opposition to Orangeism declined. Between the 1860s and the 1880s the Irish Conservatives fully embraced popular Orangeism to become, in effect, the Protestant and Unionist party. At the same time the Home Rule or Nationalist party cornered the Catholic vote, thus leaving the Irish Liberals, who had for a generation been a party of Presbyterian leaders and Catholic followers, with no basis of support.

There has been much debate over whether the initial cause of the conflict in Belfast was Protestant bigotry and Orange exclusivism or whether these forces were provoked in the first instance by local support for the Catholic nationalism of Daniel O'Connell's movement for the repeal of the Act of Union in 1830s and 1840s. In fact a militant ethnic consciousness permeated both sides increasingly deeply as the nineteenth century progressed. In the all-Ireland context it was stimulated by agrarian distress, by diaspora nationalism in the post-famine era, and later by the growth of literacy and a revolution of rising expectations. These all-Ireland factors helped to convert Catholic ethnicity into popular support for Irish nationalism in Belfast, even though their relevance to the situation of Belfast Catholics was very limited. Their existence gave added meaning on the other side to Orangeism, and helped to transform it from a pre-industrial agrarian organisation into a modern quasi-nationalist movement. Real competition within the city for housing and decently-paid jobs gave credence to what in other circumstances might have been seen as irrelevancies.

Thus Belfast politics were never able to develop in a conciliatory direction. When the Irish Municipal Corporations Act of 1840 first introduced elected councils, many expected that there would be substantial Liberal, including Catholic, representation in the city. In fact the first council, elected in 1842, consisted exclusively of 40 Conservatives, and only three Catholics were ever returned to the council prior to the Belfast Corporation Act of 1896 (Budge & O'Leary:51–3). By the latter date a sectoral pattern of ethnic residential segregation was well-established in the city, and this second major reform could do more than implement a structure which gave

Catholics control of two wards out of fifteen, or eight seats out of sixty. This of course reinforced the pattern of segregated politics and segregated living, giving no encouragement to cross-communal political appeals. The pattern of parliamentary representation was similar. The Liberals occasionally won one of the two seats in the 1830s and 1840s, but after that were successful only in the first election held under full male household suffrage in 1868, when the triumphal intervention of an independent Orange radical helped them to win the other seat. The Liberals never came close to winning a Belfast parliamentary seat again. Effectively, between 1840 and 1886, the party political cultures of Britain and Ireland went their separate ways, the one remaining Conservative/Liberal, the other becoming Unionist/Nationalist.

As elsewhere in Europe, socialism and trade unionism made earnest efforts, but proved unable to compete effectively with ethnic politics in the years before 1914. So long as trade unions remained predominantly organisations for skilled workers, the Irish labour movement had been dominated by Belfast Protestants. Thus when political Labour began in Belfast around 1900, at the same time as it emerged in Britain, it did not question Ireland's place in the United Kingdom. But after 1900 general labour unions, such as the Liverpool-based National Union of Dock Labourers, began to recruit in Belfast. A major strike of unskilled workers in the city in 1907 began as a cross-communal action for improved pay and conditions, but ended with ethnically-based disorder in the Catholic area of the city. Shortly afterwards the NUDL fell out with its strike organiser in Belfast, the Liverpool-born Jim Larkin (1876–1947). He repaired to Dublin where he formed the Irish Transport & General Workers' Union, a body which supported a militant nationalist programme and which built upon the 1907 experience to recruit strongly among Belfast Catholics. Thanks in large measure to this new union and to the ideological influence of the Edinburgh-born Irish republican socialist James Connolly (1868–1916), a separatist Irish Labour Party came into existence in 1912. One of the five Belfast branches of the British-based Independent Labour Party promptly switched affiliation to the new party. Some trade union activists among this particular generation of Belfast Protestants followed Larkin and Connolly down this route. But they were denounced by their own ethnic community as 'rotten Prods', and in 1912 about 600 of them were expelled from Belfast's main industrial workplaces along with about 2,400 Catholics (Morgan:269). 'Rotten Prod' took its place alongside 'Castle Catholic' and' West Briton' as a term of disparagement designed to stigmatise any defection from one or other ethnic monolith. By 1914 trade union militancy and Labour politics were undoubtedly well-grounded in both Belfast communities, but both had been firmly corralled into the established ethnic frameworks.

The efforts of British Liberal governments in 1886 and 1893 to pass a home rule bill, with a devolved parliament in Dublin, had twice been defeated in Parliament. Another Liberal government brought forward its third home rule bill in 1912, with the parliamentary ground better prepared, but a strongly Protestant and militantly Unionist Belfast was well-positioned to lead resistance to the measure. Massive anti-home rule rallies were held in Belfast, and a 100,000-strong Ulster Volunteer Force was formed under the leadership of sympathetic former Army officers. That Belfast had become such an important force in Irish politics was due not only to its absolute and relative population growth but also to the economic and political control which the Protestants had established in the city. This legislation passed, but was suspended for the duration of the war. The fact that the Liberal government lacked the resolve to implement its measure in the face of Ulster Unionist opposition, despite a strong majority in the House of Commons, was in large part due to the armed resistance which they anticipated from Protestant Belfast. It is true that opposition in the House of Lords delayed the finalisation of legislation until late 1914, by which time the outbreak of the First World War had caused the legislation to be postponed until the end of the war. But in fact it was already clear by the summer of 1914 that the British government, faced with rebellious mutterings from the Army, would not 'coerce Ulster', which had already begun to make convincing preparations for paramilitary resistance. In 1916, in the wake of a major republican uprising in Dublin, a convention of the moderate wing of the Nationalist party in the north voted reluctantly to accept the temporary exclusion of the north from home rule. This was done in the forlorn hope of preserving the position of the moderate nationalists in Ireland as a whole against the challenge of the revolutionary movement which was shortly to coalesce as Sinn Féin. Protestant militancy in Belfast, home to one-third of the six-county population, was central to both these decisions.

1921–72: Belfast as regional capital

After the First World War a different British government set aside the obsolete legislation of 1912–14. Through the Government of Ireland Act of 1920 it sought to implement separate devolution schemes for 'Northern Ireland' and 'Southern Ireland'. In the south guerrilla warfare continued until fuller independence – dominion status along the same lines as for Canada – was achieved in December 1921. But in Northern Ireland the scheme came into operation, with the 1920 Act as the province's constitution. Ireland was thus partitioned for the first time, and Belfast became the regional capital of Northern Ireland, a territory which was predominantly Protestant, but which included a disgruntled national minority comprising a quarter of the Belfast population and a third of the province as a whole. In the early months of 1919 Catholic and Protestant workers in Belfast were able to collaborate in a wide-ranging industrial strike over working hours and pay. But before long, in response to the IRA campaign of violence in the south and intense counter-revolutionary organisation and rhetoric from local Unionist activists, community relations in Belfast deteriorated rapidly. Beginning in the summer of 1920, and continuing until late 1922, the city experienced the highest levels of violence in its history. It remained under night curfew from July 1920 until December 1924. During these troubles Belfast sustained 469 dead, of whom a disproportionately high 58 per cent were Catholics, 33 per cent Protestants and 8 per cent members of the security forces. Additionally, between 7,500 and 10,000 were expelled from their workplaces, of whom perhaps 1,800 were 'rotten Prods', the remainder being Catholics, including about 1,800 female workers (Bardon:202; Morgan:269–70). Probably between a fifth and a third of all male Catholic workers in the city were expelled from their work.[54] With the numbers of unemployed growing rapidly from 1921 onwards, many of them were never able to return. Perhaps as many as 23,000 Catholics and 'rotten Prods' – about 5,000 households – were expelled from their homes, which again amounted to about one quarter of the entire minority community in the city. The provocation of IRA atrocities was of course an important factor in all of this. But Protestant counter-measures against innocent Catholics could be equally atrocious, a situation exacerbated as Protestant activists were increasingly given official responsibility for security.

Following elections to the Northern Ireland parliament in May 1921 a regional government was established. With the exception of a single transferable vote system of proportional representation, constitutional

---

[54] In the Census of 1911 there were 42,027 Catholic males recorded in Belfast, of whom 25,920 were members of the workforce. The number in the latter category at the Census of 1926 was not reported, but the total number of Catholic males was little changed, at 43,390. *Census of Ireland 1911: City of Belfast Report*, p.22; *Census of Northern Ireland, 1926, Belfast County Borough Report*, p.26

arrangements accorded with the standard British principles of majoritarian democracy. The local nationalist leader Joe Devlin (1871–1934) predicted that it would be 'practically an enlarged edition of the Belfast Town Council', and the outcome was government by a single party for 50 years (Hepburn 1998:233). The Unionist party won 40 of the 52 seats in 1921, and maintained a strong overall majority throughout the system's existence. Once installed it was able to use its devolved powers to adjust the system to its advantage, notably by abolishing proportional representation and reverting to a British-style first-past-the-post electoral system in both local government (1922) and regional government (1929). This ensured that an established two-party system based on the ethnic division would retain its primacy. It was a system which left no middle ground, and offered no inducement to politicians to compromise across the ethnic divide. On the 60-seat City Council for instance, the distribution of seats under PR in 1920 was Unionists 62 per cent, Nationalists and Sinn Féin 17 per cent and Labour 22 per cent. Following the discontinuation of PR, the outcome in 1923 was Unionists 83 per cent, Nationalists and Sinn Féin 13 per cent and Labour 3 per cent (Budge & O'Leary:186). The Ulster Unionist government certainly avoided the worst excesses which sometimes accompany ethnic domination, and on matters such as the funding of Catholic education it made significant concessions. It also operated skilfully to divert support from more extreme Protestant groups, and was helped in this by its decision to abolish proportional representation in elections. But the price was that in matters of symbolism, in public-sector white-collar employment, and in law and order, especially, it played safe by taking a hard line. It never attempted to reach out for Catholic support because, in electoral terms, it never needed to do so.

The new government in Belfast took over direction of the Special Constabulary – effectively an all-Protestant force – which had been created in 1920 by the British government. It also created the Royal Ulster Constabulary as a new regular police force. At first the latter recruited heavily from members of the defunct Royal Irish Constabulary, many of whom were Catholics, career policemen for whom there was no role in the Irish Free State. As these men retired however, there was little replenishment, and the proportion of Catholics in the RUC steadily declined. Internment of suspected republicans without trial continued until the end of 1924, long after overt conflict has ceased, aggravating the sense of bitterness and injustice felt by large sections of the Catholic community. The abolition of liquor licences for 'mixed traders' or 'spirit grocers', under the Licensing Act of 1923 was an early use of regional legislative power which mollified the predominantly-Protestant temperance interest at the expense of a business interest which was predominantly Catholic. Northern Ireland had been created in response to Protestant pressures, and it was inevitable that the Catholic minority would enter the new state reluctantly and resentfully. It was to be expected that reasonable security measures would be taken by the Unionist government to maintain the regime. But with hindsight we can see that this would not be enough to sustain the state in the longer term unless it was accompanied by measures designed to win Catholic acceptance. This did not happen, and perhaps was something which could not have been delivered by the majoritarian system which Britain had established in the province. Yet the British government devolved major powers to Northern Ireland, and steadfastly refused to be drawn back into the affairs of the province again, until the beginnings of its collapse in 1969.

The harsh economic climate of the inter-war period offered little opportunity for increased prosperity to take the edge off ethnic conflict. Unemployment in the city rose dramatically: for every 100 workers in shipbuilding and linen employment in 1926, there were in 1935 only 63 and 75 respectively.[55] In 1932, poor relief payments were being made to 14,000 family breadwinners in Belfast who had been unemployed for longer than six months. Single people were ineligible for this benefit. The province-wide figure in 1935 for unemployed linen workers, most of whom were women and girls based in Belfast, was 17,700 (Hepburn 1996:175). Unemployment hit the working class of both communities hard. Catholics suffered proportionately more, having a relatively larger unskilled sector, while they were to a large extent excluded from the many areas of public employment controlled by regional and local government. Whereas the proportions of Catholic and Protestant males employed in public and professional services in the city were at parity in 1901, by 1951 the Catholic share had, proportionately, fallen by a third. Belfast remained a predominantly working-class city, with non-manual employment hard to climb into, and relatively easy to skid out of. But Catholics in 1951 were more likely to have made unfavourable moves across this divide, whereas Protestants showed no deterioration (Hepburn 1996:91,110). Comparing 1901/1951 for occupational status, Catholics were more likely

---

[55] These figures are for the whole of Northern Ireland, but the overwhelming majority of such workers were in Belfast.

to be semi- or unskilled workers in 1951 than in 1901, and had experienced a proportionate decline in other occupational groups, whereas for Protestants the reverse was true. A comparison of the fortunes of Irish Catholics in Belfast with their counterparts in the British and north American labour markets shows that whereas until the late nineteenth century patterns were not dissimilar, trends thereafter began to diverge. In the USA and in Britain scholars such as Stephan Thernstrom and Lynn Lees have found clear evidence that by 1900 the economic condition of Irish Catholic migrants was tending towards the occupational distribution of the population as a whole (Hepburn 1996:71–2). In Belfast this was not happening. One reason for this was the continued operation of discriminatory Protestant employment practices, stiffened by worsening national rivalries. The other was the related fact that after 1921 the regional and well as the local state was exclusively in the hands of Protestants. In the cities of the United States and in some British centres, Irish Catholics had used political organisation and patronage to secure important footholds in various sectors of public employment. In Belfast this was not possible.

Religious residential segregation in Belfast continued throughout the twentieth century. Until further exacerbated by the protracted troubles which began in 1969, segregation levels appear to have remained little changed since 1901, when around two-thirds of the city's population lived in highly-segregated streets. The quality of Belfast's working-class housing in the late nineteenth century had compared favourably with many British industrial cities: land, bricks and unskilled labour were cheaper than in Britain, and at times the supply of houses ran ahead of demand. Thus it did not matter much at first that Belfast City Council was slower than its British counterparts to provide housing, but its historians suggest that by 1910 the City Council should have been erecting council housing (Budge & O'Leary:127). The political conservatism of an unchallenged Unionist Council – several of whose members were property developers and estate agents – meant that no council housing was built in Belfast until after the First World War, when central (and then regional) government at last required local authorities to implement housing plans. In Belfast the local authority soon got into trouble over corrupt practices regarding the supply of materials. In this situation regional government felt no binding political or ethnic loyalties: an enquiry was set up, resulting in prosecutions and senior resignations from City Hall (Budge & O'Leary:145–7).

In many Ulster towns, including the City of Derry/Londonderry,[56] the volume, location and ethnic allocation of public housing was a matter which could influence the outcome of local elections. In Belfast the large Protestant majority meant that this was not the case. Finance and a conservative ethos ensured that the volume of council housing in the city remained low until 1945, after which date regional government also built houses. In the post-1945 era Belfast city council, and to a greater extent regional government, pursued more enlightened policies in these areas. Attempts were made by planners to achieve an ethnic mix on many of the larger housing estates which were built in Belfast during this period. This policy was, in practice, brought to an end by the violence of 1969–71.

The Northern Ireland, or Stormont,[57] regime between 1921 and 1972 was regarded by the Catholic minority and by many neutral observers outside the province as inequitable, although there is some evidence that it sought to mitigate the harsher effects of ethnic oppression where it was able to do so without political risk. Certainly it maintained stability in the province for 45 years. Few in the mid-1960s would have predicted the troubles which were to follow. Apart from ten days of fierce rioting in Belfast in 1935, the period of devolved government was the longest period without a major outbreak of ethnic disorder since the mid-nineteenth century.[58] During the 1950s the cross-communal Northern Ireland Labour Party won a quarter of Belfast's seats (though none outside Belfast) in the Stormont parliament. But inequitable treatment and bitter resentment were not far below the surface. The most obvious signs of this were electoral boundaries which favoured Unionism, and an electoral franchise which favoured the better-off. Since 1945, franchise reform in Northern Ireland had ceased to keep pace with democratic changes occurring in Britain. While the right to vote in British urban council elections after 1945 extended to 99 per cent of adults, in Belfast it remained around 70 per cent (Budge & O'Leary:175). Discrimination against Catholics in

---

[56] The prefix 'London' was added to the name of the city and county following establishment of landed estates in the area by London merchant companies during the seventeenth century. Nationalists prefer to use the term 'Derry' but Unionists, especially since the troubles which began in 1968–69, have tended to make a point of using the longer version.

[57] Stormont is the district of suburban east Belfast where the grandiose parliamentary buildings were opened in 1932. The word is also used as a short-hand term for the devolved regime which operated between 1921 and 1972.

[58] The riots of 1935 resulted in ten deaths, many short-term workplace expulsions, 500 families evicted from their homes and the Army supporting the police for a week (Hepburn 1996:174–202).

housing allocation also continued to cause resentment. Drawing its inspiration from developments in the United States and given an added boost by widespread student militancy in western democracies over the Vietnam war and other issues, the Northern Ireland Civil Rights Association began a campaign of mass protests. On 5 October 1968 this came to the attention of the wider world when the RUC was shown on television to be out of control and attacking peaceful protestors, in a demonstration in the city of Derry.

This and similar occurrences might have been controlled by a Stormont government which was beginning to show signs of wishing to bring about reform. But the effective publicity secured by NICRA also provoked the beginnings of a popular Protestant backlash, so that a three-way conflict developed between moderate Protestants, extreme Protestants and Catholics. The spread of disorder to Belfast in the summer of 1969 intensified the violence greatly, taking it far beyond the control of the Stormont regime. Catholic housing shortages and related electoral gerrymandering in Derry were the most acute and blatant grievances, but the effect of this was, literally, to set Belfast ablaze. On 14 August 1969 the Stormont government had to call upon the British government to provide troops 'in aid of the civil power'. British cabinet ministers who took the decision were immediately aware that – unlike 1935 – this was not an intervention that would easily be terminated (Hepburn 1980:186). It also created a constitutional situation in which London was responsible for military forces on active service within the UK, while the political decision-making context in which those forces operated remained under the control of Stormont. This was not a sustainable arrangement. Once the Provisional IRA campaign emerged,[59] during 1970–71, it was only a matter of time before the governance of Northern Ireland was taken over by London. On 24 March 1972 the Stormont parliament was closed down and Northern Ireland came under the direct rule of Westminster.

Since 1972: rule from (mainly) Westminster again

The expansion of large cities beyond their formal boundaries, the incorporation of new suburbs as separate municipalities and the addition of formerly distinct settlements to the metropolitan area have all

---

[59] The previously-quiescent Irish Republican Army recommenced violent activity in 1970, following a breakaway by the more militant 'Provisional Executive' from the 'Official IRA'.

been characteristic of the modern city, and the bane of urban historians seeking to calculate comparisons across time. Belfast's boundaries
were extended three times during the nineteenth century, incorporat-
ing a small number of industrial suburbs and older mill villages, but
primarily drawing large areas of undeveloped land into the city. The
new boundary of 1896 caste the net very wide, and for a generation
after that statistics relating to the city proper really did embrace most
of the city's activity. In 1926, 90 per cent of the population of the
urban area still lived within the municipality, but by the 1930s Belfast
was filling up (Boal 1995:22). Working-class housing which had
seemed relatively good in 1880 was not only dilapidated but perceived
as far too small and overcrowded by contemporary standards. There
was concern about overcrowding in the inter-war period, and only the
intervention of the Second World War postponed action for so long.
Once postwar redevelopment started, expansion had increasingly to
move outside the city. The population of the municipality reached its
peak in 1951, at which time it housed 83 per cent of the wider urban
area. It subsequently declined steadily, so that by 1991 only 59 per
cent of the Belfast urban area population lived within the boundary
(Boal 1995:112). During the second half of the twentieth century there
was a widening gap between the population that lived within the city
boundary and the population that worked in it, spend money in it,
attended schools in it or even committed crimes in it. Planners and
other began to refer to 'Greater Belfast', the 'Belfast Urban Area' and
even the 'Regional City' (which included satellite towns up to thirty
miles away) to describe the wider conurbation of Belfast.

Problems of urban expansion and renewal create difficulties of transition in every metropolis, but for a city with Belfast's history there were
additional problems. The development of new neighbourhoods and
the demolition of old ones reawakened disputes over ethnic boundaries. Such questions as where Catholics and Protestants may be permitted to live, where they may freely congregate and express their
culture, which streets bands may parade along, which pubs people may
comfortably drink in, where new schools and churches may be located,
all had to be renegotiated through a variety of informal processes. It
was no coincidence that the post-1969 troubles happened during a
period when these planning issues had introduced new ethnic uncertainties into the city. The same was true in the economic sphere where
the city's main staple industries, heretofore owned in the main by
long-established local families with Unionist political connections,
contracted sharply during the 1950s. The numbers employed in textile

manufacturing, 85 per cent of whom were women, fell from 18,672 in 1951 to 10,478 in 1961 (*Census of Northern Ireland*, 1951 & 1961). These jobs were replaced, in the first instance at any rate, by man-made fibre and other industries, usually multi-nationals with no direct interest in the province's ethnic competition. Thus Belfast was experiencing the same kind of social and economic destabilisation as other western cities, just at the time when regional and global politics came together to spark off the troubles.

The general history of the Northern Ireland troubles is well known. Social and electoral injustices in the City of Derry played an important role in initiating the conflict, as did subsequent IRA activity there. In small towns and rural areas, especially those close to the border and/or with a substantial Catholic population, the conflict was also severe. But Belfast has been central to the conflict and in important ways the nature of the trouble there has been distinctive. An estimated 3,268 people were killed in Northern Ireland as a direct result of the conflict between 1969 and the end of 2001. Forty-seven per cent of these occurred within the Belfast municipal boundary, an areas which in 1971 embraced 24 per cent of the province's population, falling to 16 per cent in 2001.[60] A further 14 per cent of Northern Ireland's violent deaths occurred in the adjacent counties of Antrim and Down, of which it is safe to assume that a significant proportion occurred in the greater Belfast area. So more than half of all troubles-related deaths occurred in Belfast. But whereas in the rest of the province 37 per cent of deaths were Northern Irish Catholics and 44 per cent Northern Irish Protestants, the Belfast city figures differed significantly: 55 per cent Catholic and 34 per cent Protestant, a difference which is not explained by ethnic balances in the respective populations. Similarly, in Belfast 64 per cent of the dead were 'civilians' (i.e. neither paramilitaries nor security forces) against 42 per cent civilians among deaths outside Belfast. Whereas republican paramilitaries were responsible for 68 per cent of all those killed outside Belfast, the figure drops to 45 per cent of those killed within the city. Conversely, killings by loyalist paramilitaries, just 20 per cent of deaths outside Belfast, comprised 40 per cent of deaths in the city (Sutton 2002). Thus Belfast has been

---

[60] The five neighbouring councils closest to Belfast (Carrickgfergus, Castlereagh, Lisburn, Newtownabbey and North Down), which are now mainly suburban in nature, increased their share of the province's population from 18% to 22% between 1971 and 2001. The populations of several other council areas in the east of the province also grew, partly through satellite town development and partly through Belfast commuting.

the main locus of violent loyalist response to republican violence, just as it had been in 1912–14 and 1920–22. Belfast has also been distinguished by a higher level of violence than elsewhere in the province, by a much higher proportion of civilian deaths than elsewhere, and by a much higher proportion of Catholic deaths. All of the outcomes are related to the higher level of loyalist violence in the city and, again, reflect the old adage that the Catholics of Belfast were, as they were eighty years ago, potential hostages for the conduct of their co-religionists elsewhere.

The scale of violence over a 30-year period saw a massive increase in the number of British military on active service, a great expansion of the police force, and the development of a civilian security industry which became a significant feature of the city's labour market. Makeshift 'peace lines' consisting of corrugated iron screens and barriers gave way to more permanent constructions – high brick walls, sometimes with pedestrian gates open during the daytime – built to divide the warring communities. In West Belfast these form part of a divide between the Catholics Falls and Protestant Shankill areas which runs for several miles. In inner North Belfast, where segregation is equally intense but tends to be more micro-scale, it is less easy to make such barriers effective, and this quarter of the city has been the main centre for random killings. Army and police patrols have had some effect, but they have also constituted targets, mainly for republican paramilitaries. The British Army was initially welcomed in Catholic neighbourhoods in 1969, when it was seen as a saviour against loyalist invaders, and indeed the working-class Catholic community of Belfast had until then always provided large numbers of recruits to the British Army. But IRA provocation, and a heavy-handed approach by the Army and British government – most notably the Falls Road curfew of summer 1970 and accompanying house-to-house arms raids – quickly brought this honeymoon period to an end. From 1970 the aggressive presence of British troops in Catholic neighbourhoods gave a new credibility to Republican anti-British rhetoric. 'Brits out of Ireland' became a slogan with more resonance for ordinary people when there were armed soldiers stopping people in their streets, crouching in their front gardens or tearing up their floorboards than it has been in the 1930s or 1950s when 'the British presence' was a less tangible one.

Both Catholics and Protestants sought security through their own resources. Between 1969 and the mid-1970s there were very large movements of population within and around the city, which increased segregation levels. Much of this occurred as the result of intimidation –

direct and personal, or generalised at neighbourhood level, or simply implied or perceived – but the outcome was to harden the edges of interfaces everywhere in the city, and to consolidate communities into larger units (Darby 1986:*passim*). Later, as the troubles progressed, there was a second type of flight – on the part of people who could afford to do so – from neighbourhoods dominated by the paramilitaries of their own side, to more peaceful suburban environments in which they or their children were less likely to suffer from paramilitary bullying or be sucked into paramilitary involvement themselves. The index of Catholic–Protestant segregation by street in Belfast was 66 in 1901, rising to 71 in 1969, on the eve of the troubles, and 76 by 1972 (Hepburn 1996:49–50, 237).[61] Taking a simpler statistical measure, of streets which were more than 90 per cent occupied by either Catholics or Protestants, the overall figure increased from 67 per cent of the population living in such streets in the late 1960s to 77 per cent in the late 1970s, and it is now probably higher still. These figures include an interesting difference between private sector housing, where the percentage segregated has risen from 65 per cent to 73 per cent, and the public sector, where the figure has risen from 59 per cent to 89 per cent in the same period (Boal 1995:27–8).

The first phase of what Smith & Chambers (p.112) described as the 'ratchet' of segregation was a sharpening-up of the existing interfaces. Then it spread across the city, involving both greenfield developments, especially in working-class estates, and urban renewal projects in the inner city. Underlying all this was a major change in the pattern of ethnic demography. In the city itself, and in the newer public housing estates on the fringe, Catholic numbers were growing rapidly and Protestant numbers declining. There were several reasons for this. First, the high religious differential between the out-migration patterns of young adults, especially males, came to an end: Catholics were no longer much more likely to leave the city and province than Protestants, as labour migration became less closely linked to social class. Secondly, Protestants were considerably more like to migrate to suburbs beyond the city boundary than were Catholics, partly because

---

[61] The Dissimilarity Index will produce the maximum figure of 100 for a city where no unit (in this case the street) contained any mixing of the two communities under analysis, and a minimum of zero where every street reflected the overall city-wide proportion of one community to the other. See K.E. & A.F. Taeuber, *Negroes in Cities: Residential Segregation and Neighbourhood Change* (New York, 1965), pp. 325–7.

of increased prosperity, partly for reasons of security. Conversely Catholics seeking greater security, unless they could afford middle-class housing, were more likely to look for it within their own urban heartlands. A third factor was natural increase in the Catholic population, where a large bulge in the birth-rate in the 1950s/1960s led to an increased Catholic demand for homes from the late 1970s onwards.

Growing housing demand in Catholic neighbourhoods created pressures on the boundaries of Protestant neighbourhoods. Some new housing estates, which had not yet acquired any great symbolic significance to the Protestant community, such as New Barnsley in West Belfast, shifted totally from Protestant to Catholic occupation. In others, new boundaries were hammered out, often after periods of considerable tension involving the intervention of paramilitary groups, who sometimes became the *de facto* allocators of housing. Neither side liked any loss of symbolic territory: there was a great Unionist outcry in the late 1970s when the main Catholic sector of south-west Belfast spilled over the city boundary and – by decision of the British Labour government – a new public housing estate of 10,000 people was built on a greenfield site in the Lisburn District Council area at Poleglass. Even the maintenance of some long-established symbolic boundaries in inner-city neighbourhoods became difficult due to Protestant demographic decline. In one moment of desperation planners in north Belfast even proposed the re-alignment of a road so that local Catholic housing needs might be met without allowing the symbolic boundary of the road to be crossed (Bollens:250).

Since the 1970s city planning has mainly been the responsibility of the Westminster government, under direct rule. It has pursued a 'neutral' policy of seeking to respond to local residents' wishes, perceiving this as the best way of avoiding further exacerbation of the conflict. The focus has been on seeking the security of individuals, and of sustaining the territories of both groups, through a strategy of *de facto* local partitions. The international trend among planners and others to seek to co-operate with the institutions of civil society, through NGOs and the like, has made little impact on the local situation. In contested cities there are of course dual civil societies, so that government in Belfast has tended to work to accommodate the wishes of both, and only in a very limited way to seek the development of cross community strategies. There are two problems with this approach. First, it makes it more difficult to meet objective Catholic housing needs and secondly, through focusing on the containment of ethnic conflict in the short term, it reinforces the patterns of micro-partition, which make alleviation of the underlying social conflict harder in the longer term (Bollens:327–35). In 1986, for instance, a survey by the Policy Studies Institute found that only 19 per cent of the population of Belfast went at all often into territory they regarded as ethnically different, while 40 per cent said that they rarely or never crossed such boundaries (Hepburn 1996:240).

Some planners have pointed to Nicosia, Cyprus as an example of how total segregation/partition of two hostile populations can work, leading to an environment in which public figures are left enough space to resolve practical cross-communal matters of urban infrastructure by elite accommodation. But territorial dispositions and labour market considerations, among many other factors, make this an unattractive way forward in most cases. It really is the kind of solution which can only be implemented *in extremis* – where the scale of violence has grown so large that it is beyond the control of state power, leading to the mutual flight of populations on a larger scale than even Belfast has seen. The Belfast policy, in fact, has been based on a rather different assumption – that by dealing even-handedly with both communities, and giving each side space to develop its own civil institutions and politics, both sides will be encouraged to caste aside their fears and develop the confidence to work together. Certainly this is the assumption underlying the rhetoric of 'two traditions' and 'education for mutual understanding'. It is intended to develop mutual respect, and it may do so. The danger is that it may instead provide shields for those who want to sustain and extend hatred of the other side.

The strongest objections to full-scale micro-partition are economic. The problems of reviving the economy of a city whose traditional industries have almost disappeared, especially when that city has been afflicted by a generation of large-scale violence, are severe enough without seeking to divide the city into two self-contained units. We have seen that, as elsewhere in the western world, the linen, shipbuilding and engineering industries declined in the inter-war period, and experienced only a short-lived revival after the Second World War. The multinational phase of industrial development which followed this was a short one. Many multinationals disappeared in the early 1980s when government subsidies ended. In 1981 foreign-owned businesses accounted for 30 per cent of Northern Ireland's manufactures, but five years later the figure had fallen to 22 per cent. Efforts by British governments in 1978–83 to generate large-scale industry in Catholic west Belfast, by attracting the American car magnate John De Lorean to the city, ended in a complete debacle and an unsuccessful attempt by the British government to reclaim $1 billion of subsidies. By 1986 70 per cent of Northern Ireland's employees were public sector workers, com-pared to the overall UK rate of 42 per cent (Smith & Chambers:373–5). By 1997 only one company, the aircraft manufacturer Short Brothers, had over 4000 employees (http://cain.ulst.ac.uk/ni/economy.htm).

Unemployment has become the strongest indicator of ethnic im-balance in the labour market. The Catholic male unemployment stood at more than twice the Protestant rate for most of the 1980s and early 1990s. This became of such central importance because unemployment levels were so high: in 1986, for instance, 15 per cent of Protestants and 35 per cent of Catholics were unemployed, while figures of 50–80 per cent unemployment were cited for particular Catholic housing estates in the city. By 1997 the general upturn in western economies, and the improved condition of Northern Ireland, had reduced the Belfast unemployment rate to less than 7 per cent (http:// cain.ulst.ac.uk/ni/employ.htm). The leading analysts have demonstrated that, even aside from unemployment, the high level of structural change in the labour market has not in fact altered the pattern of Protestant : Catholic imbalance, and that continued positive action through fair employment measures would be needed. The reforms of the 1970s and 1980s did not mean that it had now become simply a matter of waiting for the impact of past discrimination to wither away (Smith & Chambers:375).

Wider political initiatives, notably the IRA and Loyalist ceasefires, which led to the Belfast (or Good Friday) Agreement of 1998, have helped to improve the general situation in Belfast. Commercial, social and cultural life in the city centre now matches that of comparable cities elsewhere in western Europe. The power-sharing ethos has, notwithstanding widespread grumbling, made some impact on Belfast City Hall: a Catholic was elected to the ceremonial position of lord mayor for the first time in 1997 and Sinn Féin members have become part of the city's political process. The powers of local authorities in Northern Ireland, including the Belfast City Council, remain very limited but even the grudging co-operation between the two sides within the Council, limited in power though it is, represents a measure of politicisation and normalisation of an ethnic conflict which had been expressed through violence for too long.

For some years now, a number of contradictory trends have been apparent in Belfast. At the media level the most visible are the incidents of street violence and intimidation: so-called 'punishment beatings' and killings, random killings, chronic low-level communal violence at the more exposed interfaces, and neighbourhood intimidation of school children and others. Part of this relates to hidden machinations within the Provisional IRA as the leadership struggles to keep the rank-and-file 'on ceasefire', and more of it relates to Protestant feelings of insecurity as they see their traditional neighbourhoods in the inner city suffering demographic decline. Increasingly, it seems, under-employed paramilitarism on both sides is degenerating into gangsterism. The appalling events which these factors generate are still important enough to threaten the destabilisation of the peace process and may yet determine the short- and medium-term future of Northern Ireland. They certainly contribute to the maintenance of very high levels of segregated living in many parts of the city. But they are paralleled by other evidence of increased inter-mixing of Catholics and Protestants: at the universities and in some of the city's most prestigious (and formerly all-Protestant) secondary schools; through intermarriage which, paradoxically, has reached higher levels during the troubles of the past generation than ever before; and through higher levels of social integration among certain sections of the middle class, such as higher civil servants and professionals.

In effect, a new division has developed in Northern Ireland between those whose daily lives are deeply embroiled in the conflict as a result of where they live, who they are, what they do for a living and what they believe, and on the other hand those who have been able – for reasons of income and status or other reasons – to shut out the troubles from their personal and family lives, and whose outlook and value-systems are little different from those found in other contemporary west European cities. It remains to be seen when and whether this element will become strong enough to alter the political culture of the city and region, or whether a long-running divide will develop such as that within the African-American community of the USA over the last generation, where on the one hand many Black Americans are more materially successful and pub-licly prominent than ever before, while at the same time drugs and vi-olence pervade the ghetto and one quarter of young Black males are in prison. In the American case only sustained economic prosperity and determinedly-targeted strategies are likely to improve this situation. In the Belfast case there is an added political dimension. Continued political stability and improved security may help to weaken paramilitaries and erode the anxieties of the most troubled areas. If they don't succeed, then the reverse is likely to be the case. What happens in Belfast in this respect is likely to determine the long-term future of the Northern Ireland region as a whole.

7

The Failure of Acute Violence: Jerusalem

... the first impression I received of walled Jerusalem in the early days ... [was] that it was an Arab city. It was as Arab as Cairo or Baghdad, and the Zionist Jews (that is the modern Jews) were as foreign to it as I was myself.

Vincent Sheean, 1935[62]

Since Jerusalem's destruction in the days of the Romans, it hasn't been so Jewish as it is now ...

David Ben-Gurion, 1948

This is how I remember Jerusalem in that last summer of British rule. A stone city sprawling over hilly slopes. Not so much a city as isolated neighbourhoods separated by fields of thistles and rocks ...

Amos Oz, *Panther in the Basement*, p.11

The conflict between Jews and Arabs over Jerusalem is a modern one, extending back no further than the late nineteenth century. Yet no city in history has been contested for as long as Jerusalem. This arid but symbolically important hill town is said to have been conquered thirty seven times. But after its capture from the Byzantines by the Arabs in 638 AD it remained, with the exception of the crusading period, under Muslim rule until 1918. The Latin Kingdom of Jerusalem

---

[62] *Personal History* (New York: Doubleday, 1935), pp.336–7. James Vincent Sheean (1899–1975) was a leading American foreign correspondent and one of the first 'book journalists'.

Map 7.1   Israel, 1949–67
Since 1967 all of Palestine has been under Israeli control
Source: B. Wasserstein, *Divided Jerusalem* (London: Profile Books, 2001) p. 166

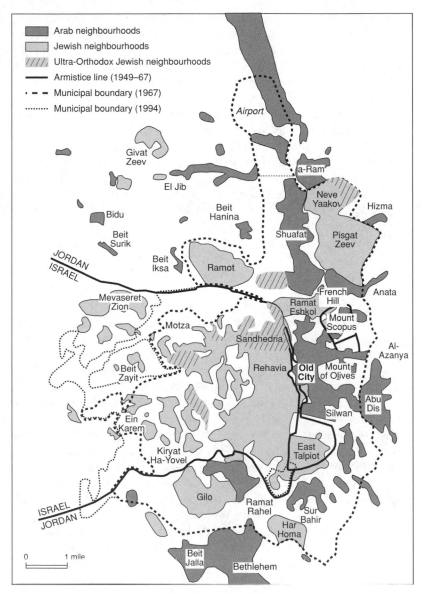

Map 7.2 Arabs and Jews in Contemporary Jerusalem
Sources: B. Wasserstein, *Divided Jerusalem* (London: profile Books, 2001) p. 214;
M. Klein, *Jerusalem: the Contested City* (London: Hurst, 2001), p. 8

ruled the city for most of the twelfth century, and briefly regained it from the Muslims during the thirteenth. Mamluk rule subsequently established the religious division of the city into the well-known Quarters – Armenian, Christian, Jewish and Muslim. In 1516 the city was captured again by the Ottoman Turks, who built the great walls which still define the Old City. Throughout the four centuries of Ottoman rule, Jerusalem remained a small, provincial backwater. Between 1919 and 1948 Britain governed Palestine under League of Nations/United Nations Mandate. Since 1949 Jerusalem has been the declared – if not internationally recognised – capital of the State of Israel, although its eastern section, including the Old City itself, was part of the Kingdom of Jordan between 1949 and 1967. Today the wider Israel/Palestine dispute remains unresolved, largely because neither Israeli Jews nor Palestinian Arabs feel able to renounce their particular claims to Jerusalem.

The city is of major importance to all three of the world's great monotheistic religions. In the Christian tradition it is the site of Christ's crucifixion. The Church of the Holy Sepulchre and the Via Dolorosa are the major sites for Christian pilgrimage, albeit that the latter was identified only in the fourteenth century. In the Muslim tradition it is the site of Mohammed's ascension into heaven. The Arab name for the city is still al-Quds, 'the holy place'. Jerusalem occupies first place only in the Jewish tradition, as the site of the Temple of David and the unchallenged spiritual centre of world Jewry. But the site claimed by the Jews as the Temple Mount has since early medieval times been, for Muslims, the Haram-al-Sharif, on which are built their own holy places, the Dome of the Rock and the al-Aqsa Mosque. For Jews the Western Wall beneath the Haram is the remnant of the Temple Mount. Long a holy site of central importance for world Jewry, its symbolic significance, especially for Israelis, has increased since it came under Israeli rule in 1967. Jews have no alternative spiritual focus comparable to Mecca or Rome. But set against the Israeli claim for precedence with regard to Jerusalem on the grounds of its unique religious importance to them is not only the Muslims' religious counter-claim, but also the more pragmatic point that Tel Aviv is Israel's largest Jewish city and real cultural centre, whereas Arab East Jerusalem is in fact the only major urban centre available to West Bank Palestinians.

All these factors are highly emotive, and have some salience in the contemporary struggle. But they are the context rather than the cause of the current conflict. The explanation for the bitterness of the past two or three generations lies, in approximate chronological order, in:

the slow collapse of the Ottoman Empire; the rise of Zionism as a response to the territorial nationalisms of east-central Europe; the lack of strategic policy direction on the part of western powers, especially Britain; the rise of Arab nationalism in Jerusalem and Palestine and the support it has found among neighbouring states, many of them newly-rich from oil revenues; and the growing role of the United States in the affairs of the region. Without these factors it is hard to see how the history of the city itself could have generated the modern conflict. In the mid-nineteenth century Jerusalem was a small city of around 15,000 people ruled by Turks (Table 7.1). Muslims, mainly Arabs, made up about a third of the population while Christians, also mainly Arabs, comprised about a quarter. By about 1840 Jews had become the largest of the three minorities, but they were mainly a population of elderly migrants living on religious charity. Jerusalem was for them not an earthly but a spiritual capital, whereas the Zionists who followed them into Palestine at the end of the nineteenth century were secular-minded people who had little interest in Jerusalem. Thus modern history does not provide compelling evidence in support of the claims of any party to the conflict. The religio-historical myths are powerful influences on millions of Jews and Arabs (as they were on many Christians in the both the twelfth and the nineteenth centuries) and must be taken into account in any attempt to resolve the problem. But they did not cause the current conflict.

While Jerusalem's contested status is plainly evident, it is less imme-diately obvious that it is a western city. Appalled by the poor condi-tion of the city and most of its inhabitants, nineteenth-century visitors from Europe certainly did not think so. But its prominence as a contested city in the twentieth century stems from two factors which are very much part of European history. First the drawn-out collapse of

Table 7.1   Jerusalem: Population and religion, 1800–1995

Year	Total population	Jews %	Muslims %	Christians %
1800	9,000 est.	25.0	44.4	30.6
1850	15,000 est.	40.0	36.0	24.0
1910	69,900 est.	64.4	17.2	18.4
1922	62,500	54.4	21.6	23.4
1946	164,400 est	60.4	20.5	19.1
1967	267,800	73.5	21.7	4.8
1983	428,500	71.5	25.3	3.2
1995	617,000	67.6	29.6	2.3

Source: Wasserstein:46

the Ottoman Empire between 1850 and 1918 raised uncertainties among all the European powers about the city's future. Even more important was the emergence of Zionism at the end of the nineteenth century, stimulating as it did a great increase in migration to Jerusalem and Palestine which continued throughout the twentieth. Zionism was in origin a European nationalist movement, arising from the same social and economic forces that produced other European nationalisms. These two factors underlay the 1917 Balfour Declaration, which stated the British Government's intention to establish a 'national home' for the Jews in Palestine. In that sense the modern Jerusalem question arises not just – or perhaps not even mainly – from the city's long history as an object of fascination for three competing religions but also from the importation from Europe of a new secular religion – nationalism – during the second half of the nineteenth century.

Ottoman rule to 1918

Jerusalem in the early modern period was a small, predominantly Arab city governed by Ottoman Turks. In 1690 it included about a thousand Jews, who made up ten per cent of the population. During the eighteenth century the Jewish 'Istanbul Committee' used its influence to restrict Jewish migration to the city so that numbers did not become financially unsupportable. As elsewhere, Ottoman rule in Palestine was tolerant of other religions, within a framework of strict Muslim control. Jerusalem Christians and Jews were not required to do military service, which was commuted to taxation, while under the *millet* system they also ran their own religious courts (Gilbert 1985:33). The *Tanzimat* reforms of the mid-nineteenth century introduced a European-style administration and a more secular emphasis in Muslim education. More stress was laid on Ottoman patriotism and use of the Turkish language. Jerusalem had an elected municipal government, on a very restricted franchise, from 1867. These developments reinforced the authority of the leading Muslim families, which always provided the mayor of the city (Wasserstein:66). The Nashashibi family was prominent in support of the reform policy, and led the political representation of the city in Constantinople. The Husaynis tended to control Muslim religious leadership in Jerusalem, flourishing in the last decades of the nineteenth century as the Ottomans sought to promote popular religion as a means of social control (Wasserstein:66; Khalidi:37–41).

A Christian visitor in 1838 reported that 'the glory of Jerusalem has indeed departed ... She has sunk into the neglected capital of a petty Turkish province'. Surrounded by barren rock and desert, without a decent water supply, Jerusalem in the early nineteenth century was still contained entirely within its walls, the gates locked at night against bandits. Its Jewish population existed mainly on external charity, or *haluka*, from European Jewry. But after about 1860 this charitable element widened from basic support for the indigent to a planned and idealistic investment in the city's infrastructure, with the provision of modern public buildings and other amenities. As early as 1840, the British foreign secretary Lord Palmerston noted that 'there exists at present among the Jews dispersed over Europe a strong notion that the time is approaching when their nation is to return to Palestine'. For several centuries the majority of Jerusalem Jews had been Sephardim, descendants of those expelled from fifteenth-century Spain, but the majority of nineteenth-century immigrants were Ashkenazim from Central and Eastern Europe. By 1845 Jews had become the largest group in the city (Wasserstein:3, 47; Gilbert 1985:7, 40, 44, 176).

At the same time the growing weakness of the Ottomans drew the European powers into more active involvement in the region. The price of their diplomatic support for the regime was the installation of powerful consuls in Jerusalem. Public concern in the west over the decrepit condition of the Christian holy places in the city lent popular support to the idea that the European powers should demand a measure of control over their holy places. But the Ottoman Government was unable to satisfy the competing demands of the Latin and Greek churches, and the conflict developed into the Crimean War, as Russia invaded Turkey. Russian defeat in the war gave the Ottomans the power to resolve the issue by allocating specific sites to specific denominations (Wasserstein:27; Gilbert 1985:23, 37, 69).

Fearing that continued demographic change would further destabilise the situation in Jerusalem, the Ottoman authorities long resisted any improvement in communication. But by 1887 a well-funded European lobby was pressing the Constantinople government to let the railway development go ahead, and in 1892 the line from Jaffa at last opened. Narrow gauge and single-track as it was, it represented an enormous advance. The journey time from the coast was reduced from two days by coach and horses to three-and-a-half hours (Gilbert 1985:210, 219). The Jews were still a small minority in Palestine as a whole, but rapid growth in the city during the previous 20 years had given them a local majority. Their European sponsors – most notably

Sir Moses Montefiore of London, supported by the Rothschild family –
had developed 'New Jerusalem' immediately to the north of the Old
City, and about twice its size, more modern in appearance than the
constrained and still-squalid Old City. The new immigration was primarily from the Russian and Austrian empires, stimulated by hostile
popular nationalisms and by developing Zionist sentiment. Whereas
the first *aliya* ('ascent to Zion', i.e. Jewish immigration) of 1882–1903
attracted relatively little Arab hostility, the subsequent second *aliya*,
following the 1905 revolution in Russia, brought more conflict, especially to Palestine's coastal plain. Driven by radical nationalist and
socialist ideas and by a more clearly-articulated Zionism, it provoked
widespread resistance from Arab peasants who found that 'their land'
was being sold by absentee landlords and that Arab workers were being
replaced by Jewish immigrants. By about 1910 this land agitation was
becoming the basis of the first links between the peasantry and a
Palestinian elite which was beginning to oppose Zionism politically
and through the press (Khalidi:110–20).

Continued growth also exacerbated conflicts within Jewry. Incoming
ultra-orthodox Jews opposed all economic development or modernisation. As late as 1914, Orthodox Jews still outnumbered secular and
Zionist Jews in the city of Jerusalem by about four to one. In the
Ottoman period Arabic was the main working language of the city,
although Turkish was widely used among the educated classes. In 1879
ultra-orthodox pressure brought to an end the teaching of Arabic and
Turkish to Jewish boys in the Jewish Orphanage and other schools. But
the introduction of Hebrew as a spoken language was also opposed by
orthodox rabbis and others, who regarded Hebrew as a language for
sacred use only. Many of them also regarded the Zionist quest for an
earthly Jerusalem as blasphemous (Gilbert 1985: 37, 60–1, 182–3;
Wasserstein:4). But in 1882 a school was opened in Jerusalem to teach
modern Hebrew as a language for everyday use. The pupils came from
homes where the everyday language was Yiddish, German, Arabic,
Russian or Spanish (Ladino/Judezmo). In 1902 a group of locally-born
Jews declared their intention to make Jerusalem 'a Hebrew city, whose
language will be the Hebrew language', while a Hebrew-language newspaper was started with financial support from the Rothschild family.
Increasingly, Zionists urged Jewish schools to adopt Hebrew as their
working language. Bitter conflicts between advocates of Hebrew and of
Yiddish continued as late as the 1940s, although the contest was virtually decided by about 1910. Hebrew – the high status literary language
of which most literate Jews had some reading knowledge – triumphed

over Yiddish, the standard popular language of European Jewry but lacking, prior to the twentieth century, any literary status. Yiddish became increasingly less useful as a Jewish lingua franca in the twentieth century. Arabic-speaking Jews from Asia and Africa found Hebrew much closer to their native tongue, while many European Jews from Yiddish backgrounds were quick to make the shift to Hebrew – in the early days for Zionist ideological reasons or, later, because it was a necessary skill for access to non-manual employment (Spolsky & Cooper:57–69).

Although more than half of Palestine's Jews still lived in Jerusalem at the end of the Ottoman period, Zionists despised the dependency of the prevailing *haluka* culture which still attached to Jerusalem and were attracted more to the coastal cities and to farming in the coastal plain. The hero of S.Y. Agnon's epic novel *Temol Shilshom*, an indecisive young man from Austrian Galicia who has 'ascended to the Land of Israel' early in the second *aliya*, moves uneasily between secular coastal society and orthodox Jerusalem as the novel unfolds. Many, like the founder of Zionism himself, Theodore Herzl, saw in 'the reeking alleys' of Jerusalem only 'the musky deposits of two thousand years of inhumanity, intolerance and foulness' (Gilbert 1985:225; Wasserstein:4). Jews at this stage constituted only about 10 per cent of Palestine's population, but the pace of growth began to cause alarm among Muslim and Christian Arabs, which was intensified following the founding of the Zionist movement in 1897. From the Ottoman point of view a dilution of Arab ethnic strength in the region had political advantages, and there were Arab protests in 1900 when Ottoman law was altered to make Jewish immigration and land purchase easier. By 1914 local Arab politicians were sufficiently concerned by 'the harm and danger awaiting us from Zionism and the Zionists' to be collaborating in the pre-emptive purchase of government land (Wasserstein:69).

As with the Jews, the Christian population of the city also increased more rapidly than the Muslim during the nineteenth century, and exceeded it in size by the end of the Ottoman period. Indeed Jerusalem, though governed by Muslims, could still give the appearance of being a Christian city, with the Easter pilgrimage the largest annual event. All this arose from the fact that the main capital inflows to the city throughout this period came not from the Ottoman government but from Jewish and Christian religious institutions. To a large extent 'religion acted as a primitive engine for economic and urban development in Jerusalem until the mid-twentieth century' (Dumper:87).

From October 1914 Ottoman Turkey was at war with the western allies. Arab nationalists were clearly suspect from the Ottoman point of view, as to a certain extent were Jews. Britain sought allies behind Ottoman lines, and may at one point have promised Palestine to Sherif Hussein of Mecca. Of more lasting significance however was the Declaration by the British Foreign Secretary, A.J. Balfour, in November 1917 (in the form of a published letter to Lord Rothschild) that the British government would use its influence to establish for the Jews 'a national home in Palestine'. A few weeks later British forces captured Jerusalem, and in May 1920 the League of Nations granted Britain a Mandate to govern Palestine. The former British cabinet minister, Sir Herbert Samuel, himself Jewish though not prominently associated with Zionism, became High Commissioner and Jerusalem became once more a capital city.

British rule, 1919–48

The Balfour Declaration and the replacement of Ottoman by British rule brought a sharp change in Jerusalem's community relations. Arab notables accustomed to representing the city in the Constantinople parliament now found that British promises of representative institutions melted away. In April 1920 the mild anti-Zionist protests of the Ottoman era gave way to fierce rioting which left nine dead and more than two hundred injured. The occasion was the annual Muslim pilgrimage of Nabi Musa. This was the beginning of a new set of conflicts revolving around holy places, which soon supplanted the older Christian–Muslim conflicts. The following year Samuel appointed to the post of Mufti, head of the Muslim religious community in Jerusalem, Haj Amin Husayni (c.1895–1974). A junior member of one of the leading Jerusalem families, Haj Amin had been an Ottoman army officer, but had switched to the pro-British Arab side in 1917. In 1920, however, he was sentenced in his absence to a long prison sentence for a strongly anti-Zionist speech which he had made at the time of the Nabi Musa riots. This sentence was rescinded in the following year, and he returned to an influential role in Jerusalem's religious politics. Previously a pan-Arabist who had sought to minimise the Zionist challenge through the anticipated incorporation of Palestine into Greater Syria, he began to articulate a specifically Palestinian nationalism once Syria was placed under a French Mandate in 1920. Haj Amin set out to counter the Jewish advance in Jerusalem by building up the city's religious status in the Islamic world: with international help he had the two mosques on the Haram-al-Sharif magnificently restored. In 1931, however, he failed in his bid to establish a Muslim university in Jerusalem, just as the British authorities had failed to establish an 'English' university in the previous decade. The Jews, meanwhile, were in 1925 at last able to implement their pre-war plans for opening a Hebrew university in the city, on Mount Scopus (Khalidi:187; Gilbert 1996:104–7, 111–12; Mattar:17–20; Wasserstein:43, 100–7).

Until the early 1930s Jerusalem's Arab elite worked to keep the peace. Ragheb Nashashibi (1882–1951) was a moderate mayor of the city from 1920 until his electoral defeat in 1934, while the Mufti also took a pragmatic line during these years, co-operating with the British administration while strongly opposing Zionism. But throughout the 1920s Arab–Jewish relations on the ground steadily worsened. Residential segregation greatly intensified. As the Nazis assumed power in Germany, Jewish immigration to Palestine grew more rapidly, from 10,000 during 1932 to 62,000 in 1935 (Nashashibi:32). Arab protests intensified, including a general strike and rioting throughout Palestine. The Mandate authorities reduced the quota of Jewish immigrants, but there was no glimmer of improvement in community relations, and in April 1936 far more serious Arab riots broke out. On the Jewish side a paramilitary group, the Irgun Zvai Leumi, also commenced terrorist operations. After 1929 the Mufti had become more directly involved in political as well as religious activity. As Jewish immigration and Arab unrest both continued, the Husaynis, Nashashibis and other Palestinian notables buried their differences and came together in an Arab Higher Committee. In 1937 this body was proscribed and the British exiled the Mayor of Jerusalem, who had always by custom been an Arab. The Deputy Mayor, by custom always a Jew, took over as Mayor for an extended period, which was not customary. Other Arab councillors were similarly dealt with, so that a *de facto* Jewish majority emerged on the city council for the first time. Arab members boycotted the council until the appointment of a new Arab Mayor. The Mufti was deprived of his position as President of the Supreme Muslim Council. He took sanctuary on the Haram, and later fled to Lebanon.[63] For a brief period in 1938 Jerusalem and Palestine's other main cities were in the hands of the rebels, but there was no effective leadership and the

---

[63] He did not return to Jerusalem or Palestine until 1966, and then only for a brief visit in the context of King Hussein of Jordan's efforts to retain Palestinian support.

revolt was crushed. Between 1936 and 1939, 500 Jews and150 Britons had been killed by Arabs, while more than 3,000 Arabs were killed – including 2,000 by British forces and about 1000 by extremists on their own side. Britain abandoned any further attempt to work with the Mufti, who in turn no longer regarded collaboration with Britain as a worthwhile means of resisting Zionism. From 1939 he sought allies in Nazi Berlin (Gilbert 1996:119–37; Mattar:65–85).

Beginning in the 1890s, but developing more rapidly during the Mandate period, an important shift in migratory patterns took place. Although Jews had been a majority in the city of Jerusalem since the late nineteenth century, at the end of the Ottoman period they were still outnumbered 2:1 in Palestine as a whole. But by the late 1930s the Jewish population of Tel Aviv was double that of Jerusalem: 177,000 to 82,000, notwithstanding a westward extension of the municipal boundary of Jerusalem by the British authorities in 1927 which max- imised the Jewish population of the city. Jerusalem had in fact ceased to be the main centre of Jewish population in Palestine. In 1932 the Jewish Agency, the formal voice of Jewish opinion under the Mandate, proposed the division of the city into two boroughs – a Jewish west, based in the New City, and an Arab east based on the Old City – in the hope of achieving greater local security. At that stage the British gov- ernment rejected partition of the city. But in 1937, in the midst of the worst riots, the government's Peel Commission recommended the par- tition of Palestine into an Arab territory, comprising the West Bank, Gaza and the Negev, to be merged with Transjordan, and a Jewish state consisting of Galilee and the coastal plain. Peel proposed that Jerusalem should be excluded from both these states and remain under the British Mandate, with a corridor linking it to the Mediterranean. On the Arab side the Nashashibis – who had Jordanian links – showed some interest, but the Mufti and the young radicals leading the revolt were beyond any compromise with Zionism. The Nashashibis resigned from the Arab Higher Committee and the British attempted to move against the Mufti, but the Commission report was not implemented. Most Zionists would at this stage have been prepared to accept a Jewish state without Jerusalem, although Jewish opinion in Jerusalem itself was predictably less flexible. Jews now made up 60 per cent of the city's population, and on the death of the mayor in 1944 they called for an end to the custom of always having an Arab mayor. The British govern- ment proposed a rotating system, which the Jews accepted but the Arabs rejected. The Jewish Deputy Mayor therefore remained on as acting Mayor until July 1945, when the British High Commissioner suspended the municipality altogether (Gilbert 1996:142–50,168; Mattar:80–1; Wasserstein:110–12).

Anxious not to lose Arab support in the impending conflict with Germany, the British government agreed in 1939 to restrict Jewish immigration to 75,000 over the following five-year period, after which the people of Palestine would have the right to veto any further immigration. But with Nazi forces in Crete and western Egypt by the end of 1941, the bulk of Jewish opinion continued to be pro-British in its general outlook. Von Ribbentrop declared that the 'obliteration of what is called the Jewish National Home' was a firm aim of Nazi policy. Mainstream Jewish opinion solidified behind the Allies in November 1942 when the first news reached Jerusalem of Nazi gas chambers in Poland, although the Lehi or 'Stern Gang', a breakaway group from the Irgun, continued its campaign of violence against British forces throughout the war (Gilbert 1996:159–60, 167). Arab opinion was split between supporters of the Mufti, who broadcast from Berlin during the war, and a pro-Allies wing.

The war ended with Jewish demands for the right to immigration of all survivors of Nazi Europe still opposed by most Arabs and by Britain. A sustained Jewish campaign of bombing and shooting developed, including an Irgun bomb at Jerusalem's King David Hotel in July 1946 which killed 92 people. A new British proposal in 1945, based on local government partition, brought agreement no nearer: the Fitzgerald plan was well-constructed but it depended politically on securing a measure of local support and on a continued British presence to hold the ring, neither of which were forthcoming (Wasserstein:122). In March 1947 the British government announced its intention to surrender the Mandate. The United Nations Special Committee on Palestine, UNSCOP, then proposed the partition of Palestine into two sovereign Arab and Jewish states with an economic union, which would be democracies with safeguards for minority protection. Jerusalem would become a *corpus separatum* – a neutral, demilitarised city, an international trusteeship – administered by a neutral United Nations Governor and police force.

The UNSCOP plan differed from Fitzgerald's scheme in its definition of 'Jerusalem'. Although the Jerusalem municipality in 1947 comprised 99,320 Jews and 65,000 Arabs, the proposed separated area under UN control was to include many outlying towns and villages, including Bethlehem, so that it would have a slight Arab majority of 105,000 to 100,000 Jews. This was especially important inasmuch as a referendum was to be held for the Jerusalem area after 10 years, to see whether its inhabitants wished international status to continue or be modified. Although the Arabs were in a majority, it was agreed early on in the detailed planning that new Jewish immigration to Jerusalem would be permitted. The Arab Higher Committee, supported by some of the major Arab states, opposed the plan, and reiterated its call for a unitary, independent Palestine. Palestinian Arab leadership, however, was fragmented between the rival elite families, with the absent Mufti still the most influential figure, and it had no effective military power other than the armed forces of the neighbouring state of Transjordan.[64] The Jewish Agency agreed to the UNSCOP proposal. At this stage majority Jewish opinion was still prepared to concede control of Jerusalem, home to almost one-sixth of all Palestine's Jews, in order to get some kind of Jewish state established. Understandably, Jerusalem Jews were less enthusiastic, but in November 1947 the UN General Assembly approved the UNSCOP plan by 33 votes to 13, with Britain among the 10 abstainers (Wasserstein:124; Gilbert 1996:174–9).

Again this proposal was nullified by opposition on the ground. In the absence of any international force to implement the UN's decision, warring Jewish-Israeli and Arab-Jordanian forces became the effective decision-makers in the area. By tacit agreement both sides in practice preferred a bilateral partition of the city, to be fought out between themselves, rather than admit the intervention of outside forces. The UN decisions were simply ignored. Jordanian forces took the Old City, but could not dislodge the Israelis from a tiny outpost on Mount Scopus. Fighting continued mainly in rural areas, but strategy was dictated by the wish to control access to Jerusalem. At the Arab village of Deir Yassin, just outside Jerusalem overlooking the Jaffa Road, on 9 April 1948, an attempt by Irgun and Lehi members to drive out the inhabitants was resisted, resulting in the deaths of 254 people in a morning, almost all of whom were local Arabs. By way of reprisal, Arab forces ambushed a Jewish convoy in Jerusalem, killing 77. In the five months to 3 May 1948 an estimated 3,469 Arabs, 1,256 Jews and 152 Britons were killed (Gilbert 1996:192–208).

The British civil and military authorities withdrew from Palestine three months ahead of schedule, on 14 May 1948. That afternoon Ben-Gurion announced the establishment of the Jewish State of Israel. Within hours the governments of Lebanon, Syria, Iraq, Transjordan and Egypt ordered their armies into Palestine, many expecting to

---

[64] After its acquisition of Palestinian territory on the west bank of the Jordan river in 1948 the state became known as Jordan.

over-run it within days. More cautiously King Abdullah ordered Glubb Pasha, the British Army general in command of Transjordan's Arab Legion, to take Jerusalem and secure the Old City. Neither Israelis nor Jordanians were now prepared to allow their own extremists – the Irgun/Lehi and the Mufti/Husayni faction – to gain the initiative in the city (Wasserstein:151;Gilbert 1996:213). Britain and the USA began to lose interest in the *corpus separatum* proposal, the main defender of which became, rather tellingly, the Vatican (Wasserstein:170). The manner of Britain's withdrawal was influenced by a wish to maintain good relations with the Arab world through avoiding any appearance of responsibility for partition. In fact, however, Britain had discreetly facilitated partition between the Zionists and the Jordanians. One attraction of this outcome was that it left the supporters of the Mufti out in the cold. Another was that it undermined the UNSCOP plan, thereby avoiding the Foreign Office's *bête noire* of another Danzig, or 'city state' option (Wasserstein:134–8).[65]

The United States quickly recognised the State of Israel. A few days later the Jews besieged in the Jewish Quarter of the Old City finally surrendered to the Arab Legion, and 1,300 refugees left the Quarter for West Jerusalem. The Jewish community lost access to the Western Wall for the first time in many centuries. The cease-fire was signed on 11 June 1948. Three hundred and sixteen Jews, including 199 civilians, had been killed in Jerusalem during the previous five weeks. But Arab attempts to break out of the Old City into West Jerusalem were not successful, and Jewish forces managed to secure the corridor to the coast: all 35 Arab villages in the corridor were overrun, and 50,000 refugees fled to Arab-controlled territory. Stalemate had at last been reached, and a second truce was established in Jerusalem on 17 July 1948 (Gilbert 1996:224–33).

In August Israel proclaimed West Jerusalem as Israeli-occupied territory and formally rejected the internationalisation of the city. The announcement a few months later by the UN General Assembly of its intention to establish a permanent international authority to govern a demilitarised Jerusalem had the remarkable effect of uniting Israel and Transjordan in support of the *status quo*. On 2 February 1949 the Israeli

---

[65] Commenting on an earlier proposal to create a separate Jerusalem state under either British or international control the British Foreign Office had observed that in view of the state of Arab–Jewish relations in the city, it was unlikely that 'the Jerusalem State ... will turn out to be a credit to its founder'(Gilbert 1996:161–5; Wasserstein:116–18).

Government announced the incorporation of West Jerusalem into Israel, and on 17 March King Abdullah established Jordanian civil authority in East Jerusalem. An Israel–Jordan armistice was signed on 3 April 1949, under which Jerusalem was formally partitioned along the cease-fire line. The hospital and university on Mount Scopus remained an isolated Israeli enclave (Gilbert 1996:237–41; Dumper:31).

The British Mandate did end in the establishment of Balfour's promised national home for the Jews in Palestine, but it was scarcely a political triumph. The path to it was destructive and bloody, and prospects for future peace and stability were greatly damaged. Part of the problem was Britain's lack of clarity regarding long-term goals. Like many First World War promises, the Balfour Declaration contained little indication of its intended scope, extent and timescale, or proposed means of implementation. Different British governments through the 30-year period took different views, in changing circumstances, of the relative importance of conciliating Arab and Jewish opinion in the region. Meanwhile Jews continued to immigrate, and Arabs increasingly objected. British governments came up with various neat constitutional structures, but appear to have given far less thought to means of implementation. Weakest of all, there seems to have been no co-ordination between political and constitutional policy on the one hand, and the shaping of facts on the ground on the other. If Britain played any part in the ultimate establishment of Israel it was mainly by default: the existence, structure and boundaries of the new state were thrashed out between the local powers.

Partitioned Jerusalem: 1949–67

Israel and Jordan remained formally at war throughout the period of the city's partition, but 'a strange diplomatic symbiosis grew up between them' (Wasserstein:179). In December 1949 the Israeli cabinet declared that Jerusalem was the capital of the new state, and the Knesset [parliament] moved there permanently from Tel Aviv. With very few exceptions the international community continued to maintain its embassies in Tel Aviv, to avoid giving recognition to Jerusalem as the capital. Capital or not, West Jerusalem during the 1948–67 period remained a dead-end, a divided frontier city supported by public money at the closed end of a long, narrow corridor, while the real centre of government remained in Tel Aviv. No government figure in Israel prior to June 1967 called for an irredentist policy towards East Jerusalem, and the decision in the early 1960s to re-site both the major institutions which had been cut off in the Mount Scopus enclave – the Hadassah Hospital and the Hebrew University – in West Jerusalem suggested acquiescence in the partition of the city (Gilbert:243–45, 264; Wasserstein:199, 204–5; Dumper:21).

The length of the 1947–49 military campaign had intensified Arab–Jewish segregation. This was particularly the case in West Jerusalem, where over 30,000 Christian and Muslim Arabs fled, leaving the Israeli sector of the divided city as 99 per cent Jewish. By contrast, somewhat larger Arab minorities continued to live in Israel's coastal cities. The first years of independence saw further demographic changes. One side-effect of the declaration of the State of Israel in 1948 was an increase in anti-Jewish feeling in Arab countries, which brought many thousands of poor Jews from Iraq, Turkey, Yemen and Morocco to Jerusalem in the 1950s and later. This inflow of middle eastern and north African Jews amounted to more than half of new Jewish immigration to the city. In comparison to migrants from Europe they brought with them more familiarity with Arab society, but also more bitterness (Dumper:58, 71–2; Karmi:3; Gilbert 1996:259). Thus West Jerusalem, although now totally Jewish, in fact became more of an ethnic mix than before.

East Jerusalem presented more of a problem for the government of Jordan. Amman had been the state's capital since 1921, whereas Jordan's connection with East Jerusalem began only in 1948. During the fighting an estimated 57,000 Arabs, many from comfortable suburbs, fled from West Jerusalem. Large numbers of them settled in Amman, where they played a crucial role in transforming it from a small desert town into a modern city, from a population of 22,000 in 1948 to 250,000 by 1961. The development of Amman contrasted sharply with stagnation in East Jerusalem. Under Jordanian rule the Muslim population of East Jerusalem rose only slowly. A university was established in Amman but not in East Jerusalem, and government offices were transferred from East Jerusalem to Amman. The young King Hussein declared that Jerusalem was 'the alternative capital of the Hashemite Kingdom [of Jordan]'. But he had seen his grandfather King Abdullah shot dead by a Palestinian militant on the steps of the al-Aqsa Mosque in July 1951, and in practice the Jordanian regime was determined to weaken the influence of its Husayni rivals and their East Jerusalem power base. It rejected efforts by the Mayor of East Jerusalem to extend the municipal boundaries, it abolished the Supreme Muslim Council and it allowed the festival of Nabi Musa to lapse. In 1959 the Jordanian government agreed to change the status of East Jerusalem from an ordinary 'municipality' to an *'amana'*, which gave it the same formal status as Amman, but in practice little changed. Many East Jerusalem leaders wanted to seek alternative alliances with the more militant governments of Egypt and Syria. Having failed in that they sought the overthrow of Hussein in 1963, and in 1964 the Palestine National Council was inaugurated in East Jerusalem, leading to the foundation of the Palestine Liberation Organisation (PLO). Hussein made efforts to counter these developments by upgrading the Jerusalem-Jericho-Amman road, by building an Intercontinental Hotel on the Mount of Olives and a royal palace to the north of the city, by once again creating a golden dome for the Dome of the Rock, and even by welcoming the ageing Mufti back to Jerusalem. But the Mufti was a spent force, while the investments addressed the symptoms rather than the cause of Jerusalem Arab discontent, which was to do with power-lessness and lack of status (Gilbert 1996:244–53, 266–7; Wasserstein:83, 188, 192; Dumper:34).

The relative size of the Christian population more or less held through the Mandate period. But during the second half of the twenti-eth century the Christian proportion of the Jerusalem population fell precipitously, from about 30,000 in 1946, almost matching the number of Muslim Arabs, to 14,000 in 1995, of whom more than 3,000 were non-Arab expatriates. Many departed during the warfare of 1947–49, but many of these who initially stayed on came to feel they had no place in either Jewish West Jerusalem or what became increas-ingly, in practice, Muslim Arab East Jerusalem. Christians left steadily for Lebanon, Europe or the USA. This communal collapse reflected the decline in the role of 'the Christian powers' in Jerusalem, a role which had developed during the era of the consuls in the mid-nineteenth century and continued through the Mandate period. The Orthodox Church lost state support after the Russian revolution of 1917, while the Vatican's influence declined as the commitment of the west European powers weakened after the Second World War – first to the loud but toothless calls for 'internationalisation' of the Holy Places in mid-twentieth century, and then to recognition by the end of the century that it had scarcely any significant role at all (Wasserstein:267).

On the outbreak of the Six Day War in June 1967 Israel sought to ensure Jordanian neutrality, but an unenthusiastic Hussein was unable to resist Egyptian pressures to join the war. His doubts were quickly confirmed. Within 24 hours Israeli counter-attacks had taken most of East Jerusalem and all of the West Bank of Jordan fell to Israel, as did the Egyptian-controlled Gaza strip. The *Jerusalem Post* declared that the division of the city had been 'a painful and expensive anomaly', that the United Nations could not be depended on for access to the Old City and other areas, and that 'some entirely new solution to this problem will have to be found' (Gilbert 1996:272–82). That day Israeli forces captured the Old City, and the battle for Jerusalem was over after three days, in contrast to the long struggle of 1948. The death toll in the city was about 200 Israelis and over 600 Arabs, a third of whom were civilians. 'We have returned to our holiest of holy places, never to part from it again' declared Defence Minister Moshe Dayan. Jerusalem's significance for Israel and world Jewry was transformed: 'it was only after the capture of East Jerusalem that the ancient city assumed retroactively the status of *terra irredenta* for Israel', wrote an American observer. The transformation of the cramped Western Wall area into a massive plaza, by the demolition of a small Arab neighbourhood, in effect created a new holy place in the heart of the Old City (Dumper:162; Wasserstein:208).

United Jerusalem? 1967 to the present

Unlike in 1948, when protracted warfare caused population transfer and resettlement on a large scale, the reunited city now included a large Arab minority. Israel also took over *de facto* responsibility for the Old City and for the holy places of three major religions. The physical signs of partition were quickly removed. West Jerusalem Mayor Teddy Kollek invited co-operation from the local Arab regime in the provision of essential services, and many posts continued to be held by their previous Arab holders. In some ways Kollek did a remarkable job as Mayor (1965–93), achieving technical and practical unification of the city quickly, making courageous reconciliatory gestures such as securing the erection of a memorial to Arab war dead and finding ways to minimise individual Arab hardships in the face of official non-collaboration by their community. But the state's policy of massive Jewish immigration into East Jerusalem, which the municipality generally supported and implemented, undermined and negated any effective reconciliation. 'The object', admitted Kollek in 1968, 'is to ensure that all of Jerusalem remains a part of Israel ... and we need Jewish inhabitants to do that' (Wasserstein:218). Although there was no repeat of the Arab exodus of 1948–49, East Jerusalem was steadily encircled by large, strategically-sited Jewish suburbs, some built on expropriated Arab land, and all contributing 'facts on the ground' in support of the case for Israeli sovereignty over an undivided Jerusalem.

Arab suburbs grew too, especially to the north of the city, but an Israeli pattern was imposed on the city as part of a concerted demographic plan. Only about 2 per cent of East Jerusalem Arabs accepted Israeli citizenship. The remainder hold identity cards which distinguish them from West Bank Arabs and admit them to state welfare benefits (Gilbert 1996:305–7; Klein:312).

A decade after reunification Jerusalem was no longer the interface between a Jewish cul-de-sac and an Arab backwater but a rapidly growing and thriving, if contested, capital city. The Muslim Arab population grew from less than 60,000 in 1967 to 92,000 in 1979 and 130,000 in 1985. With an Arab minority approaching 30 per cent, post-1967 Jerusalem differed sharply in character from Tel Aviv and Haifa, 4 per cent and 9 per cent non-Jewish respectively (Sharkansky:120). From being Israel's least Arab city, Jerusalem overnight became its most Arab city. In 1992 the city boundary was extended substantially westwards. This created the potential for enhanced economic links with the coastal plain, but politically it was a recognition that, although the city needed more land, extension in any direction other than westward would have had the effect of increasing the Arab proportion of the municipal population. Kollek had opposed earlier government plans to intensify Jewish settlements in the north-eastern sector of the city, but on his defeat in the mayoralty race in 1993 his victorious Likud opponent Ehud Olmert announced a plan to 'fill in the gap' and complete a belt of Jewish housing running several miles north east from the central city (Gilbert 1996:327–8, 354–9; Dumper:52).

By the mid-1990s the Israeli policy of creating 'facts on the ground' had succeeded in the sense that the Jewish population of East Jerusalem – close to zero in 1967 – had reached 160,000, almost matching the Arab population. On the other hand it had failed, notwithstanding the settlements policy, in the sense that the Arab proportion of the city's population had increased from 28 per cent to 32 per cent since reunification. The Arab rate of natural increase exceeded that of Jews in the city by 34 to 27 live births per thousand, while government investment in the creation of an infrastructure to promote Jewish immigration acted as an economic magnet drawing further Arab labour to the city. A second factor is the in-flow of *haredim* (ultra-orthodox Jews). They seek full segregation from Arabs and other Jews through the establishment of *eruvs*, or neighbourhoods designated as religiously observant. The neighbourhoods which they occupy make up about a third of Jerusalem's Jewish area and population, while the proportion of pupils in religious (as distinct from secular) schools increased from

45 per cent to 61 per cent between 1972 and 1992.[66] The growing strength of these groups has caused something of an exodus of secular Jews from Jerusalem in recent years, to western suburbs outside the boundary or to the coast, in what has been seen as a move analogous to 'white flight'. This growth in the number and consciousness of ultra-orthodox groups has more than offset the potentially unifying trend within Jewry promised by the narrowing of the socio-economic gap between Ashkenazim and Sephardim, and the intermarriage rate of about twenty per cent across this divide. It has also accentuated long-established differences in voting patterns for the Knesset: Labour and the left in Jerusalem ran further behind their national voting levels in 1992–2003 than they had done in the 1970s, while Likud and the right performed relatively better in Jerusalem than elsewhere. In particular, support for extreme right-wing religious and secular parties in Jerusalem increased by more than 100 per cent across this period while increasing less than 50 per cent, from a lower base, in Israel as a whole (Dumper:203–6; Sharkansky:126–36; Wasserstein:356; www.election-world.org/ election/israel.htm).

UN Security Council Resolutions 242 and 252 called for a restoration to Jordan of the lands lost in 1967 and declared invalid the actions taken by Israel to change the status of Jerusalem. These were the first of many international protests to be ignored by the Israeli government. Any hopes of reconciliation in Jerusalem quickly faded. Most alarming to Arabs was the great scale of Jewish expansion: on the one hand the massive growth of western Jerusalem as an international political and commercial capital, with up to forty major projects being considered at one point in 1973; on the other the determined encirclement of the city by new Jewish suburbs. Arab political parties and candidates boycotted elections in the reunited city. Later Kollek invited some East Jerusalem Arabs to serve on city council committees, but they withdrew their names as soon as the matter became public knowledge (Wasserstein:229; Gilbert 1996:303–16). Having failed to draw the Arab elite into any kind of participation in electoral politics Kollek developed a 'boroughs' plan which, while keeping the city entirely under Israeli sovereignty, would have given the Arabs local autonomy. It went down well with international opinion, but it did not attract Arab support, and it was never taken up by either Labour or

---

[66] More dramatically, while the proportion of pupils in state religious schools in Jerusalem fell from 28 to 19%, the proportion in independent religious schools rose from 17% to 42% (Sharkansky:127).

Likud governments. In practice Kollek ran East Jerusalem using a very traditional strategy of elite accommodation through a group of about 60 *mukhtars* (traditional village leaders). This kept the peace for 20 years, but was 'fraught with tensions between appearance and reality' (Hasson & Kouba:123).

Urban policies have not reunited the city in the way that Kollek had hoped. They have, however, made an independent impact on the development of the Jerusalem question, albeit that that they have been determined as much by central as by local government. These policies, implemented to further the goals of political control and national security, have been pursued through the drawing of boundaries, demographic planning and patterns of public spending favourable to Jewish neighbourhoods. In practice they have increased ethnic instability, widened the area of conflict and decreased the personal security of many individual Jews. Israeli planners have been expected to give priority to maintaining the 72:28 population ratio of Jews to Arabs in the city, which means that planning decisions have been taken in a frankly partisan way, and also that there have been ongoing disparities in municipal spending. While Arabs comprise about 30 per cent of the city's population, expenditure in Arab neighbourhoods is estimated at somewhere between 4 per cent and 17 per cent of city expenditure. Secondly, planners have been expected to maintain the population ratio at the same time as they have been required to locate Jewish development strategically, both in direct military terms (e.g. on high ground) and in the sense of preventing the development of any large, contiguous Arab areas, especially where these might link up with the West Bank. Thirdly, as the process has continued, the cultural balance of the Jewish population of the city has been altered by the new immigration, and the Jewish residents of East Jerusalem and the adjacent West Bank settlements have developed a militant political voice which has become in itself a significant factor.

In this context it has been very difficult for Palestinian institutions of civil society to develop in the city. After the Yom Kippur War of 1973, even though Jordanian neutrality meant that Jerusalem was not in the front line, violent incidents there increased. Some were acknowledged by the PLO, while later more extreme Muslim fundamentalist groups, Hamas and Islamic Jihad, became active. To date the favourable economic and security conditions enjoyed by East Jerusalem Arabs in comparison to inhabitants of the West Bank have helped to ensure that support for the extremist groups has remained relatively low. The bulk of Arab violence in Jerusalem over the past 30 years has been carried out by people from outside the city. But as Israel finds it increasingly difficult to maintain the economic and security distinctions between Arab East Jerusalem and adjacent West Bank areas within the greater metropolis, there is a real danger than the situation could change and that extremist groups will fill the gaps left by the absence of working institutions of civil society (Bollens:307–24).

During the period of Jordanian rule in East Jerusalem, the local political elite worked in very much the same way that it has done during the Mandate period. Land, capital and status remained the basis of power, while politics was organised to a great extent through the *hamula*, or extended family, legitimated by tradition and religion. The Husaynis, the Nashashibis (who were close to the Jordanian royal family) and the Jarallahs were the most prominent, with histories of rivalry for the posts of Mayor and Mufti going back to the nineteenth century. After 1967, with growing modernisation, urbanisation and education, this began to change. Individual members of the leading families, including Yasser Arafat, continue to be prominent, but the PLO has succeeded in organising Palestinian politics around ideology and political institutions. It was aided by financial and political support from the Arab world, by the energies of a rising middle- and lower-middle class of students and graduate professionals, and by its creation of 'popular organisations' which provided welfare, youth, sport and health facilities. The older elites were by and large co-opted into this structure. The Arab elite in Jerusalem became more heterogeneous, and post-1967 immigrants, especially Hebronites, became prominent within it. Education was one of the areas after 1967 where Palestinian civil resistance in Jerusalem had some effect. The initial Israeli intention of assimilating the East Jerusalem public school system to the Israeli Arab curriculum failed in the face of strikes and other means. By the mid-1970s the Israeli government had in effect accepted that Arab schools in East Jerusalem would continue to operate under the Jordanian curriculum that was used in the West Bank (Klein:183–5; Wasserstein:225; Dumper:44).

Kollek and the Jewish moderates in local government after 1967 laid their emphasis on the actual and potential benefits to all of Jerusalem's inhabitants of the restored unity of the city, in contrast to the negative impact for both communities of the partition years. But despite their sincere and considerable efforts, the city has not come together in any meaningful way. Public institutions in Jewish and Arab Jerusalem function separately. Arabs and Jews speak different languages, have different days of rest, different currency laws and different legal status.

Whereas 'Israeli Arabs' (i.e. Arabs domiciled within Israel's pre-1967 borders) tend to have a good knowledge of Hebrew, Palestinians in the high school system of East Jerusalem tend not to, and are prepared for higher education in Arab countries. Religious, linguistic and national differences re-enforce one another. Despite close physical proximity, daily economic encounters and the absence of physical barriers, there is a very high level of micro-segregation. There are no mixed areas and scarcely any cases of mixed individual identity (Kotek 1996a:108; Sharkansky:124; Klein:13; Romann & Weingrod: *passim*).

City ordinances require that a Hebrew sign must be displayed, on its own or with others. But in Arab East Jerusalem most signs are in Arabic and English only. Hebrew is an elective language, just like any other foreign language, in Arab schools and at Al-Quds University.[67] Israeli institutions functioning in these districts have in practice to use Arabic. Banks and road signs are usually trilingual. Shops and businesses are open, and buses run on the Jewish sabbath and holidays, unlike in West Jerusalem. The Jordanian dinar was a prominent currency in East Jerusalem until its value slumped in 1991. Cultural and media provision is Arab and Palestinian, though subject to Israeli censorship. In public education, the symbols and organisation are Israeli, but the curriculum and examinations were overseen at first by Jordan and now by the Palestinian Authority. Religious schools are even less closely linked to Israel. Al-Quds University operates in East Jerusalem without a permit and without Israeli oversight. There are in effect two parallel, non-competing public transportation systems. Jordan has effectively surrendered to nominees of the PLO the administration of the Haram-al-Sharif, which (until Ariel Sharon's intervention in the autumn of 2000) in practice operated outside Israeli sovereignty (Klein:310–7).

The employment patterns of Jews and Arabs are very different. In part this arose from past economic and other differences between the eastern and western sectors of the city. We have seen that East Jerusalem's growth was very sluggish during the period of Jordanian administration. There was a heavy dependence on tourism, mainly

---

[67] Al-Quds University, billed on its website as 'The Arab University in Jerusalem', began as a number of individual colleges in the 1970s. It came together as a University in 1995, and has more than 5,000 students. It is located at suburban Abu Dis, on a site which straddles the new, extended city boundary, although it has also operated at out-centres within the city. It is tolerated rather than supported by the State of Israel. There are also four Arab universities in the West Bank, the best known of which is Bir Zeit.

from Muslim countries, which dried up after 1967. East Jerusalem Arabs, though comprising 26 per cent of the overall population at that time, accounted for only 16 per cent of the city's labour force and 6 per cent of its purchasing power. Twenty-five per cent of Jews completed 13 years of education but only 7 per cent of Arabs did so. Over the following quarter-century there were significant absolute increases in Arab employment levels and standard of living, but little if any narrowing of the differentials between Arabs and Jews. Economic necessity and some complementarity of skills provide a basis on which Arabs and Jews do work together to a significant extent. But employment practices and behaviour mean that relationships are asymmetrical and the labour market is far from open or unified. In general Arabs will work with Jews, but Jews will tend to avoid employing, or being employed by, Arabs wherever possible. The main exceptions to this are those tasks which are informally categorised, usually because of low status and/or low pay, as 'Arab work'. There are also certain Arab work niches, such as car maintenance and the building trade. Jewish firms will subcontract work to the Arab sector of the economy where savings can be made, and Jewish professionals will provide their services to Arab firms. But it is very rare for Jews to be employed by or work under Arabs. In general Jews are relatively independent of the Arab sector, but Arab labour is a significant part of the Jewish sector of the economy. The prevailing Arab attitude of *sumud* ('steadfastness') has meant that, with relatively little stigma, Arabs can accept politically controversial work such as building Israeli settlements. In 1994, 64 per cent of Jerusalem Jews were concentrated in managerial and professional occupations, against only 19 per cent of Arabs. Most Arabs were blue-collar workers or engaged in petty commerce or tourism-related activities. Only 7 per cent of Arab women were in paid work compared to 42 per cent of Jewish women (Romann & Weingrod:99–100, 123–5; Hasson & Kouba:113).

Although tourism remains important as always, Jerusalem's economy continues to be very heavily dependent upon government spending. In the mid-1990s 44 per cent of the city's population was employed in the public services and only 10 per cent in industry. By comparison the figures for Tel Aviv are 21 and 19 per cent and for Haifa 28 and 22 per cent. In addition government investment in house-building programmes for Jews in East Jerusalem and the West Bank represents a further very important economic intervention by government. Growth has arisen mainly from such building activity, i.e. arising from the 'facts on the ground' programme. Ironically, this work has been a major source of Arab employment. In this and other ways the Arab sector of the labour market is heavily dependent on the Jewish sector. Multinational companies have not been greatly attracted to Jerusalem or Israel in general because of the trade boycott maintained by most of its Arab neighbours, and the fact that Israel itself is a very small market. What Israel, and Jerusalem in particular, needs is access to trading markets in the Arab world, which it will not get without a peace settlement acceptable to the Palestinians (Sharkansky:128–9; Dumper:208, 227).

In 1976 the Labour party, which had governed Israel since its foundation, was replaced by the more aggressively nationalist Likud. In 1980 the Likud, opposed by one third of the Knesset, formally annexed East Jerusalem to the State of Israel. The measure was symbolic, intended to ensure the exclusion of Jerusalem from any future scheme for Palestinian autonomy in the West Bank (Gilbert 1996:328–9). Attempts by Egyptian President Sadat to re-establish Arab sovereignty in East Jerusalem during the Camp David talks of 1978 came to nothing, and the 1980s saw no new ideas. Israeli policy during these years was restricted to the creation of demographic facts on the ground. Jewish building in East Jerusalem went ahead rapidly, while Arab building was discouraged. Neither, at this stage, did the PLO give great priority to the Jerusalem issue, which was not mentioned in the 1964 or 1968 versions of its National Charter. Only from the late 1970s did East Jerusalem Arabs begin to develop a more strongly nationalist outlook (Wasserstein:237–8, 250, 252).

Whereas the Arabs who had remained in Israel after 1948 were mainly rural, traditional and lacking in leadership, the East Jerusalem Arabs who were incorporated into the State of Israel in 1967 were none of these things. They also tended to have active personal links to the West Bank, and consequently did not accept annexation in the way that the Israeli Arabs of 1948 had done. The outbreak of the *Intifada* at the end of 1987 made it more difficult for Israel to maintain the distinction it had sought to sustain since 1967 between the occupied territory of the West Bank and the 'reunified' city of Jerusalem, as rising opposition forced it to apply the same harsh tactics in both places. The *Intifada* rather took the PLO leadership by surprise, but the result was to give a considerable boost to a flagging movement. Average incomes in Arab Jerusalem were higher than in the West Bank and Gaza, and the *Intifada* in the city was said to derive its strength mainly from the refugee camps and the external suburbs of the West Bank. But a key effect of the *Intifada* was to link East Jerusalem more closely to the

West Bank and to widen the gulf between it and Jewish Jerusalem. It was, therefore, more effective in achieving its objectives than were Israeli efforts to make East Jerusalem Jewish. The *Intifada* in fact strengthened Jerusalem's role as the centre of Arab Palestine. 'The situation in Jerusalem has changed in a fundamental way', said Teddy Kollek. The renunciation by King Hussein in 1988 of Jordan's territorial claims in Palestine, and his recognition of the PLO demand for an independent state, further increased the trend towards independent Palestinian action. Shortly afterwards the PLO formally voiced for the first time its demand for Jerusalem as Palestine's capital. The *Intifada* continued fiercely for five years.[68] Preliminary discussions between successive Israeli Governments and the PLO, which began at Madrid in October 1991, at last brought it to a halt early in 1993. Hamas and Islamic Jihad, however, rejected the peace process, and sporadic violence continued (Klein:24, 80–7; Khalidi:200–3; Wasserstein:239, 255–60; Gilbert 1996:346–55).

In 1988 the PLO had proclaimed a Palestinian State, with 'Holy Jerusalem' as its capital. But for the government of Israel, insistence on Jewish rule over Jerusalem united orthodox and secular Jews, the Ashkenazi elite with the growing Sephardi and oriental majority, and the State of Israel itself with the Jewish diaspora. Jerusalem therefore emerged as the most difficult aspect of the Israeli–Palestinian dispute, regarded by both sides as their capital and the location of their holiest and most emotive places. Whether this means that it is the problem that should be tackled first, or left until last, is a matter which had been much debated (Gilbert 1996:336; Dumper:2).

On 13 September 1993, Israel and the PLO signed the 'Oslo accords' in Washington, thereby approving the establishment of a 'Palestinian Authority' in the West Bank and Gaza. Jerusalem was excluded from the initial settlement, but the Palestinians continued to press for East Jerusalem to be made their capital. They wanted it to be an undivided city, with the eastern half of it under Palestinian rule and security matters a joint responsibility of both regimes. Israel agreed that East Jerusalem Palestinians could vote in the elections for the Palestinian Authority, but stipulated initially that offices of the Palestinian Authority could be located only in Jericho and Gaza, and not in Arab Jerusalem. In practice, however, the local PLO leader Faisal Husayni

---

[68] During the *Intifada* 697 Arabs were killed by Israeli forces in the West Bank and Gaza, of whom 78 were aged 14 or under; 528 Arabs were killed by other Arabs; and 25 Israelis were killed.

(1940–2001) was permitted to develop quasi-governmental activities at Orient House, in East Jerusalem. By September 1995 it housed 11 institutions of the Palestinian Authority, effectively government departments, notwithstanding Israeli protests. Israel at that time would have preferred either Ramallah or Bethlehem as the Palestinian capital (Gilbert 1996:349–54). Yasser Arafat at that stage also wished to prioritise progress towards a Palestinian State rather than concentrate on Jerusalem as the Palestinian capital, believing that a Palestinian State would guarantee obtaining Jerusalem as a capital, rather than the other way round. Both the Israeli right and the 'external' PLO of Yasser Arafat were therefore uneasy about Orient House. There was a low-key struggle between the local and national PLO which continued over the next few years. At first the popularity of Orient House favoured the Husayni group, but the more hawkish attitude of Netanyahu's Likud government after 1996 boosted Arafat and the national PLO leadership (Klein:196–201).

The deterioration of Arab–Jewish relations in Jerusalem continued through the 1990s, exacerbated by the growing number of ultra-orthodox Jews in the city. These two factors led to the ousting of Kollek from the mayoralty in 1993 after twenty-eight years, easily defeated by the Likud candidate Ehud Olmert. Kollek's policy has been described as the 'quiet, creeping annexation of East Jerusalem and its surroundings' (Klein:255). Olmert, however, adopted an opposite tactic, making the settlements policy noisy and overt, and seeking to make life difficult for the Rabin Labour government whenever it attempted to apply the Oslo Accords in Jerusalem. Potential sites for a quasi-Jerusalem capital of the Palestinian State, such as suburban Abu Dis, were soon surrounded by new Jewish settlements which were built both inside and outside the municipality.

By the mid-1990s, Palestinians were attempting to develop practical counter-measures to resist the settlements policy. For the most part they were spontaneous and private – not only without planning permission from the Israeli authorities, but also without much co-ordination or planning on the part of the national or local Palestinian leadership, beyond *ad hoc* encouragement. After 1997 they were backed up by attempts of the Palestinian Authority to issue its own building permits. The sum effect of this has been to create some contiguity between Arab neighbourhoods, mainly in the north of the city – rival 'facts on the ground' which threaten to cast a spoke in the wheel of some Israeli encirclement plans. Illegal Palestinian construction, declared Olmert, 'is a cancer that is a clear and present danger to

Israel's sovereignty in Jerusalem'. Israeli authorities responded by destroying unlicensed Palestinian buildings and revoking Jerusalem residence permits of Arabs who moved outside the municipal boundary. In the hope of reversing the current demographic trend, they have also adopted a plan to draw the Jewish settlements in the West Bank into a greater Jerusalem umbrella municipality, with planning and construction powers over an expanded metropolitan area. Local Arab protests, especially against the Har Homa development in1997, forced the national Palestinian leadership to bring the struggle against settlements, and the Jerusalem issue in general, to the forefront of its activities (Klein:271, 281, 323).

Between Autumn 1993 and Spring 1995 the Israeli deputy foreign minister in the Rabin Labour Government, Yossi Beilin, and a leading PLO figure known as 'Abu Mazen' held about 20 secret meetings to try to break the impasse.[69] They agreed plans for a Palestinian State which would control over 94 per cent of the West Bank and Gaza, with security arrangements acceptable to the Israeli government. Their most interesting proposals related to Jerusalem. They agreed that it should remain undivided, with free access to members of all faiths, and that the existing municipality should be divided into a number of Israeli and Arab boroughs in a 2:1 proportion. These would in effect comprise two cities, to be known as Yerushalayim and al-Quds respectively. Each group of boroughs would come under a sub-municipality with devolved powers regarding housing, education, local taxes and services. There would be a unified umbrella municipality which could be expected to elect a Jewish mayor, but decisions which it took regarding the two sub-municipalities would be subject to the consent of the Israeli or Palestinian government, as appropriate. Sovereignty was therefore divided to the extent that the Palestinian government would have control over what went on in al-Quds. Ultimate sovereignty over the whole territory of Jerusalem however – which was to be expanded somewhat in area – remained with Israel. Just days before the Beilin-Abu Mazen agreement was signed Prime Minister Rabin, the first Israeli prime minister to have been born in Jerusalem, felt obliged to stress to the Israeli people that 'there are not two Jerusalems. There is only one

---

[69] 'Abu Mazen' is the *nom de guerre* of Mahmoud Abbas. In March 2003, following American and Israeli pressure, he was designated by a reluctant Arafat to the new post of prime minister of the embattled Palestinian Authority, but he resigned in September 2003 following protracted disputes with Arafat over control of Palestinian security agencies.

Jerusalem. For us, Jerusalem is not subject to compromise, and there is no peace without Jerusalem'. Notwithstanding this attempt to moderate Israeli perceptions of the agreement, Rabin was assassinated in Jerusalem ten days later by a Jewish extremist. His caretaker successor, Shimon Peres (to whom Beilin was close), was demonised in the ensuing general election by the Likud opposition as planning to 'divide Jerusalem' and the Beilin–Abu Mazen plan sank with Peres' defeat. The incoming Likud government sought to reverse Labour's policy by turning Jerusalem into 'the essence of the dispute, rather than a separate issue', in order to get off the track of the Oslo Accords. Later that winter Hamas suicide bombers killed a total of 45 people in Jerusalem, and the future of the peace process hung in the balance (Wasserstein:290–6; Klein:292; Gilbert 1996:360).

Direct recognition of any degree of formal or symbolic Palestinian sovereignty in Jerusalem was politically impossible for Israel. But in practice the situation in the later 1990s was rather different. Although the Palestinian Authority had no power in Jerusalem, East Jerusalem Arabs were permitted to vote in its elections. By this time the Authority had acquired a significant level of practical control over many aspects of public life in Arab Jerusalem, including the Muslim religious establishment and its property, the private schools, which were attended by 40 per cent of Palestinian pupils, the Arabic press, and the collection of some taxes. Al-Quds University operated in central Jerusalem, without authorisation from the Israeli ministry of education, as well as from its headquarters in the West Bank suburbs. As early as 1994 Orient House had begun to operate as something like a city hall for East Jerusalem. In the run up to the 1999 general election the Likud Government vowed to close down Orient House, but the election result meant that this did not happen (Wasserstein:298–9, 307).

The return to power of Ehud Barak's Labour-led government in 1999 re-opened the door to general peace negotiations, and the Camp David summit followed in 2000. The main points at issue in this crucial and tragically unsuccessful negotiation focused on a cluster of disputes over Jerusalem. These included the management of the Temple Mount/Haram al-Sharif and of the Old City in general, and the future of the crescent of Palestinian neighbourhoods to the north, east and south of the Old City, which represent the heart of Arab Jerusalem. There was tacit recognition at Camp David that the Jewish city would be larger than that defined by Israel immediately after 1967; that the Palestinian city would grow to include the new suburbs which had been disconnected villages in 1967; and that 'an international border, in the common sense of the word, would not run through' Jerusalem. The Americans advocated a modified version of the Beilin-Abu Mazen proposals, under which Israel would withdraw from 91 per cent of the West Bank, with the remaining 9 per cent – mainly the Israeli settlements in the greater Jerusalem fringe – being annexed to Israel, while Arab areas of the fringe would become part of Palestine, including suburban Abu Dis, which would become the Palestinian capital. Both East and West Jerusalem would remain under Israeli sovereignty, including the Old City, but its Muslim and Christian Quarters would be administered in some way by Palestine as would the 'Arab boroughs' in the city. Arafat, however, felt that it would be impossible for him to relinquish his demand for sovereignty over Arab Jerusalem. It was the Jerusalem question, therefore, which blocked a general settlement. Soon afterwards, following serious incidents on the Haram-al-Sharif, the Israelis elected an uncompromising right-wing government under Ariel Sharon, while the Palestinians began a second *intifada*. Since the beginning of the al-Aqsa *intifada* in autumn 2000, 92 per cent of Palestinians now say that peace is impossible without Jerusalem as capital of the Palestinian State (Klein:3; Wasserstein:314–6).

Whether measured by United Nations resolutions or by attempted great power interventions, international factors have long been important in the development of the Jerusalem issue. From 1947 to around 1990, the Arab–Israeli dispute was a component in the cold war. Major happenings in Jerusalem became the subject of international attention. The Arab loss of East Jerusalem in 1967, together with the increasing power of oil-rich Arab states, meant that the city also became the single most important element in the growing antagonism between Islam and the West. But there were important political divisions within the Arab world. Most Arab states, for instance, never recognised Transjordan's incorporation of East Jerusalem and the West Bank, 1949–67, favouring instead the internationalisation of the city. Jordan thus had little support from other Arab states during its tenure of East Jerusalem. After 1967 there was more Arab support for Palestinian Jerusalem. But the withdrawal from the conflict by Egypt, the largest Arab nation, in 1978, was another blow to Arab unity on the issue (Dumper: 229–31, 250–7). While the United States Congress – if not always its State Department – is a strong supporter of Israel, it is not likely to go all the way in support of Israel's demand for a recognition of a united Jerusalem under direct sovereignty, except in the context of a general Israel–Palestinian settlement.

The most recent major study of the Jerusalem problem, by Menachem Klein, argues that contrary to general opinion, several pragmatic steps have in fact been taken towards a solution. First, international bodies no longer have a significant mediating role to play. Secondly, both Israeli and Palestinian leaderships are determined to keep the Jerusalem question a political rather than a religious matter. The growth of ultra-orthodox Judaism in the city may even be more of a threat to this than Hamas and the other Islamist groups. Thirdly, the approach which postpones the Jerusalem question to the end of the peace process is the right one, but it needs to be noted that issues impacting significantly on this question can be discussed piecemeal as the peace process continues. Fourthly, Israel cannot and in reality does not exclude Jerusalem from discussion, and the Palestinian leadership does in fact acknowledge that a resolution of the East Jerusalem question will be along lines distinct from what is agreed for the West Bank and Gaza. Both sides now recognise that neither the pre-1967 partition line nor the current municipal boundary can become international borders, because of the high level of interdependency between the city and 'its Palestinian hinterland' (Klein:331–5).

Jerusalem, most especially the Old City, is a place where the warring communities are divided by language in addition to everything else. Israeli Arabs learn Hebrew, but West Bank and East Jerusalem Arabs are less likely to know it except insofar as they need it for employment. Jews are less likely to know Arabic that used to be the case. A century ago the official Turkish language lacked the strength in Jerusalem to threaten the vernacular use of Arabic, Ladino and Yiddish. Modern Hebrew, however, has a more formidable presence. Any limitation on its power arises not from counter-pressure on Hebrew-speakers to learn Arabic but from the spread of English, in Jerusalem as in so many other world cities, as an alternative means of Arab–Jewish communication. Research on bitterly-contested cities, however, suggest that linguistic conflicts of this kind reflect rather than cause the existence of deeper problems. Minor changes in language policy are likely to follow social and political change rather than vice versa (Spolsky & Cooper:148–50).

A recent projection of Jerusalem's population in 2020 estimates an overall growth to 947,000, of whom as many as 38 per cent would be Arabs. For the metropolitan area as a whole, the Jewish:Arab balance is already about equal. If all of this area came under Israeli sovereignty it would embrace about a third of the population of the West Bank. The settlements policy which has created a ring of Jewish settlements outside the municipal boundary, together with the economic pull of

Jerusalem for West Bank Arabs, has created the concept of a 'greater Jerusalem' which blurs the line between Israel and the West Bank and thereby blurs the Jerusalem sovereignty issue. Demographically, Israeli is in a cleft stick. The logic of its policy is security through demographic expansion, which requires additional space. But the recent expansion of planning and construction powers, to embrace the wider area of metropolitan Jerusalem, has had three disadvantages for Israel. It has extended housing competition into territory where Israeli controls are weaker; it tacitly acknowledges that the 1967 annexation lines are no longer relevant; and it thereby helps the national Palestinian leadership to penetrate Jerusalem and to be seen to be leading the Palestinian cause, at the expense of the local leadership (Klein:326–7). The achievement of territorial control in Jerusalem in the way that the Israelis have set out to do tends, of its nature, to become an unending process. (Wasserstein:357; Dumper:3, 24, 54; Klein:326–7; Bollens:328).

Thus the long-established Israeli strategy of making the municipal/ annexation line a permanent border, delineating a united Jerusalem and severing it completely from the West Bank, has not worked. Equally, economic imperatives are stimulating the further growth of a greater Jerusalem within West Bank territory, which attracts more and more West Bank Arabs to the area, which in turn draws Israel into further settlement initiatives. The aspiration implicit in the long years of Teddy Kollek's regime in Jerusalem, that peace would develop 'from below', from practical coexistence in the city, and that the Palestinians would accept Israel's annexation, has not happened. It is true that local politics are also shaped by local factors such as the patterns of segregation and interaction and the general relationships between the communities, which in various ways are specific to Jerusalem and differ from those of the West Bank or Gaza. But Jerusalem is now, if it has not always been, central to the broader Israeli–Palestinian conflict, so that the city politics of Jerusalem are in an important sense an extension of national politics. A local solution to the Jerusalem problem now seems highly unlikely. Any effective resolution is likely to come only in the context of a national settlement. Outside powers may be able to apply very important pressures and offer inducements, but the problem of Jerusalem essentially will have to be resolved at the level of the state and its constituent nations.

8
Conclusion

> You know what changed my whole life? ... Finding out at age
> fourteen, not till then, I was part black ... and if you're part,
> man, you're all.
>
> Elmore Leonard, *Get Shorty* (London:Penguin, 1991) p.102

Most historians and social scientists agree that ethnic difference is a
social construct. Even in the case of an observable physical difference
such as skin colour, some societies attach particular significance to
gradations of colour, while in others people who do not appear to be
entirely 'white' are deemed to be, or deem themselves to be 'black'.
Today we tend to regard skin colour, or 'race', as the most potent and
enduring ethnic marker. Yet it may have been the case in the Britain
of 1,500 years ago that hair colour was an equally salient indicator.
Hair colour remains one of the most commonly-used personal descrip-
tors among people of European origin, but any ethnic significance
which may have once attached to it evaporated long ago. The objective content of ethnicity in the cases studied in this book has been
either language difference or religious difference, or a combination of
both. All of these cases confirm the centrality of the social and the
circumstantial.

The main distinguishing label in Belfast is religious denomination.
But disputes arising from Catholic–Protestant religious differences have
in practice not been difficult to resolve. The modern conflict draws its
energy not from religion but from conflicting national aspirations
arising out of different senses of history and group memories of different languages and cultures. In Jerusalem religious issues are part of the
conflict in a more practical way. This is true both in the general sense

that the city has strong spiritual meaning for many people on all sides of the conflict and in the specific sense that serious disputes exist over control of particular sites. On the other hand the most commonly-used juxtaposition for the main protagonists, 'Jews' and 'Arabs', indicates that the conflict is not perceived entirely as religious in nature. Differences in language, in culture and in racialised perceptions of the culture of the other, are also important. The Jewish ideological goal of 'ascending to the Land of Israel', whether simply to die in the earthly Jerusalem in the hope of attaining the heavenly Jerusalem or to help to achieve the goals of secular Zionism, could not have been implemented without a set of social, economic and political circumstances specific to a particular time in European history. Likewise the merging of Arab nationalist and Islamic identities is something that has developed mainly from events which occurred in Palestine, especially in Jerusalem, between 1920 and 1948. Religion is thus only an ethnic marker in certain contexts. Being a Presbyterian in Preston or a Jew in Jarrow may involve no more than individual religious practice. Being a Presbyterian in Belfast or a Jew in Jerusalem normally also means being a member of a ethnic group, with implications and constraints as to residence, workplace, associational activities, political views and general outlook.

The other case studies in this book have dealt with ethnic conflicts in which difference has been defined by language. But ethnolinguistic identity is also to some extent a subjective, rather than objective indicator of ethnicity. Many specialists in language learning believe that bilingualism is seldom if ever a natural acquisition, but something which the human brain naturally tries to reject, and which can 'cause conflicts of ethnic identity'. Bilingualism in this view is distinct from second-language acquisition. The latter can be beneficial to mental development where the mother-tongue is sufficiently 'well-rooted' to establish 'precedence between the [individual's] dominant and the subordinate languages' (Laponce:20–1). But even if this view is correct, problems often still arise when we attempt to classify people into objective and exclusive linguistic categories by language. In part this is a problem of obtaining reliable data. More crucially, ethnolinguistic identity is also to some extent a subjective matter. It is affected by a range of social factors, most notably power, as expressed through a variety of means such as workplace languages, and the urban *visage* or public face. Whatever the psychological and psycho-physiological dimensions of language acquisition, people in linguistically-contested cities have both to make their own choices and to operate in the context of choices made by others. Language is thus no more reliable an indicator of ethnicity than is religion. It is true that mother-tongue may often be an intrinsic and exclusive carrier of identity. But at a practical, everyday level language may be primarily a tool of communication, a skill which may be learned. Language shift may be accepted and achieved by many individuals in a contested city and which, furthermore, may be seen as reversible or as an addition to an existing identity. A religious conversion by contrast, though easier in practical terms, is an exclusive and stark choice where moral pressures, both internal and external, are likely to be greater. An ethnic identity based on religion is thus in one sense harder to change than one based on language. On the other hand we must also note Laponce's point (p.159) that whereas the protection of a religious minority is something that can be safeguarded through individual rights, the protection of a language can only be accomplished through a group rights approach: individual linguistic rights cannot be considered in isolation from the group, inasmuch as they cannot be exercised unless group facilities can be maintained at a certain level.

What is the specific impact of the urban *milieu* on ethnic conflicts? Spolsky & Cooper (p.147) argue that urbanisation, paradoxically, promotes both linguistic diversity and linguistic uniformity. Cities act as magnets which attract an ever-widening ethnic mix of peoples, as transport provision improves and becomes more widely accessible. Within the city occupational specialisation and social stratification are greater, and so permit more linguistic diversity. On the other hand the urban environment puts people in closer physical proximity to others, while the extension of state and municipal activity encourages uniformity of language through education systems and other public services. There is a tension between the need to communicate, which pulls towards linguistic unification, and the instinct to protect sub-group identities, which tends to sustain ethnic languages (and religions). Proximity does not necessarily help to improve ethnic relations. When the peasants come to the city or move into a new occupational stratum in sufficient numbers, they may be able to reverse or, if they are of the other persuasion, reinforce patterns of ethnic supremacy. Where this does not happen they often send an enhanced ethnic awareness back to a homeland where ethnic identity was previously unchallenged and therefore taken for granted. A striking number of leaders of the Irish revolution of 1916–22, for example, worked in white-collar jobs in Dublin or London, but hailed from peasant backgrounds in the ethnically-homogeneous south-west of Ireland. A similar pattern emerged from a survey conducted in two contrasting cities in the province of Quebec. It found that young Francophones in bilingual Hull, immediately across the river from Ottawa and therefore very close to Anglophone Ontario, had a considerably higher level of contact with English-language culture but a considerably less favourable opinion of Anglophones than did an equivalent group in Quebec City, deep in the heart of unilingual French Quebec (Laponce:41). Similarly indicators of violence in Northern Ireland, as well as the general tenor of ethnographic and other studies, have always suggested that the close proximity of the other side in Belfast relative to the rest of the province has produced more hostile rather than less hostile ethnic relations (Darby 1986, 1997; Burton; Bruce; Harris). On the other hand, what relevant evidence there is from Danzig and from inter-war Trieste suggests that these relatively harsh ethnic regimes were quite effective in converting incomers to the dominant language, with resistance more likely to be sustainable in outlying suburbs and villages. In the Brussels case Flemish ethnic consciousness first developed not in the capital but in Flanders, although more in the Dutch-speaking cities of Antwerp and Ghent than in rural areas.

Since the nineteenth century cultural factors, rather than economic ties or physical geography or the requirements of military strategy, have come to define what the peoples of western cities regard as their 'hinterland'. The relationship between contested cities and their hinterlands is important, and often mutually reinforcing. Ethnic groups in the modern world need a metropole, as a centre and showpiece for their culture, and as a focus for urbanisation. To the extent that urbanisation in the modern world is inevitable, an ethnic group without a city is in trouble. Magyar Budapest was the main centre for urban Slovaks at the end of the nineteenth century, as was Italian Trieste for Slovenes: Bratislava and Ljubljana had to be invented – or at least developed – as regional capitals in double-quick time in 1918. In earlier times cities could, almost by definition, be outposts of a different culture, the leading edge of acculturation/assimilation. In some cases this was reversed by demographic pressure: Prague, Dublin and Helsinki are examples of this. Elsewhere reversal was less straightforward, for reasons of demography, geography or state policy: Slovenes in Trieste were unable to compete demographically with Italians. In Danzig and Breslau a combination of demographic and state power prevented any reversal, until it was achieved by massive external intervention in 1945.

In some contexts the ambivalent status of the contested city-metropole has continued. Sometimes it has been regarded as a threat, as the strike-force of the dominant culture, thereby generating an anti-urban ethos within the non-dominant community. In other contexts the metropole has been seen as a prize to be 'captured' or 'regained'. In the case of Brussels, the nationalist movement of Flanders has been determined not to relinquish its aspiration for linguistic reclamation, partly because of the city's Flemish past and partly because of its modern importance. This, notwithstanding the fact that alternative, if more modest, metropoles such as Antwerp are already in Flemish possession. A similar situation in Bosnia appears to have been resolved differently: the Constitution of Republika Srpska states that multi-ethnic Sarajevo (in effect the Serbian suburb of Pale) is its capital, but since 1997 a less confrontational Bosnian Serb regime has moved the seat of government away to the mainly Serb-populated city of Banja Luka. Until half a century ago Quebec nationalism tended to reject urbanism altogether as an anglicising and corrupting influence, but in the past half-century it has shown great determination to extend the French face of Montreal. Likewise, Palestinian nationalism will not give up its claim to some part of Jerusalem, because it has no alternative metropole available to it. Israel on the other hand, although it also has the considerably larger Jewish metropole of Tel Aviv, is not willing to concede any part of Jerusalem, because of its immense symbolic significance. Belfast's status is not the subject of any challenge independent of the wider question of the existence of Northern Ireland. But its existence as a Protestant citadel has been of immense importance, both in the development of an Ulster Protestant sense of identity and in the practical sense that the British state has been unwilling to risk overruling the wishes of the majority in such a volatile city. On the other side, the existence of a large Catholic minority in Belfast has constituted one of the main practical arguments against any repartition of Ireland. Trieste and Danzig were rather different cases, but between 1918 and 1945 Trieste was important to the Italians of the region as the protector of the Italian coastal towns of nearby Istria: if Trieste was lost, the smaller towns further along the coast would certainly be lost.

Rival ethnic groups in contested cities mark out their territories in a variety of ways, sometimes defending what they see as their sector of the city, at other times seeking to mark the city itself as theirs. Symbols, myths, edifices and interfaces of various kinds may all be summoned into action for this purpose. Jews prayed at the Western

Wall of Jerusalem's Temple Mount for centuries if not millennia, until it ended up on the wrong side of the partition line in 1949. It was, however, simply a wall running along one side of a narrow street in a poor neighbourhood. Its recapture in 1967 was a signal for the immediate demolition of the neighbourhood and the creation of a massive plaza with the Wall as its focus. In religious terms nothing had changed, but in practice an entirely-transformed holy site had been created, which plays an important part in reinforcing Israel's popular will and political determination to retain control of the Old City. On the Muslim side, the same is true of efforts to raise the status of their own holy places, above the Wall on the Haram al-Sharif, which were initiated by the Mufti in the 1920s. It is a battle for the symbols of the Old City, in which the Israeli identification during the 1990s of an historic tunnel *under* the Temple Mount/Haram al-Sharif is only the latest example of archaeology in the service of politics. In Montreal 'The Main', the St Lawrence Boulevard, was long the symbolic frontier between English and French Montreal: Mayor Drapeau's public building plans were a deliberate Francophone effort to break that barrier. There are many other examples, from all of our case studies. Italian nationalists in Habsburg Trieste rejoiced when new road tunnels exposed the more Slavonic parts of the city to urban *italianitá*. Later they destroyed the Slovene National House and, as in Belfast, would permit nationalist cultural manifestations only in back streets and out-of-the-way neighbourhoods. In Belfast, indeed, even streets running through now-derelict areas retain their significance as ethnic frontiers.

A dominant group may seek to assimilate a non-dominant group, or marginalise and ghettoise it, or even expel it. A non-dominant group may seek assimilation, or may seek to reverse the balance of power. Either or both groups may seek a pluralist settlement, although these can on occasion be, implicitly, half-way houses on the road to some more drastic change. Strategies on both sides can alter with the passage of time and changed circumstances. A shift in the demographic balance or a widening of the electoral franchise can alter the two sides' assessments of their respective situations. Party politics may thereby become 'ethnicised' where previously they were not so. This became the case in Belfast and Ulster by the 1880s and in Trieste a little later. In Brussels in did not become so until the 1960s and in Montreal, in a slightly different way (reflecting a different demographic balance) at about the same time. In Jerusalem democratic politics did not really appear until after 1948, by which time minority numbers were very marginal to the party political culture of the state. Sometimes minority ethnic parties can benefit from playing a role in coalition politics, but this in itself is influenced to a great extent by the level of intensity of the conflict. In modern Finland, where the level of conflict has been low, the Swedish People's Party has been able to defend Swedish culture more effectively than its weak electoral position might have suggested was possible. Quebec, rather differently, has developed a party political culture in which one major party is strongly ethnic while the other is a fully-mixed ethnic coalition. Party-political co-operation in more bitterly-contested cities such as Belfast or Jerusalem, however, has tended to lead to a rapid decline in the fortunes of parties which attempt it.

What social mechanisms do non-dominant groups develop in such contexts? Where prospects for the non-dominant group appears poor, a quietist strategy has been common. In Montreal it was *la survivance*, for two centuries down to 1960; in Palestine it was *sumud* ('steadfast-ness'), at least until the emergence of a more modern form of national-ism in the mid-1960s; in 1950s Belfast the novelist Joseph Tomelty wrote of 'the awful fatalism of the Falls Road', the city's main Catholic neighbourhood (Hepburn 1996:14); the opportunistic ethnic identity of Jan Bronski in Grass's *The Tin Drum* is a similar response. In rural Flanders and in rural Ireland in the late nineteenth century similarly stoic values, opposed to both emigration and urbanism, were urged, especially by the Catholic Church. In Brussels, the city-born Flemish working class was remarkably quiescent until galvanised by incomers from Flanders in the post-1945 era. But again, groups which have been acquiescent in one period of history can become militant in another.

In urban settings one might expect intermarriage to erode the bound-aries between groups. In nineteenth-century Montreal this happened to some extent between working-class French and Irish Catholics, the off-spring of such marriages normally being brought up as French-speakers. There is also some evidence of a more upwardly-mobile type of intermar-riage in Montreal where the outcome was anglicisation of the French partner, but religious and communal pressures worked to discourage all but the most determined. In Brussels marriage across the language divide was more common, and was customarily associated with mobility into the dominant group. There was less communal opposition than in Montreal and, crucially, no religious barrier. It is probable that this was also the case in Trieste, and in Danzig. Where religion was at the centre of an ethnic divide, intermarriage was far less likely. The level has always been minimal in Jerusalem. In contrast to the association of intermar-riage with upward mobility into the dominant group in Brussels and to some extent Montreal, in Belfast the opposite has been the case: mixed marriages were non-dominant marriages. They were Catholic marriages in the eyes both of the Protestant mobs which expelled them from their neighbourhoods, and of the Catholic Church, which required the children of such marriages to be brought up as Catholics. Religious shift, or conversion, has occasionally been an aspiration of Protestant missionaries in Belfast, but neither there nor in Jerusalem has it ever occurred on a significant scale.

Language shift, on the other hand, has occurred on a significant scale in many contexts. David Laitin (p.315) has made an interesting distinction between total dominance or 'language hegemony', and the more limited 'language standardisation/rationalisation'. He suggests that the latter is quite commonly achieved, but without full hegemony the possibility of a reversal remains, as happened in nineteenth-century Prague and Helsinki. In the Brussels case it has been suggested that the similarity of the Brabant dialect of Flemish/Dutch to Belgian French, coupled with the gap between the Flemish dialects and standard Dutch, means that upwardly-mobile Flemings in Brussels have found it easier to replace their local dialect with a standard form of French rather than standard Dutch. Probably the truth has less to do with such linguistic technicalities than with the fact that aspiring, upwardly-mobile Brussels Flemings, at least before the mid-twentieth century, were simply more exposed to standard French than to standard Dutch.

Many of the cases studied or referred to in this book raise questions relating to the role of local dialects. *Brusseleir* is a Dutch-based dialect with many signs of French influence; *Triestino* is a very thriving Italian dialect with many Slovene words; Kaszubian and Alsatian are other examples. These widely-used and locally-based dialects, although ultimately based within one language group rather than another, were both practically easier for incomers to use and symbolically more acceptable than standard versions of alien national languages.[70] In late nineteenth-century Prague, on the other hand, there were both German- and Czech-based local dialects, while in Jerusalem in the same period advocates of Hebrew were struggling to establish it as a common language to unite Jews, both local and incoming, whose first

---

[70] There may be some similarity between this phenomenon and the practice of koineisation – dialect-levelling or the development of a new common dialect by e.g. disparate groups of migrants into a new town – identified in socio-linguistics (Kerswill:1–13).

language was Yiddish or Ladino or Arabic. In this case a local (or at least a locally-developed and modernised) language was used not to bridge an ethnic divide but to strengthen ties within one of the competing ethnic groups. There was an equally valid practical case in Ottoman Jerusalem for making Arabic the common language of the city's Jews: the fact that this did not happen probably had as much to do with the determination of European Ashkenazi Jews that they, rather than the predominantly non-European (and often Arabic-speaking) Sephardim, should lead the development of Jewry in the region as it did with any concern to exclude Arabs.

What is the relationship between ethnicity and economy, between ethnic division and occupational structure, in a contested city? What is cause and what is effect? In cities where language shift has been associated with upward social mobility the problem, is, in effect, resolved by assimilation (although those who are not upwardly mobile remain unassimilated, so that the outward appearance of an asymmetric occupational structure remains). Thus in Brussels the dominant Francophone society put up no barriers against Flemings, provided that they spoke French; indeed they were welcomed as converts. In Montreal, where there was less interest in conversion, the average Anglophone salary in 1961 was 50 per cent higher than for Francophones. In both these cities the picture has changed since 1960. Brussels saw the development of a newly-educated and culturally-self confident class of incoming Flemish professionals and white-collar workers. The driving force was supplied, not by established Brussels Flemings, but by new immigrants from an economically-revived Flanders, rising as post-industrial Wallonia drifted towards 'rustbelt' status. Similarly, as the state-led cultural and economic revival of Francophone Quebec gathered pace, the median income of those who spoke French at home rose from 28 per cent below that of Anglophones in 1970 to 1 per cent above them in 1995 (Germain & Rose:251). In Trieste the pattern was different. There the small Slovene middle class was nationalist from an early stage, and confined to providing professional services to the minority. Slovene workers were over-represented among day-labourers in general, in the hardest and dirtiest jobs, and in the lower echelons of the public sector. They were largely unrepresented among apprentices in industry. In these respects there was considerable similarity between Trieste and Belfast. In Danzig, partly because of the ruthlessly assimilationist approach of the Prussian/German state and partly because of the weak national identification of the Kashubians, the pattern of development prior to

1918 was closest to the early Brussels model. During the inter-war period, on the other hand, the presence of a revived Polish state meant that ethnic barriers were more consciously maintained on both sides. In Jerusalem on the other hand the cultural and economic differences had become considerable by the end of the nineteenth century, as Zionism began to draw young, frequently urban, Europeans into contact with a traditional, rural Arab society. This cultural division of labour has been immensely strengthened by developments since 1948.

Levels of housing segregation have varied considerably. In Brussels and Trieste certain neighbourhoods have been associated with an ethnic minority but, statistically, levels of segregation have remained quite low. In Montreal there has been a sharp divide between the Francophone east and the Anglophone west of the city, with micro-level segregation in the industrial districts of the south-west. More recently, high-status Francophone suburbs have developed in the west among English neighbourhoods. In Belfast and Jerusalem levels of segregation have also been very high, maintained by violence, intimidation and fear. Violence is in fact another means by which urban ethnic groups seek to regulate their relationships. Time and again, periods of rioting in Belfast included trouble over new housing. The extreme example of violence-induced segregation is the partition of a city, as in Jerusalem between 1949 and 1967, or in Nicosia since 1974. Such an outcome is seldom regarded as final however, and tends to cause more problems – not least those to do with a city's physical and economic infrastructure – than it solves.

Another important dimension is the impact of third party immigration. In the Montreal case Francophone militancy in the 1960s was exacerbated by the increasing anglicisation of Italian and other immigrants. In this and other cases, the openly-acknowledged ethnic rivalry between the main groups also created a climate in which overt hostility to third-party incomers could be manifested in a way that, in other contexts (especially in the post-Nazi era) has not been regarded as acceptable. Thus some elements of Quebec nationalism have in the past been frankly anti-Semitic and, more recently, hostile to Black Francophone immigrants. In Brussels we have seen that the increase in support for the extreme-right Vlaamsblok has had less to do with a new found working-class enthusiasm for traditional Flemish nationalism than with a nativist opposition to new immigration. Several of the cities studied have included Jewish minorities as a third group. The general pattern has been for the Jews to assimilate, linguistically and to a degree culturally, to the dominant group. This has been especially true in Montreal, where the Jewish community is large in absolute terms, in Trieste where it was small but mainly middle-class and, on a much smaller scale, in Belfast. In central Europe a linguistic factor has cut across the religious factor: in Danzig and other cities German Jews sought to integrate to one community whereas Polish, Russian and other Jews integrated in the other direction. We have seen in the Danzig case how the Jewish community coped with this division in its last years. In Jerusalem one might even regard the recent large-scale immigration of ultra-orthodox Jews as a 'third group' phenomenon. Certainly the impact of ultra-orthodox communities in Jewish Jerusalem has been at least as significant as the impact of new immigrants to Montreal in the 1960s.

What may be said about the prospects for resolving contested city issues? The order in which problems are addressed may be important. In wider cases of regional ethnic conflict, it is often the case that the contested metropolis is the hardest part of the problem to resolve. This has certainly been true in the case of Palestine and Jerusalem, where the opinion of most experts has been that it should be left until the end of the wider negotiation. It was indeed the main factor on which the Camp David talks of 2000 broke down. In Belgium, too, Brussels has been the most difficult problem to deal with, although a viable solution was at last implemented in 1989. The Trieste case after 1945 is slightly different, inasmuch as the outcome was a two-stage division of its hinterland between Italy and Yugoslavia. But it, too, is an example of leaving the urban centre until other matters have been resolved.

Partition of the city has on occasion been tried, and can be a tempting course of action where the level of urban segregation is, or has suddenly become, very high. It was, thus, possible to partition Jerusalem between 1949 and 1967, while Nicosia has remained partitioned since 1974. But such an approach is not really practicable unless the location of the city lies close to the partition line of the wider territory. Even where it has been tried it has not been regarded as a satisfactory or long-term answer. In Belfast, where segregation is very high, the location of the city within Protestant rural and suburban heartlands means that the wider repartition of Ireland is not a practical proposition. Indeed, the existence of a large and visible Catholic minority in Belfast is probably the main reason why proposals for more feasible adjustments to the Irish border have not aroused much interest: Belfast is central to the problem, and border realignments would not help. In Montreal what amounted to a partition scheme was proposed in the early 1970s, but it found little support.

Conflict can sometimes be alleviated by the presence of cross-cutting issues, important public concerns over which people align themselves in ways other than along the ethnic divide. Trade unionism, socialism and communism have on occasion demonstrated the best potential for cross-cutting. From the Austro-Marxists of Trieste to the 'rotten Prods' of the Belfast shipyards there are many examples of the political left seeking to lead working people away from ethnic entrapment. But achievement has not matched aspiration. All over ethnic Europe in the decade prior to 1914 labour movements were splitting into ethnically-based sub-units. Representatives of non-dominant minorities came to feel, for a variety of reasons, that the wider movements of which they had been a part did not adequately cater for their needs. 'International' came to be read as meaning 'imperialist'; ideologists advanced arguments linking the class and national struggles. On the other side, 'internationalist' socialism failed to recognise the particular concerns of ethnic minorities. Non-dominant minorities found themselves transformed into the tail of nationalist movements, while worker elements from the dominant group sometimes ended up in movements associated with fascism or national socialism. The issue was perpetuated by the development of Communism in eastern Europe. In Trieste and any other places, anti-Slavism transformed itself with remarkable facility into anti-Communism. Conversely, Communism was not slow to take advantage of the national question where it was convenient to do so. But whereas in Trieste after 1945 it could reasonably be argued that what appeared to be about class ideology was really about ethnicity, Hamalainen's work on the Helsinki case has suggested that what appeared to be about ethnicity was really about class conflict.

To what extent can state power, at any level, affect this kind of conflict? It used to be said that Teddy Kollek's conciliatory policies as mayor of Jerusalem in the years after the 1967 reunification mitigated the impact of the wider conflict on the city, preserving it as a relative island of calm for some years. Certainly services were effectively reorganised across the reunited city in a way that was beneficial to all. But resource allocation between the two sides was not established on a fair basis, and the wider policies of the state predominated on key issues such as settlements policy. Ultimately, municipal government proved unable to isolate the city from the wider conflict. In late nineteenth-century Trieste the concept of *municipalismo*, the belief that the city government had the capacity to embrace people from a variety of different cultural backgrounds, was gradually eroded not by any central state but by the growing power of Italian nationalism in local politics.

In inter-war Danzig, Free City government proved as incapable as Germany itself of resisting the advance of Nazism. In Belfast, before local government was shorn of most of its powers in 1973, the city government proved *less* capable than regional government of resisting partisan pressures. In Montreal, city government was, until very recently, greatly restricted both in geographical area and in the range of services under its control. In Brussels too, most of the key decisions affecting ethnic relations in the city have in the past been taken at a higher level. But since the granting of regional status to Brussels-Capital in 1989 this has changed, and the extended city now has formidable powers, drawing its authority direct from the Belgian constitution. The question in the longer run is whether it will be able to maintain ethnolinguistic stability in an urban territory where the boundaries are permanently frozen.

The role of regional and national states has been significantly greater than that of municipal governments. In Brussels it was the power, initially, of the central state – under popular pressure in Flanders – which created a framework for reversing the decline of Dutch in the capital. In Quebec, provincial government brought about a remarkable and apparently lasting transformation of ethnolinguistic trends in Montreal. Israeli central government has gone so far as to make control of the united city of Jerusalem a symbol of its authority. In Belfast a 50-year experiment with majoritarian regional government ultimately failed to manage ethnic conflict effectively, both beginning and ending in near-civil war conditions. Along the German–Slav interface the retention of Danzig's (and Breslau's) Germanness in the late nineteenth century, at a time when Austrian-ruled cities like Prague were becoming increasing non-German in ethos, owed much to the style of government emanating from Berlin.

The weapons used by governments have ranged from mobilising the resources of the state to create new 'facts on the ground' to the manipulation of educational provision, while language laws have been devised to control the use of language in all kinds of contexts, from the army and the police force to hospital and welfare provision and even signs in shops. The best known example of facts on the ground is of course the Israeli settlements policy in and around east Jerusalem, which has made any kind of territorial repartition difficult if not impossible. The Polish creation of Gdynia as a rival to Danzig in the 1930s, the centre-piece of Poland's efforts to 'polonise' the Polish corridor, was another successful example, while Mussolini's attempt during the inter-war period to 'italianise' the South Tyrol left a more limited permanent imprint. An example of failure to create facts on the ground is the unsuccessful attempt made by the German government in the generation before 1914, in association with patriotic voluntary bodies, to strengthen German's demographic position in the German East and to reverse the *ostflucht*.

The harshest approach to education policy, apart from the open brutality of the fascist period, has been that of the German state in Danzig and elsewhere at the end of the nineteenth century, when German instruction was made compulsory and Polish banned throughout the schools system. More frequently, dominant regimes have been reluctant to develop minority education provision in urban areas, and less willing to provide it at higher than at elementary level. This arises from their vision of the city as an assimilative organ: rural people in minority areas might be permitted to obtain elementary education in their own language, but that should be the limit of concession. 'It is often necessary and desirable that any special language of the peasantry should be recognised and used as the language of instruction in elementary and primary schools, but not in higher places of education', wrote the British diplomat James Headlam-Morley in 1919 (Hepburn 1978:179). Where minority-language education did penetrate the city it tended to be restricted to minority suburban areas, as in Trieste. Where minority languages have thrived in the urban context religious difference, especially Catholicism, has often been the key factor. Even where language difference has been salient, as with French in Montreal, it has in fact been religious difference and the existence of a Church organisational structure which has preserved separate education. In many western countries the Catholic Church has had sufficient organisation and wealth to provide secondary education for at least a proportion of the minority population, more or less independently of the state.

In higher education protracted battles have been fought, partly because of the higher cost of separate provision at this level. The main reason, however, has been reluctance to create a channel which would perpetuate the non-assimilation of the elite of the non-dominant community. This has frequently been cloaked in arguments *a lá* Headlam-Morley about the minority language being of 'interior cultural value'. The Belgian state resisted the creation of any Dutch-language university until after the First World War, and did not establish one in Brussels until 1970. Likewise in Montreal the prestige university has always been the English-language McGill. Laval University in Quebec City was for a long time the only Francophone equivalent, until in

1969 its branch in Montreal was given independent status, following a failed demand by students for the *francisation* of McGill.[71] In Trieste the Italian government resisted establishing even an Italian-language university in the city until 1938. Slovenian-speaking students tended to study instead at the University of Ljubljana, but have not been permitted to teach in Slovene schools in Italy unless they have also undertaken some of their study in Trieste. In the Free City of Danzig things worked the other way round: Poles from northern Poland, together with Danzig Poles, constituted a third of enrolments in the Technical University in 1930. They were later expelled by the local Nazi regime, which regarded their presence not as potentially assimilative to German culture but as a step towards 'polonisation'. In Belfast the Queen's University, founded in 1908, was intended by government to be Presbyterian in ethos. After partition the number of Catholic students who chose to attend it rather than go south to Dublin or elsewhere increased. Queen's created a separate department of scholastic philosophy and, much later, a chair of Irish history, but for many years most Catholic doctors in the city trained at University College, Dublin where Catholic medical ethics were taught. Likewise, until the 1940s there was no Catholic teacher-training provision for men in Northern Ireland, most students going to London. In Jerusalem, the Arabs, Jews and British all attempted to establish universities in the 1920s, but only the Jews had sufficient organisation and support to succeed. Very recently, and with a certain amount of discouragement from the Israeli state, an Arab university has been established in the Jerusalem area.

Where a city's division is an ethnolinguistic one, language laws have often been used by central or regional governments to reinforce or reverse patterns of language usage. Sometimes this is a matter of power and pride, where people who can perfectly well understand one language demand to be dealt with in another. But in other contexts it is a more serious matter of people not understanding what is said to them in hospitals, government offices or the armed forces. During the first half-century of its existence the Belgian state gave legal backing to the status of French as the sole official language of the country. In the twentieth century, essentially since the extension of the franchise and

---

[71] In 1970 the prestigious Catholic University of Louvain/Leuven (in Flanders but very close both to Brussels and to the national language border) once strongly Francophone and then for some time bilingual, became exclusively Dutch-speaking, as the Francophones were required under the revised Belgian constitution to decamp across the language line to what became Louvain-la-Neuve.

the beginnings of Flanders' economic revival, language legislation in Belgium has worked in the opposite direction, to support and defend Dutch. In this, and in other cases, it is important to note the distinction between law and practice: many Belgian language laws were not effectively enforced by the state prior to the 1960s; in Helsinki language laws concerning the right to use Swedish in dealings with the public services exist, but in the current social context many Swedes take the pragmatic view that their command of Finnish is likely to be better than officials' command of Swedish. Some language rights are therefore unasserted in Finland, where the issue may be losing its salience. The Swiss capital of Berne, notwithstanding the legal rights enjoyed in the city by civil servants from Francophone cantons, is in practice becoming a more thoroughly German-speaking city, with the position of French weakened further by the rise of English as the international second language (Laponce:176). In Montreal, on the other hand, social processes which favoured English have been reversed since the mid-1970s by tough enforcement of language laws. The drive for this has come essentially from Quebec's regional government, with strong popular support in the Francophone areas of Montreal. The federal government has also acted to give Canada a bilingual *visage*, with improved opportunities for Francophones in the federal services, but this has been essentially a response to changes in power and attitude at the regional level.

In summary therefore, the role of the state has been a mixed one. In some contexts the regional state, especially, has made a powerful difference. In others it has been less effective, or has simply reinforced – or been superseded by – informal social processes. It is hard to draw a line between the two, for in democratic societies the doings of the state and the social processes developed by its citizens are not entirely independent of one another. Ethnic relationships, and changes in ethnic relationships, are brought about by the exercise of power, or by changes in the distribution of power – the latter brought about by economic change, social and educational change, demographic change or changes in the electoral system.

The most obvious manifestation of power in influencing the development of contested cities is international intervention. This may take the form of protection, invasion, occupation or an imposed settlement. It may consist of promises or pledges – public, secret or even false – given by outside powers to one of the protagonists. It may take the form of some kind of intervention by an international body. Or it may consist of the balancing of two competing forces in a city by an imperial power – technically a state intervention, but one external to the main parties to the contest. In a few cases, such as Montreal, and to a slightly lesser extent Belfast, international intervention has been unimportant. In other cases, like Danzig and Trieste, outside intervention has been decisive. In Jerusalem, outside interventions were a crucial determinant of events for a century, from the Crimean War through the Balfour Declaration and beyond. Since the end of the British Mandate however, there has been a plethora of *attempted* international interventions, but the reality is that the role of outsiders has been reduced to that of facilitation between the main protagonists.

In cities such as Danzig/Gdańsk, Wroclaw/Breslau and Thessaloniki, social processes and state policies have counted for nothing in the face of massive international upheaval. Short of genocide – which of course brutally and tragically ended the Jewish presence in many European cities – expulsion is the harshest means of attempting to resolve contested city issues. Effectively, German Danzig no longer exists because the Nazi intervention failed to reverse the decisions of 1919, provoking instead an overwhelming backlash against the people of the German East. German Breslau, if Churchill's account is to be accepted, came to an end essentially because the British electorate discharged him from office in the general election of 1945. The Trieste case is similar in some respects. The western allies had less direct interest in keeping Trieste out of Italy than Russia and Poland had in keeping Gdańsk out of Germany. Had Slovene and Croat migration into late-nineteenth-century Trieste been both greater in volume and more resistant to *italianitá* at an earlier stage, *and* had the Italian fascist state not then had more than two decades to reinforce *italianitá* by harsh measures, Trieste might have been more convincing as a Slav city during the weeks when Tito controlled it in 1945. Had this been the case, it seems likely that the western allies would have been less determined to keep the city out of Yugoslavia (and later to take it into Italy) than they in fact were. But the decisions on Trieste, and on the location of Italy's nearby boundary in the region, were ultimately taken by the western allies in negotiation with Tito, without Italian state involvement.

A final question to be considered is whether there are any circumstances in which contested cities would be better off without their overarching states. Where the conflict at the level of the regional or central state broadly shares the same parameters as the conflict in the city this is inherently unlikely. Belfast, for instance, while its violent history and bitterly-divided present would render an imposed settlement a hazardous enterprise, is not a different issue in kind from the rest of divided Ulster. In Montreal, the urban partition implied in the West Island City scheme of the 1970s would have necessitated special treatment for the metropolis, distinct from the policy direction taken by the various governments of the Province of Quebec over the past generation. But in Brussels, something close to urban independence, or at least to constitutionally-irreversible devolution, appears to be happening. Here the two competing sides are evenly balanced – the one side predominating in the state as a whole, the other predominating in the city. The guarantors of the arrangement, through the Belgian Constitution, are in effect Flanders and Wallonia. It is also important to remind ourselves that although ethnolinguistic conflict in Brussels goes back to the foundation of the Belgian state and earlier, there is scarcely any tradition of serious violence associated with the conflict but, on the contrary, a long tradition of problem-solving by political means.

When we look at more formal and internationally-sponsored attempts to address contested city problems by separating them from a wider state, there is a dismal record of failure. Danzig was made a free city in 1919 because, while ethnicity pointed to its return to Germany, economic links, earlier history and the outcome of the war dictated otherwise. The Free City of Danzig failed, of course, because Nazism destroyed the Versailles peace settlement and because the League of Nations lacked the power and will to stand over the structure for which it was supposed to be the guarantor. The ethnic majority in the city, furthermore, failed to develop the economic and political relationship with Poland which might have prevented the latter's creation of a rival port at Gdynia. But Danzig was at least a free city scheme which was intended, by most of its proponents, to work.[72] In the case of the Free Territory of Trieste even this is questionable. The spectre of Danzig's failure hung over it, and at no stage was it suggested that the newly-created United Nations should take responsibility. Through the period of uncertainty from 1945 to 1954, allied thinking on the city's future was determined by cold war perspectives: first, what Stalin could be expected to swallow; then what a non-aligned Tito could be persuaded to accept; and always, in the background, how the Trieste situation might affect the prospects for resisting Communism in Italy. By the time of Tito's departure from the Comintern

---

[72] Although it is possible that some of the Versailles diplomats involved in the Free City's creation were sufficiently out of touch with the nationalist spirit of the age to believe their own rhetoric about its being a stepping stone back into Poland, after 125 years of separation.

in 1948 it was clear that the British-American allied military government wanted to unload its Adriatic responsibility, did not want to pass it over to international control, and was looking for an opportunity to return Trieste city to a pro-western government in Italy as soon as that could be achieved. The FTT was never much more than an interim or transitional arrangement. In an international climate such as this, the 1947 United Nations plan for Jerusalem looked like the no-hoper which it has turned out to be. The UN, following on – it has to be admitted – from previous British proposals which never left the drawing board, proposed that the territory of Palestine be partitioned between Jews and Arabs, but that the city of Jerusalem and a chunk of surrounding territory be excluded and remain under permanent United Nations control. This became known as the *corpus separatum* proposal. It failed to get off the ground for the same reason as the previous British schemes, and for the same reason that the Free City of Danzig had failed: lack of both political will and available international force. As we have seen, even in the midst of a bitter war with one another, Transjordan and the nascent State of Israel could at least tacitly agree that Jews and Arabs would rather fight the matter out between themselves than agree to third-party arbitration. More than half a century – and many more tragedies – later, this still appears to be the position. It may well be that international diplomatic pressure will at some stage play a crucial role in facilitating an Israel–Palestine settlement. But it would be a major surprise if the outcome involved anything like a free city solution for Jerusalem.

An historical case-study approach has been adopted here in order to bring out fully the differences as well as the similarities which exist between different examples of the phenomena being studied. This book has set out to analyse the various factors which may affect the development of contested cities, using the broad themes of international intervention, various levels of state intervention, and a wider range of demographic, economic, social and cultural activities which have been summarised as social processes. If there is one central conclusion from these studies it is that socio-economic determinism and what used to be called 'the uniqueness of the historical event' are not alternatives, but partners in a constantly changing relationship. The social processes which are apparent in all these studies work in very similar ways, and are central to our understanding of historical change. In each case, however, there are factors – whether of location, human agency or chance – which interact with these processes to produce a particular and distinct outcome.

Bibliography

* indicates a novel

1 Contested Cities: Social Change, State Action and International Intervention

General and comparative

Ascherson, N. *Black Sea: the Birthplace of Civilisation and Barbarism* (London: Jonathan Cape, 1995)

Berger, S. & A. Smith (eds) *Nationalism, Labour and Ethnicity, 1870–1939* (Manchester: University Press, 1999)

Engman, M., F.W. Carter, A.C. Hepburn & C.G. Pooley (eds) *Ethnic Identity in Urban Europe* (Aldershot: Dartmouth Publishing/New York University Press, 1992)

Gee, M., T. Kirk & J. Steward (eds) *The City in Central Europe: Culture and Society from 1800 to the Present* (Aldershot: Ashgate, 1999)

Hepburn, A.C. (ed.) *Minorities in History* (London: Edward Arnold, 1978)

Hroch, M. *Social Conditions of National Revival in Europe* (Cambridge: University Press, 1985)

Hroch, M. *In the National Interest: Demands and Goals of European National Movements of the Nineteenth Century* (Prague: Charles University, 1996)

Ignatieff, M. *Blood & Belonging: Journeys into the New Nationalism* (London: BBC Books, 1993)

Kerswill, P.E. & A. Williams, 'Mobility and social class in dialect levelling: evidence from new and old towns in England', in K. Mattheier (ed.) *Dialect and Migration in a Changing Europe* (Frankfurt: Peter Lang, 2000)

Kotek 1996a: J. Kotek, S. Susskind & S. Kaplan (eds) *Brussels and Jerusalem: from Conflict to Solution* (Jerusalem: Truman Institute, 1996)

Kotek 1996b: J. Kotek, (ed.) *L'Europe et ses villes-frontiéres* (Bruxelles: editions complexe, 1996)

Laponce, J.A. *Languages and their Territories* (London: University of Toronto Press, 1987)

Lehan, R. *The City in Literature* (Berkeley: University of Californian Press, 1998)

Lynch, J. *A Tale of Three Cities: Comparative Studies in Working Class Life* (Basingstoke: Macmillan – now Palgrave Macmillan – 1998) [Belfast, Bristol, Dublin]

Minority Rights Group, *World Dictionary of Minorities* (London: MRG, 1990)

Mitchell, B.R. *International Historical Statistics, 1750–1988* (3rd edn New York: Stockton Press, 1992)

Preston, P. & P. Simpson-Housley (eds) *Writing the City: Eden, Babylon & the New Jerusalem* (London: Routledge, 1994)

*Roth, P. *American Pastoral* (London: Jonathan Cape, 1997)

Smith, P., K. Koufa & A. Suppan (eds) *Ethnic Groups in International Relations* (Aldershot: Dartmouth Publishing/New York University Press, 1991)

Wright, F. *Northern Ireland: a Comparative Analysis* (Dublin: Gill & Macmillan, 1987)

Other cities

Cohen, G.B. *The Politics of Ethnic Survival: Germans in Prague, 1861–1914* (Princeton: University Press, 1981)

Davies, N. & R. Moorhouse, *Microcosm: Portrait of a Central European City* [Wroclaw] (London: Jonathan Cape, 2002)

Gardner-Chloros, P. *Language Selection and Switching in Strasbourg* (Oxford: Clarendon Press, 1991)

Glettler, M. 'The Slovaks in Budapest and Bratislava, 1850–1914', in M. Engman *et al.* (eds) *Ethnic Identity in Urban Europe* (Aldershot: Dartmouth Publishing, 1992)

Gounaris, B.C. 'Thessaloniki, 1830–1912: history, economy and society', in I.K. Hassiotis (ed.) *Queen of the Worthy: Thessaloniki, vol. 1 History and Culture* (Thessaloniki: Paratiritis, 1997)

Hamalainen, P.K. *In Time of Storm: Revolution, Civil War & the Ethnolinguistic Issue in Finland* (Albany, NY: State University of New York Press, 1979)

Henderson, K. *Slovakia: the Escape from Invisibility* (London: Routledge, 2002)

Laitin, D.D. 'Linguistic revival: politics and culture in Catalonia', in *Comparative Studies in Society and History*, 31 (1997), pp. 297–317

McRae, K.D. *Conflict and Compromise in Multilingual Societies: Finland* (Waterloo, Ontario: Wilfrid Laurier University Press, 1997)

Petridis, P.B. 'Thessaloniki, 1912–40: a period of political and social transition', in I.K. Hassiotis (ed.) *Queen of the Worthy: Thessaloniki, vol. 1 History and Culture* (Thessaloniki: Paratiritis, 1997)

Papagiannopoulos, A. *History of Thessaloniki* (Thessaloniki: Rekos, 1982, 1997)

Rubes, J. 'The case of Prague: a frontier city of the past', in J. Kotek, S. Susskind & S. Kaplan (eds), *Brussels and Jerusalem: from Conflict to Solution* (Jerusalem: Truman Institute, 1996)

Sayer, D. 'The language of nationality and the nationality of language: Prague, 1780–1920', in *Past & Present*, 153 (November 1996), 164–210

Schoolfield, G.C. *Helsinki of the Czars: Finland's Capital, 1808–1918* (Columbia SC: Camden House, 1996)

Siguan, M. *Multilingual Spain* (Amsterdam: Swets & Zeitlinger, 1993)

Woolard, K.A. *Double Talk: Bilingualism and the Politics of Ethnicity in Catalonia* (Stanford: University Press, 1989)

Zafiris, C. *The Thessaloniki Handbook* (Athens: Exandas Books, 1997)

2   From Danzig to Gdańsk

Askenazy, S. *Dantzig and Poland* (trans. from Polish. Engl. edn London: Allen & Unwin, 1921)

Bacon, G.C. 'Danzig Jewry: a short history', in *Danzig 1939: Treasures of a Destroyed Community* (New York: The Jewish Museum, 1980)

Burleigh, M. *Germany Turns Eastward: a Study of Ostforschung in the Third Reich* (Cambridge: University Press, 1988)

Chwin, Stefan, *Hanemann* (Gdańsk: Wydawnictwo Marabuk, 1995, Engl. edn forthcoming: Harcourt)

Cieślak, E. & C. Biernat, *History of Gdańsk* (Gdansk: Wydawnictwo Morskie, 1988)

Davies, N. *God's Playground: a History of Poland*, 2 vols (Oxford: Clarendon, 1981)

Donald, R. *The Polish Corridor and its Consequences* (London: Thornton, Butterworth, n.d. c.1929)

Friedrich, K. *The Other Prussia: Royal Prussia, Poland and Liberty, 1569-1772* (Cambridge: University Press, 2000)

Gayre, G.R. *Teuton and Slav on the Polish Frontier* (London: Eyre & Spottiswoode, 1944)

*Grass, Günter, *Unkenrufe: ein Erzählung* (Göttingen: Stedl, 1992); English edn: *The Call of the Toad* (London: Secker & Warburg, 1992)

*Grass, Günter, *Die Blechtrommel* (1st edn 1959). Engl. edn *The Tin Drum* (London: Secker & Warburg, 1962)

Grass, Günter, 'The Jewish community of Danzig, 1930–39', in *Society*, 29, vi (Sept.1992), pp. 69–83

Hagen, W.W. *Germans, Poles and Jews: the Nationality Conflict in the Prussian East, 1772–1914* (Chicago: University Press, 1980)

Headlam-Morley, J. *A Memoir of the Paris Peace Conference, 1919* (London: Methuen, 1972)

Holtom, P. 'Kaliningrad and the Versailles experiment: a warning from Danzig' (Centre for Russian and East European Studies, University of Birmingham, www.crees.bham.ac.uk, 2001)

*Huelle, P., *Weiser Dawidek* (1st edn 1987) Engl. edn *Who was David Weiser?* (London: Bloomsbury, 1991)

Jerzak, K. 'The City that is no More, the City that will Stand Forever: Danzig/Gdańsk as Homeland in the Writings of Günter Grass, Pawel Huelle and Stefan Chwin', in M. Cornis-Pope & J. Neubauer (eds), *History of the Literary Cultures in East-Central Europe: Junctures and Disjuntures in the 19th and 20th Centuries*, vol. ii (Amsterdam: John Benjamins, 3 vols, forthcoming)

Kimmich, C.M. *The Free City: Danzig and German Foreign Policy, 1919–34* (New Haven: Yale University Press, 1968)

Kulczycki, J.J. *School Strikes in Prussian Poland, 1901–07: the Struggle over Bilingual Education* (New York: Columbia University Press, 1981)

Levine, H.S. *Hitler's Free City: a History of the Nazi Party in Danzig, 1925–39* (Chicago: University Press, 1973)

Mallek, J. 'A political triangle: ducal Prussian estates, Prussian rulers and Poland. The policy of the city of Königsberg versus Poland, 1525-1701', in *Parliaments, Estates and Representations*, 15 (1995), pp.25–35.

Mason, J.B. *The Danzig Dilemma: a Study in Peacemaking by Compromise* (Stanford: University Press, 1946)

Nelson, H.I. *Land and Power: British and Allied Policy on Germany's Frontier, 1916–19* (London: Routledge & Kegan Paul, 1963)

Pollmann K.E. 'The parliamentary representation of the national minorities in the German *Kaiserreich*, 1867–1918', in G.Alderman *et al.* (eds) *Governments, Ethnic Groups and Political Representation* (Aldershot: Dartmouth, 1993)

Schenk, D. *Hitlers Mann in Danzig: Albert Forster und die NS-Verbrechen in Danzig-Westpreußen* (Bonn: J.H.W. Dietz, 2000)

Stone, G. 'The language of Cassubian Literature and the question of a literary standard', in *Slavonic & East European Review*, 50 (1972), pp.521–9

Szermer, B. *Gdańsk Past and Present* (Warsaw: Interpress Publishers, 1971)

Tighe, Carl, *Gdańsk: National Identity in the Polish–German Borderlands* (London: Pluto Press, 1990)

Twersky, I. (ed.) *Danzig, Between East and West: Aspects of Modern Jewish History* (Cambridge, Mass: Harvard University Press, 1985)

Wandycz, P.S. *The Lands of Partitioned Poland, 1795–1918* (Seattle: University of Washington Press, 1974)

Ward, P. *Polish Cities: Travels in Cracow & the South, Gdańsk, Malbork and Warsaw* (Cambridge: Oleander Press, 1988)

Whomersley, C.A. 'The international legal status of Gdańsk, Klaipeda and the former East Prussia', in *The International and Comparative Law Journal*, 42, iv (Oct. 1993), pp.919–27

3   Resistance: the survival of Italian: Trieste

Ara, A. 'Italian educational policies towards national minorities, 1860–1940', in J. Tomiak (ed.), *Schooling, Educational Policy and Ethnic Identity* (Aldershot: Dartmouth, 1991)

Ballinger, P. *History in Exile: Memory and Identity at the Borders of the Balkans* (Princeton: University Press, 2002)

*Berger, J. *G: a Novel* (London: Weidenfeld & Nicolson, 1972)

Cattaruzza, M. 'Slovenes and Italians in Trieste', in M. Engman *et al.*, *Ethnic Identity in Urban Europe, 1850–1940* (Aldershot: Dartmouth, 1992)

Cattaruzza, M. *Trieste nel'Ottocento:Le Trasformazioni di una Società Civile* (Udine: Del Bianco Editore, 1995)

Duroselle, J-B. *Le Conflict de Trieste, 1943–54* (Brussels: L'Université Libre, 1966)

Gardner, M. 'War shadow in Trieste', in *Times Higher Education Supplement*, 20 May 1994

Hametz, M. 'The Carabinieri stood by: the Italian State and the "Slavic Threat" in Trieste, 1919–22', in *Nationalities Papers*, 29, iv (2001), pp.559–74

Hametz, M. *A Central European Port-City and an Italian Border Town: Trieste, 1918–54* (Woodbridge: Boydell & Brewer, forthcoming 2003–04)

McCourt, J. *The Years of Bloom: James Joyce in Trieste, 1904–20* (Dublin: Lilliput Press, 2000)

Mazzolini, A. 'Italy's foreign policy and Italian minorities in Slovenia and Croatia' (University of Bradford MA thesis, 1995)

Melik, V. 'The representation of Germans, Italians and Slovenes', in G. Alderman *et al.* (eds), *Governments, Ethnic Groups and Political Representation* (Aldershot: Dartmouth, 1993)

Mihelic, D. *The Political Element in the Port Geography of Trieste* (University of Chicago: Department of Geography, 1969)

Moodie, A.F. *The Italo-Yugoslav Boundary: a Study on Political Geography* (London: Philip, 1945)

Morris, J. *Trieste and the Meaning of Nowhere* (London: Faber, 2001)

Novak, B.C. *Trieste, 1941–1954: the Ethnic, Political and Ideological Struggle* (Chicago: University Press, 1970)

Rabel, R.G. *Between East and West: Trieste, the United States and the Cold War, 1941–1954* (London: Duke University Press, 1988)

Rusinow, D. *Italy's Austrian Heritage, 1919–1946* (Oxford: Clarendon Press, 1969)

Sluga, G. 'Trieste, ethnicity and the cold war, 1945–54', in *Journal of Contemporary History*, 29, ii (1994), pp. 285–304

Sluga, G. *The Problem of Trieste and the Italo-Yugoslav Border: Difference, Identity and Sovereignty in Twentieth-century Europe* (Albany: State University of New York Press, 2001)

Stranj, P. *The Submerged Community: an A-Z of the Slovenes in Italy* (Trieste: Editoriale Stampa Triestina, 1989. Rev. Engl. Edn 1992)

Webster, R.A. *Industrial Imperialism in Italy, 1908–15* (Berkeley: University of California Press, 1975)

Whittam, J.R. 'Drawing the line: Britain and the emergence of the Trieste question, Jan.1941–May 1945', in *English Historical Review*, 419 (April 1991), pp. 346–70

www.eblul.org:8080/eblul. Search site for 'Trieste' (reports by S.T. Jobbins, R. Heinola, A. Cameron and R. van Ditzhuyzen)

4   Peaceful Reconquest: Montreal

Bélanger, C. *Quebec History* website, Marianopolis College, Montreal (http://www2.marianopolis.edu/quebechistory, 2000)

Bradbury, B. *Working Families: Age, Gender and Daily Survival in Industrialising Montreal* (Toronto: McClelland and Stewart, 1993)

Copp, T. *The Anatomy of Poverty: the Condition of the Working Class in Montreal, 1897–1929* (Toronto: McClelland and Stewart, 1974)

Germain, A. & D. Rose *Montréal: the Quest for a Metropolis* (Chichester: John Wiley, 2000)

Heintzman, R. 'The political culture of Quebec, 1840–1960', in *Canadian Journal of Political Science,* 16, i (March 1983)

Jenkins, K. *Montreal: Island City of the St. Lawrence* (New York: Doubleday, 1966)

Laponce, J. 'The City centre as conflictual space in the bilingual city: the case of Montreal', in J. Gottman (ed.) *Centre & Periphery: Spatial Variation in Politics* (Beverley Hills, Ca.: Sage Publications, 1980)

Levine, M.V. *The Reconquest of Montreal: Language Policy and Social Change in a Bilingual City* (Philadelphia: Temple University Press, 1990)

Lewis, R. 'The segregated city: class residential patterns and the development of industrial districts in Montreal, 1861 and 1901', *Journal of Urban History* 17, ii (Feb 1991), pp. 123–52

Lewis, R. *Manufacturing Montreal: the Making of an Industrial Landscape* (Baltimore: Johns Hopkins University Press, 2000)

*MacLennan, H. *The Two Solitudes* (Toronto: McClelland & Stewart, 1945)

McRoberts, K. *Quebec: Social Change and Political Crisis* (Toronto: McClelland & Stewart, 3rd edn 1988)

McRoberts, K. *Misconceiving Canada: the Struggle for National Unity* (Oxford: Oxford University Press, 1997)

Marsan, J-C. *Montreal in Evolution* (Montreal: McGill-Queen's University Press, 1981)

National Library of Canada website (2002), http://www.nlc-bnc.ca/primeministers
Prévost, R. *Montreal: a History* (Toronto: McClelland & Stewart, 1993; orig. French edn 1991)
Richler, M. *Oh Canada! Oh Quebec! Requiem for a Divided Country* (Harmondsworth: Penguin, 1992)
*Roy, G. *Bonheur d'occasion* (Montreal: Editions Pascal, 1945). English edn: *The Tin Flute* (Toronto: McClelland & Stewart, 1980)
*Roy, G. *Alexandre Chenevert* (Montreal: Beauchemin, 1954). English edn: *The Cashier* (Toronto: McClelland & Stewart, 1955)
Rudin, R. *The Forgotten Quebecers: a History of English-speaking Quebec, 1759–1980* (Quebec: Institut québécois de recherche sur la culture, 1985)
Sancton, A. *Governing the Island of Montreal: Language Differences & Metropolitan Politics* (Berkeley: University of California Press, 1985)

5 Peaceful Contest: Brussels

Buyst, E. 'Economic aspects of the nationality problem in 19th & 20th century Belgium', in A. Teichova, H. Matis & J. Patek (eds) *Economic Change & the National Question in Twentieth-Century Europe* (Cambridge: University Press, 2000)
De Lannoy, W. 'The Brussels urban region in the twentieth century: a socio-geographical analysis', in E. Witte & H. Baetens Beardsmore (eds) *The Interdisciplinary Study of Urban Bilingualism in Brussels* (Clevedon: Multilingual Matters, 1987)
De Metsenaere, M. 'The impact of geolinguistic and social processes on the language siutation in Brussels', in E. Witte & H. Baetens Beardsmore (eds) *The Interdisciplinary Study of Urban Bilingualism in Brussels* (Clevedon: Multilingual Matters, 1987)
Deprez, K. & L. Vos (eds) *Nationalism in Belgium: Shifting Identities, 1780–1995* (Basingstoke: Macmillan – now Palgrave Macmillan, 1998)
Detant, A. 'The Flemings in Brussels', in J. Kotek, S. Susskind & S. Kaplan, (eds) *Brussels and Jerusalem: from Conflict to Solution* (Jerusalem: Truman Institute, 1996)
De Vriendt, S. & R. Willemyns, 'Linguistic Research on Brussels', in E. Witte & H. Baetens Beardsmore (eds) *The Interdisciplinary Study of Urban Bilingualism in Brussels* (Clevedon: Multilingual Matters, 1987)
Donaldson, B.C. *Dutch: a Linguistic History of Holland and Belgium* (Leiden, Martinus Nijhoff, 1983)
Favell, A. & M. Martiniello, 'Multi-national, multi-cultural and multi-levelled Brussels: national and ethnic politics in the "Capital of Europe"', ESRC Transnational Communities Working Paper Series WPTC-99-04, April 1999, available on-line at www.transcomm.ox.ac.uk
Falter, R. 'Belgium's peculiar way to federalism', in K. Deprez, & L. Vos (eds) *Nationalism in Belgium: Shifting Identities, 1780–1995* (Basingstoke: Macmillan – now Palgrave Macmillan, 1998)
Govaert, S. 'A Brussels identity? A speculative interpretation', in K. Deprez, & L. Vos (eds) *Nationalism in Belgium: Shifting Identities, 1780–1995* (Basingstoke: Macmillan – now Palgrave Macmillan, 1998)

Hasquin, H. 'Brussels, the Francophone point of view', in J. Kotek, S. Susskind & S. Kaplan (eds) *Brussels and Jerusalem: from Conflict to Solution* (Jerusalem: Truman Institute, 1996)

Hermans, T (ed.), *The Flemish Movement: a Documentary History, 1780–1990* (London : Athlone Press, 1992)

Louckx, F. 'Ethnolinguistic enclosure patterns in post-war Brussels', in E. Witte & H. Baetens Beardsmore (eds) *The Interdisciplinary Study of Urban Bilingualism in Brussels* (Clevedon: Multilingual Matters, 1987)

Lorwin, V.R. 'Linguistic pluralism and political tension in modern Belgium', in J.A. Fishman (ed.), *Advances in the Sociology of Language* vol. 2 (The Hague & Paris: Mouton, 1972)

McRae, K.D. *Conflict & Compromise in Multilingual Societies: vol. 2 Belgium* (Waterloo, Ontario: Wilfrid Laurier University Press, 1986)

Obler, J.L. 'Assimilation and the moderation of linguistic conflict in Brussels', in *Administration*, 22 (Winter 1974), pp.400–32

Pas, Wouter 'Institutionalising ethnic diversity in post-conflict situations: working paper on the case of Brussels' (www.peaceproject.at/PPdocs)

Polansky, J.L. *Revolution in Brussels, 1787–1793* (Hanover, NH & London: New England University Press, 1987)

Saey, P., C. Kesteloot & C. Vandermotten, 'Unequal economic development at the origin of the federalisation process, in K. Deprez & L. Vos (eds) *Nationalism in Belgium: Shifting Identities, 1780–1995* (Basingstoke: Macmillan – now Palgrave Macmillan, 1998)

Van Velthoven, H. 'The process of language shift in Brussels: histrocial background and mechanisms', in E. Witte & H. Baetens Beardsmore (eds) *The Interdisciplinary Study of Urban Bilingualism in Brussels* (Clevedon: Multilingual Matters, 1987)

Vos, L. 'The Flemish national question', in K. Deprez, & L. Vos (eds) *Nationalism in Belgium: Shifting Identities, 1780–1995* (Basingstoke: Macmillan – now Palgrave Macmillan, 1998)

Witte 1987: E. Witte, & H. Baetens Beardsmore (eds) *The Interdisciplinary Study of Urban Bilingualism in Brussels* (Clevedon: Multilingual Matters, 1987)

Witte 1992: E. Witte & M. De Metsenaere, 'The Flemings in Brussels', in M. Engman *et al.* (ed) *Ethnic Identity in Urban Europe* (Aldershot: Dartmouth, 1992), pp. 13–38

Witte 1999: E. Witte, & H. Van Velthoven, *Language and Politics: the Situation in Belgium in an Historical Perspective* (Brussels: VUB Press, 1999)

Witte 2000: E. Witte, J. Craebeckx & A. Meynen, *Political History of Belgium from 1830 Onwards* (Brussels: VUB Press, 2000)

http://www.vub.ac.be/POLI/elections (2003)

Zolberg, A.R. 'The making of Flemings and Walloons: Belgium, 1830–1914', in *Journal of Interdisciplinary History*, 5, ii (Autumn 1974), pp.179–235

6   The Failure of Chronic Violence: Belfast

Bardon, J. *Belfast: an Illustrated History* (Belfast: Blackstaff Press, 1982)

Boal, F.W. *Shaping a City: Belfast in the Late Twentieth Century* (Belfast: Institute of Irish Studies, Queen's University, 1995)

Bollens, S.A. *On Narrow Ground: Urban Policy and Ethnic Conflict in Jerusalem and Belfast* (State University of New York Press, 2000)

Bruce, S. *The Red Hand: Protestant Paramilitaries in Northern Ireland* (Oxford: University Press, 1992)

Buckland, P.J. *The Factory of Grievances: Devolved Government in Northern Ireland, 1921–39* (Dublin: Gill & Macmillan, 1979)

Budge, I. & C. O'Leary, *Belfast: Approach to Crisis. A Study of Belfast Politics, 1613–1970* (London: Macmillan, 1973)

Burton, F. *The Politics of Legitimacy: Struggles in a Belfast Community* (London: Routledge & Kegan Paul, 1978)

*Caulfield, M.F. *The Black City* (London: Jonathan Cape: 1952)

Darby, J. *Scorpions in a Bottle: Conflicting Cultures in Northern Ireland* (London: Minority Rights group, 1997)

Darby, J. *Intimidation and the Control of Conflict in Northern Ireland* (Dublin: Gill & Macmillan, 1986)

Elliott, M. *The Catholics of Ulster* (London: Allen Lane, 2000)

Farrell, S. *Rituals and Riots: Sectarian Violence & Political Culture in Ulster, 1784–1886* (Lexington: University Press of Kentucky, 2000)

Gray, J. *City in Revolt: James Larkin & the Belfast Dock Strike of 1907* (Belfast: Blackstaff Press, 1985)

Griffin, B. *The Bulkies: Police & Crime in Belfast, 1800–1865* (Dublin: Irish Academic Press, 1997)

Harris, R. *Prejudice and Tolerance in Ulster* (Manchester: University Press, 1972)

Hepburn, A.C. *The Conflict of Nationality in Modern Ireland* (London: Edward Arnold, 1980)

Hepburn, A.C. *A Past Apart: Studies in the History of Catholic Belfast, 1850–1950* (Belfast: Ulster Historical Foundation, 1996)

Hirst, C. *Religion, Politics & Violence in Nineteenth-century Belfast: the Pound and Sandy Row* (Dublin: Four Courts Press, 2002)

Howe, S. *Ireland and Empire: Colonial Legacies in Irish History and Culture* (Oxford: University Press, 2000)

Jones, E. *A Social Geography of Belfast* (London: Oxford University Press, 1960)

*McLaverty, M. *Lost Fields* (London: Jonathan Cape, 1942)

*McLaverty, M. *Call my Brother Back* (London: Longman, 1939)

Maguire, W.A. *Belfast* (Keele: Ryburn Publishing, 1993)

*Moore, B. *The Lonely Passion of Judith Hearne* (London: André Deutsch, 1955)

Morgan, A. *Labour & Partition: the Belfast Working Class, 1905–23* (London: Pluto Press, 1991)

Phoenix, E. *Northern Nationalism: Nationalist Politics, Partition and the Catholic Minority in Northern Ireland, 1890–1940* (Belfast: Ulster Historical Foundation, 1994)

Smith, D.J. & G. Chambers, *Inequality in Northern Ireland* (Oxford: University Press, 1991)

Sutton, M. *'Bear in mind these dead': an Index of Deaths from the Conflict in Ireland, 1969–93* (Belfast: Beyond the Pale Publications, 1994), updated to the end of 2001 on *cain.ulst.ac.uk/sutton* (2002)

*Tomelty, J. *The Apprentice* (London: Jonathan Cape, 1953)

Wright, F. *Two Lands on One Soil: Ulster Politics before Home Rule* (Dublin: Gill & MacMillan, 1996)

7 The Failure of Acute Violence: Jerusalem

*Agnon, S.Y. *Temol Shilshom* (1st edn 1945). Engish edn: *Only Yesterday* (Princeton: University Press, 2000)

Bollens, S.A. *On Narrow Ground: Urban Policy and Ethnic Conflict in Jerusalem and Belfast* (State University of New York Press, 2000)

Dumper, M. *The Politics of Jerusalem since 1967* (New York & Chichester: Columbia University Press, 1997)

Gilbert, M. *Jerusalem: Rebirth of a City* (London: Chatto & Windus,1985)

Gilbert, M. *Jerusalem in the Twentieth Century* (London: Pimlico, 1996)

Hassan, S. & S. Kouba 'Local politics in Jerusalem', in J. Kotek, S. Susskind & S. Kaplan (eds) *Brussels and Jerusalem: from Conflict to Solution* (Jerusalem: Truman Institute, 1996)

Karmi, G. (ed.) *Jerusalem Today: What Future for the Peace Process* (Reading: Ithaca Press, 1996)

Khalidi, R. *Palestinian Identity: the Construction of Modern National Consciousness* (New York: Columbia University Press, 1997)

Klein, M. *Jerusalem: the Contested City* (London: Hurst & Co. 2001)

Kotek 1996a: J. Kotek, S. Susskind & S. Kaplan (eds) *Brussels and Jerusalem: from Conflict to Solution* (Jerusalem: Truman Institute, 1996)

Mattar, P. *The Mufti of Jerusalem: Al-Hajj Amin al-Husayni and the Palestinian National Movement* (New York: Columbia University Press, 1988)

Nashashibi, N.E. *Jerusalem's Other Voice: Ragheb Nashashibi and Moderation in Palestinian Politics, 1920–48* (Exeter: Ithaca Press, 1990)

*Oz, A. *Panther in the Basement* (London: Vintage, 1997)

Parfitt, T. *The Jews in Palestine, 1800–1882* (Woodbridge: Boydell & Brewer, 1987)

Romann, M. & A. Weingrod *Living Together Separately: Arabs & Jews in Contemporary Jerusalem* (Princeton: University Press, 1991)

Sharkansky, I. *Governing Jerusalem: Again on the World's Agenda* (Detroit: Wayne State University Press, 1996)

Spolsky, B. & R.L. Cooper *The Languages of Jerusalem* (Oxford: Clarendon Press, 1991)

Wasserstein, B. *Divided Jerusalem: the Struggle for the Holy City* (London: Profile Books, 2001)

Index